THE NEW UNTOUCHABLES

THE NEW UNTOUCHABLES

Immigration and the New World Worker

NIGEL HARRIS

I.B.TAURIS PUBLISHERS
LONDON · NEW YORK

Published in 1995 by I.B.Tauris & Co. Ltd
45 Bloomsbury Square, London WC1A 2HY
175 Fifth Avenue, New York, NY 10010

In the United States of America and Canada distributed by
St Martin's Press, 175 Fifth Avenue, New York, NY 10010

A full CIP record for this book is available
from the British Library

Library of Congress catalog card number 95–060076
A full CIP record for this book is available
from the Library of Congress

ISBN 1 85043 956 7

Set in Monotype Baskerville by Lucy Morton, London SE12
Printed and bound in Great Britain by WBC Ltd,
Bridgend, Mid Glamorgan

Contents

Preface

In the late 1970s I started work on an attempt to understand why from the 1960s international migration became a significant factor in the European and American labour markets. I realized that to understand this phenomenon one needed to locate it in the changing structure of the world economy, in the idea of a world labour force. That led to an attempt to identify the emerging world economy, to provide a cartoon of the main structure and trends (published by Penguin in 1983 as *Of Bread and Guns: The World Economy in Crisis*). The main thesis – which has by now become commonplace – was that an integrated world economy was superseding its national parts, that the process of economic integration which occurred most rapidly between 1840 and 1870 had been resumed in the 1960s, this time outside the framework of empire. In between had been a century dominated by the rivalries of the Great Powers, by nationalism and étatism; unwinding the structures of that period is a central theme of our age, ranging from the modest projects of structural adjustment of national economies to the foundering of the mighty Soviet Union and its allies.

These preoccupations led then to an examination of what was happening in the developing countries, the heirs to the traditions of economic nationalism and étatism in the developed countries of the 1930s and 1940s (published by I.B. Tauris and Penguin in 1986 as *The End of the Third World: Newly Industrializing Countries and the Decline of an Ideology*). From there I pursued the thread of political nationalism, the reasons for its rise and the conditions of its decline, and its relationship to an integrated global economy (again, published by I.B. Tauris and Penguin, as *National Liberation*, in 1990).

In *The New Untouchables* I have at last returned to the starting point, international migration. Had I known when I started that the project would have taken so long and involved four volumes instead of one (although each book is designed to stand alone), I would not have had the temerity to embark upon it; nor would my publishers have mustered the courage or indulgence to tolerate it. However, from my point of view, the excursus has been immensely valuable, allowing me to explore a framework for the understanding of the main lines of modern economic and political history, cutting across the ancient battle lines of right and left. The form of national capitalism which dominated perceptions for the past century has now come to appear not as a final destination but as only a way-station on the road to a global economy, or – to change the metaphor – as an incubator for birds that, once mature, abandon the national nest.

In this context, the international movement of workers assumes special significance, since not only is it propelled by the economic integration of the world (and the partial emergence of global labour markets); it also collides directly with the prerogatives of political sovereignty, the power of the state. The new and the old are set in collision, and – whatever the resolution – will determine whether the old political form of the system, the state, will succeed in sacrificing the growth of the world economy, and the jobs and incomes of its citizens, to the defence of its old power.

The climate of opinion has also changed since I set out on this project, particularly among governments. The number of official meetings and conferences on immigration – 60 were recorded in the first half of 1992 – and the flood tide of studies, reports and books, threatens to engulf us more completely than any movement of migrants could. This growth reflects much wider doubts about the decline of the old world. The new agonies of the Europeans over whether to create a European state, or the worries of Americans about free trade with Mexico, exhibit the fears sharply. Such fears are often based upon a myth: that the good old days of simple national power were a time of security. For, after all, the past includes the Great Depression and mass unemployment, and two world wars. Yet the insecurities are no less real, even if the explanation is false.

The fears are automatically generated by processes of violent economic change which seem to render worthless whole industries, cities and individual lives. The misery of the unemployed and the low-skilled in the developed countries is painfully visible in the great cities, nearly as painful now as the poverty of the developing countries. Protest against such conditions, which simultaneously reaffirms a fundamental loyalty to the old national state, has always needed to invent the myth of malevolent foreigners to blame for current disasters (then national governments are blamed for being the creatures of these foreign interests). The political establishments likewise need easy targets in order to deflect any popular anger which might be directed against them, even though in an integrated world system the power of governments to have a major impact upon domestic economic conditions is in decline. The myth of the foreigner is a vital part of the shadow play. And immigrants are not only foreigners; they also occupy despised roles in society. The poor immigrant is thus cast in an extraordinarily heroic role: the source of social discontent, the lightening conductor of society. Few governments can resist the temptation to blame the immigrant. Only the profound implausibility of the diagnosis checks such madness.

This book is mainly about the international migration of those who become unskilled workers in the developed countries (the 'brain drain' receives little attention, refugees somewhat more). The reasons for this choice of theme are explained in the text. The book is also about the relationship between what have hitherto been the heartlands of the system and the developing world. Even with this delimitation, the subject is vast and growing at speed. The account is not country-specific. Examples are chosen to illustrate points without being concerned as to representativeness. However, for reasons of language and accessibility, more are drawn from the experience in the United States and Britain than from elsewhere (although the situation in many more countries is discussed). This weakness may prompt premature generalization on too narrow a basis of information; if this is so, I owe the reader an apology.

The account starts from demand in the labour market, not from the supply of labour or the troubles of governments (the normal entry point). Despite the certainties of many who write on this subject, I have seen no convincing evidence that the bulk of migrant workers (as opposed to refugees) are driven out of their countries by deprivation, and much evidence that the movement and its composition (skills, education, gender, age) are highly sensitive to the demand for workers at the destination. The approach assumes implicitly that governments have only limited powers to prevent market demand operating – as limited as in other fields where market demand is strong.

The attempt to locate migration in the demand for workers is not always successful, since many of the key expressions of this demand are unknown. Take, for example, the labour brokers who simultaneously search out new markets and new sources of supply and organize the linkage between them. They are like termites, boring through the walls of state power. Yet they are almost unknown, particularly because their activity is often clandestine or illegal. The account suffers also because we are currently in a period of transition from national economies to a single global one, from a state-dominated to a market-led system. The old national concepts and assumptions cling to the main modes of analysis, yet they become increasingly arbitrary or blurred, undermined by new global factors. The 'national interest' grows equivocal.

The book's structure attempts to follow the logic of the central argument. The introductory chapter seeks to provide a swift overview of migration under capitalism, the reasons for the emergence of immigration controls, the features of the postwar period of high growth, and the characteristics of the emerging world economy. Chapter 2 identifies the sectors of the developed countries – with special reference to the United States and Britain – where the demand for low-paid workers remains high and where immigrants, legal or not, are increasingly required to fill the jobs abandoned by the native-born. Chapter 3 suggests something of the potential of developing countries to provide a home for the world's labour-intensive processes, now become increasingly difficult in the developed countries. There is also a case study of the creation of an instant cosmopolitan workforce in the oil-producing Middle East, with a suggestion of the creation of occupational specializations defined by nationality. For the high-growth developing countries (the cases are Malaysia, Korea, Hong Kong, Taiwan and Singapore), labour shortages have emerged swiftly in the late 1980s, inducing significant illegal immigration; there is a discussion of the efforts of governments to fight against this inevitable by-product of high economic growth (while still pursuing high growth).

In Chapter 4, we confront the issue of state power in the developed countries (particularly the United States, Europe and Japan) as the central problem for the movement of labour. This is pursued through an examination of the policies and practices of governments in their efforts to reconcile economic growth with the defence of what has come to be seen as a necessary condition for the exercise of sovereignty and the definition of nationality (there is also some account of refugee movement here). In Chapter 5, we stand back a little from the main thread to look at some of the social effects of emigration on the countries which export labour. Chapter 6 embodies a more theoretical explanation of movements from developing to developed countries, predicated on the different costs of the reproduction of labour and different average levels of productivity. From this there follows an outline of why migration to the developed countries must almost inevitably increase due to the particular type of labour demand emerging (even if it goes with increased emigration).

Chapter 7 is a manual of the more common arguments against immigration, with an overview of the evidence to help evaluate such propositions. Finally, Chapter 8 seeks to draw the threads together to reiterate the argument as to why modern capitalism is driven in this period to integrate capital flows, trade flows – and, increasingly, labour flows.

I am conscious that the argument is long and heavy with detail. It is also, whether valid or not, an exceedingly unpopular argument. A better writer or scholar would no doubt have been able to render the account more attractive and more persuasive, but one has to learn to live, regretfully, with one's deficiencies and hope that readers will not be too irked by them. In so far as the book escapes some of these deficiencies, it is in no mean measure attributable to the perseverance of ill-tried friends in correcting the text. Anna Enayat of I.B. Tauris did far more than is customarily called for in the line of a publisher's duty. I am most grateful also to Alasdair McAuley and Jo Beale for many suggestive insights and corrections (I have not, I fear, always been able to meet their exacting standards), to Tirril Harris for the sheer hard slog of putting some sense into muddled thought, and to Duncan Hallas for his erudite overview of the work. Thanks are also due to Frankie Liew for his excellent work on the graphics. As always and sadly, the errors of fact and judgement are exclusively my own.

THE NEW UNTOUCHABLES

I

Introduction: Capitalism and Migration

Introduction

Immigration in Europe and North America has become one of today's most sensitive issues of public policy and opinion. Yet the prominent place it occupies in political debate and in the media is no testimony to the truth of the fears it evokes. There are few areas of political life where opinions at variance with the known facts are advanced with such confidence and by people supposedly in authority. Everyone regards themself an expert in this field, and the fictions which so often pass for common sense are allowed free rein. Constant reiteration of these fictions ensures that, at least for some of the time, a majority of people are persuaded that immigration is a serious problem. This was not so in the past. Before the nineteenth century, rulers usually welcomed immigrants and the skills and capital they brought with them. An expanding population was a sign of expanding power, and princes rejoiced at the misfortune of their fellow monarchs in losing their subjects. Today, immigrants attract no welcome; and for refugees, compassion, let alone economic interest, has disappeared.

Increased migration is inevitable in an integrating world economy. In developed countries, trade and capital beat the paths of integration followed by workers. But to most people imports and foreign investment are abstract and remote phenomena, whereas foreign faces seen on the street and the foreign tongues heard in shops or on buses are an immediate, tangible reality. Few make the connection between the foreigners they encounter in such public places with the workers who staff the hospitals, till the land, cut the coal, drive the buses. And when they do, it is all too often to accuse foreigners of stealing work that should rightfully be done by natives, even though the natives have long rejected many of these jobs. Most people's fears, however, are not only about work but also about a threat to the political order – the right of citizens to determine national affairs. It is not accidental that the arrival of migrant workers is so often described as 'an invasion', even though immigrants are usually both small as a proportion of the population and among the poorest.

Although the idea of impoverished Mexicans seizing Washington and assuming control of the United States is laughable, in their rhetoric, governments and political leaders trade on such absurd fears – and, indeed, perhaps share the nightmare. Yet increasingly their public embrace of anti-immigration fantasies is in practice tempered with realism. For economic growth very often leads to demand for workers at a given wage exceeding local supply. So immigration rules are eased to admit, say, agricultural workers, domestics, entertainers, nurses. And the illegal movements often required (though to an unknown extent) to equilibrate the domestic labour market are quietly tolerated. In addition, governments always make special exceptions for the highly skilled and the rich. They cannot afford to impede the activity of multinational corporations and the increasing numbers of their staff who are required to move for extended periods between countries or the armies of consultants and other businessmen who constantly cross borders. Already by the mid-1990s, the trans-border paths have been beaten down, despite the continuing illusion that the norm of social life is national isolation.

This contradiction – between segregated national spaces and the increasing international movement of workers driven by the world labour market – is the theme of this book. We begin, however, with the background to the current situation, looking briefly at how the cross-border demand for labour has expressed itself historically, and at the origins in this century of efforts to control international migration.

Capitalism Historically Considered

Governments in the past were, when they considered such matters, more concerned to prevent emigration (and the export of capital) than immigration. If immigration increased the power of the state, emigration supposedly reduced it. However, emigration could be encouraged in certain circumstances: for example, as an instrument of colonization. Despite Britain's experience with its rebellious American colonies, emigrants were seen, up to very recent times, as a means of spreading political influence and expanding markets. Furthermore, as the capitalist economic system spread, migration came to be seen as a means of making up for an inadequate supply of labour in the colonies. Between

10 and 20 million Africans were snatched from their homes in West Africa and forced to cross the Atlantic to man the plantations of North and South America. From 1800 up to 1930, some 60 to 70 million Europeans followed the pioneers to the New World; about a quarter of them subsequently returned. In the second half of the nineteenth century, and especially during the two decades preceding the First World War, the movement expanded to an unprecedented flow – taking about one-fifth of the 1840 European population; some 60 per cent of them went to the United States (Carr-Saunders, 1960). Possibly some 50 million Indians and Chinese (between 1840 and 1930) were recruited by the gangers of empire for work in California, the Caribbean, Southeast Asia and Africa. By 1930, possibly 30 million Indians had gone to work abroad, about 24 million of them subsequently returning home (Tinker, 1977).

As trade expanded – by a factor of 25 in the century before 1913 – capital flowed round the world to create the sinews of a new world economy. Yet the demand for labour seemed continually to exceed the supply, and this forced increases in productivity. This was true even in the European heartlands where labour shortages were less obvious than in the Americas or European possessions in Africa and Australasia. In the leading countries of industrializing Europe, labour demand continued to spill over the national borders to neighbouring countries. Even as emigrants were escaping in large numbers, especially from the countryside, immigrants from abroad were moving into the cities. The British depended heavily upon workers from Ireland. The French drew in Belgians, Italians, Poles, Spaniards (Cross, 1983), as well as workers from the French possessions abroad, particularly the Maghreb in North Africa. Belgium recruited Italians, Germany recruited Poles (Castles and Miller, 1993). Especially during the two world wars, the appetite for workers was prodigious – in the case of Germany, something in the order of 8 million foreign workers were forced into the country to work in the Second World War.

Thus, up to the 1970s, the historical record would suggest that any reasonable level of economic growth in Europe would lead to labour demand exceeding local supply. Far from Europe being sharply distinguished from the Americas – the so-called 'countries of immigration' – all advanced industrializing powers required immigration to sustain growth. The past cannot tell us what will happen in the future, but it is important not to forget that immigration is by no means a modern phenomenon. Everyone in Europe is ultimately descended from immigrants, some more recently than others.

The Socialized State

If economic expansion came so swiftly to rely on an inflow of foreign workers, how did governments come to jeopardize economic growth by imposing immigration controls? The drive to control came from sources quite distinct from the needs of the labour market. It was, rather, a product of the creation of a new polity.

Historically, the mass of the population in Europe were not regarded by their rulers as part of a nation, the foundation of society. That privilege was reserved for the class of great landowners, the aristocracy. The business magnates and bankers, where they existed, might claim financial leverage over the monarchs; and the more fortunate among them governed independent city-states, some of which, like Venice, might rival the great territorial lordships. Only in Holland, after a long-drawn-out popular war against Spanish imperial government, did the perimeter of the nation begin to extend beyond the rich. In the new United States, after the War of Independence against British imperial control, and in France, following the Revolution, the idea of the nation for the first time came to include most of the population, now transformed from 'subjects' to free 'citizens'.

However, much of Europe retained the old forms. Only in the second half of the nineteenth century did most of the European states come to emulate the same process, one symbolized by the gradual extension of the franchise (since the right to vote was the fundamental mark of the citizen; subjects were required only to obey). The process was impelled, we can speculate, less by a conversion to liberalism on the part of the ruling orders of Europe than by the simultaneous conjuncture of several processes:

(1) The rise of new business classes, which demanded equal access to the old corruption that was the state, and a reduction in the favouring of landed interests.

(2) The emergence of populist nationalism, created in part by new national markets and business classes, with the affirmation that sovereignty should be embedded in the willing concurrence of the mass of the population.

(3) The increasing use of intensive systems of production that required an educated labour force and conscious participation in the process of manufacture. The creation of mass educational systems, a popular press, open electoral contests between rival political parties, the extension of trade unions – all were thus both cause and effect of the rise of mass involvement in the political process. Inevitably,

the issue of popular welfare could no longer be excluded from the national political debate.

(4) The increasing rivalries between the Great Powers and the arrival of the era of total war obliged governments to foster much higher degrees of social unity than had been required hitherto. This was an urgent question since industrialization itself had, it seemed, generated among the new industrial working class a much higher degree of social alienation than ever before; unlike the old peasantry, the new workers were strategically located in the new economy with the power to bring it to a halt.

The new nations had to be fashioned from the heterogeneity that pertained in most countries. The socialized state required an identity, whether it be symbolized in a common set of physical features (racial descent), a culture, language, religion or some combination of these. Members of the old cosmopolitan aristocracy were also forced to acquire a vernacular identity, to become quasi-citizens of one country rather than proud members of a European caste (with relatives scattered across the map of Europe, regardless of the new boundaries). Furthermore, the 'nationalization' of the population required the subordination of the 'cosmopolitan bourgeoisie' (Jones, 1987); in material terms, business-men now became increasingly dependent upon alignment with one or other of the competing states. National capitalism became the norm.

Every major state endeavoured to instil social homogeneity in its people, to force their unruly shape into a predetermined corset of national identity – as witnessed in the social marginalization of languages and accents not recognized as socially acceptable. The French revolutionaries set out to destroy regional languages. The Prussian monarchs endeavoured to Germanize the Polish inhabitants of their eastern domains (and, when the Poles resisted, tried to drive them out and resettle the lands with German subjects). The Austro-Hungarian emperors found themselves trying to Germanize the empire, while the Magyar gentry attempted to Hungarianize their southern Slav depend-encies: in each case, the effort to homogenize intensified the disinte-gration of the empire, thereby encouraging heterogeneity. Even the Russian autocrats, the tsars, tried to Russify their polyglot populations, and in so doing instituted the fearful anti-Semitic pogroms of the 1890s.

The enterprise automatically created minorities – those who were excluded on one or other ground from the newly invented national identity. Jews, gypsies and others, who had been no more than a component in the social mosaic of Europe, suddenly found themselves isolated as foreigners. Indeed, their newly invented foreign character was a key factor in creating the social unity of everyone else – without their existence, ruling orders would have been obliged to invent them. It was the historical role of Polish and Russian Jewry to be the vital means for the invention of a new Poland and a new Russia.

Embedded in this process was an important, if implicit, bargain – a social contract. In allowing the mass of the population to enter the nation, the state demanded the complete loyalty of its new citizens. In return, the state promised to protect its citizens, and in some cases to offer them a measure of guaranteed welfare against want. The social contract seemed to work. Despite the appalling conditions of nineteenth-century capitalism, the major part of the population did not rebel. Furthermore, through two world wars and, in the 1930s, the Great Depression, the sorely tried peoples of the developed countries remained astonishingly loyal to their respective states. The state system thus held (despite the brief rebellion of the Russians in 1917) in the face of un-precedented devastation and popular deprivation.

The creation of the new socially exclusive states had powerful impli-cations for the ancient patterns of movement of people. In the nine-teenth century, outside the domains of the Russian tsars, travel across borders was generally free of legal restrictions – passports, visas, resi-dence and work permits were not required. It was still possible as late as 1889 for an International Emigration Conference to declare:

> We affirm the right of the individual to the fundamental liberty accorded to him by every civilized nation to come and go and dispose of his person and his destinies as he pleases. (Thomas, 1961: 9)

The arrival of the socialized state – the compact between state and citizens – not only identified minorities; it also made those from abroad a problem. By the First World War, virtually all the Great Powers were seeking to control movements across their borders. War itself provided a crescendo of hysteria on the issue, sufficient to reverse long-standing commitments and practices relating to the freedom to move. By the 1920s, most governments had taken powers to control movement. In the two decades that followed, these powers were of limited value. Economic stagnation and the Great Depression damped down labour demand and led to long-term unemployment. Few wanted to migrate, and indeed international movement fell to very low levels.

The Resumption of Economic Growth

By 1950, opinion in the developed countries took for granted a world composed of separate national economies, managed by governments in part as if they were giant diversified corporations. In the empires, it was thought that independence of the possessions would bring about a replication of the same form of national economy. There was still much intellectual clearing up to be done to reconcile this historically unusual role for governments with an inherited liberal and market tradition. But such puzzles preoccupied a minority of intellectuals. For the rest, a social-democratic conception ruled parties of both right and left in much of Europe: a society, governed by a powerful state, managed through great representative corporations (business, the trade unions, professional associations), and founded on a popular sovereignty based upon a social contract between government and governed. Even in the United States, a similar conception had infected public opinion considerably more than official doctrines acknowledged.

Even as this intellectual orthodoxy was being established, growth in the developed countries took off on a scale and for a duration that were without precedent. As in the earlier phase of sustained growth, between 1840 and 1870, a cosmopolitan capitalism reasserted itself, but this time outside the political framework of empires. The governments of the developed countries found it increasingly necessary, in order to benefit from sustained growth, to dismantle the machinery of protection and state direction which had been constructed over at least the 30 years up to 1950, and to open up to external markets, to the free flow of goods and, to a lesser extent, of capital. In so doing, governments purchased growth at the cost of power to shape their domestic economies.

Even when growth was checked in the first major recession of the postwar period (1973–75), the process of integrating the national economies was not reversed. Indeed, the great surge of integration of world capital was still to come, in the 1980s. There was no retreat into national (or, as before, imperial) autarky, as had occurred under the impact of the Great Depression of the early 1930s. And there was no plunge into war, as there had been before; on the contrary, one of the contenders in the great conflict between East and West that dominated the postwar period, the Soviet Union, imploded under the impact of the new global economy.

The spread of reform, of 'structural adjustment', extended from Europe and North America to developing countries and to the former members of the Eastern bloc. It seemed as if all governments were obliged to open up to world markets and to dismantle formerly strategic parts of the state's role in the domestic economy. The results of reform were very uneven, not least in the developed countries as they began to dismantle the old social contract. However, in East and Southeast

8 THE NEW UNTOUCHABLES

Asia, a group of economies – including China – attained extraordinarily high rates of growth, creating for the first time a new source of world growth.

International Migration

After the Second World War, Europe experienced population movement on an extraordinary scale as the new political order settled down. Some 25 to 30 million moved westwards. West Germany was particularly affected, with 8 or 9 million people claiming German descent ('ethnic' Germans) arriving up to 1956, and a further 5.5 million up to 1989 (including a large concentration in the years before the 1961 closure of the border between East and West Germany). There were also major movements in other parts of the world. The partition of old British India into Pakistan and India led to the estimated flight of between 15 and 17 million people. Some 6 million Japanese returned to their traditional homeland from Japan's possessions abroad (particularly Taiwan and Korea). Arabs fled from the Palestinian territories appropriated by the new State of Israel. The old order in China fled the victorious Communist armies to Taiwan.

In Europe, there was an extraordinary process of economic growth in the late 1940s and 1950s. In the five years to 1958 (that is, after the period of recovery from the war), European industrial output increased by 30 per cent – 50 per cent in West Germany, 48 per cent in France, and 40 per cent in Italy. The newcomers thus rapidly found jobs. Indeed, so high was the continuing demand for labour that employers competed to make their job offers more attractive. There followed unprecedented increases in wages and improvements in conditions of work, and extraordinary improvements in living standards.

There was also a radical reorganization of the labour force in both Europe and America, away from the old labour-intensive sectors of production. Agriculture, for example, experienced a rapid decline in its employment share (see Figure 1.1). Married women were drawn out of the home into paid employment (an issue discussed later). Sellers of labour-intensive manufactured goods dispatched buyers abroad to find new sources of supply, since wage rates were making production at home too expensive; and they were instrumental in stimulating the spread of manufacturing to other countries, in particular to what became known as the four 'Asian tigers' – Hong Kong, Taiwan, South Korea and Singapore – and later to Southeast Asia and China.

Yet the appetite for workers was still not satisfied. Employers and

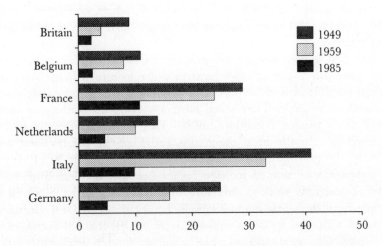

Sources: 1949 and 1959 – ECE, 1964: 28, Table 29; 1985 – Bean, 1989: 205–55.

Figure 1.1   Share of agriculture in total employment, 1949–85 (%)

governments in Europe became preoccupied from the mid-1950s with finding new sources of supply. West Germany, with the most prodigious increases in output and demand for labour, signed agreements to obtain workers from Italy (1955 and 1965), Greece and Spain (1964), Morocco (1963), Portugal and Turkey (1964), Tunisia (1965), Yugoslavia (1968), and even Korea (1962). Given the turnover of workers – some returning home – the stock had reached some 2.5 million each for France and Germany by 1973 (10 to 11 per cent of the respective labour forces), and 600,000 for Switzerland (30 per cent of the workforce). The total for Europe was some 11.5 million (Payne, 1974), of which about 9 million were from developing countries.

The labour market was highly competitive. For example, Turkish miners, brought to Belgium's Borinage area, were wooed by German employers to desert for the Ruhr; 12,000 Moroccans were promised tied housing to leave France for Belgium, The Netherlands and Germany. Originally, the Luxembourg authorities did not grant Italian miners the right to settle, but they were subsequently obliged to reverse the decision in order to keep the miners' services. In the same way, the German government was obliged to change its policy of recruiting single workers to allow the entry of their families – and employers were eager to take on spouses; by 1968, about one-fifth of foreign workers in Europe were women, and three-quarters of foreign-born wives were in paid employment.

The first generation of immigrant workers in manual occupations were generally eager to work hard in order to return home with the largest possible sum of savings. They therefore avoided unemployment as much as possible. They saved hard, surviving on inadequate diets, living in the poorest conditions, undertaking the worst jobs – often the night-shifts – in the most dangerous and high-risk occupations, and working the maximum amount of overtime (Bourguignon et al., 1977). As a result, they tended to have higher sickness, accident and death rates. Immigrant workers therefore allowed many native workers to escape from the worst manual labour. For example, in West Germany between 1961 and 1968, 1.1 million Germans left manual occupations for white-collar jobs, and over half a million foreign workers replaced them. Thus the 'structural adjustment' of economies was accelerated by the availability of foreign-born workers.

The manual occupations most concerned were in agriculture and mining in the 1950s, and in construction by the early 1960s. By the late 1960s, in Germany, 45 per cent of immigrant workers were employed in manufacturing – three out of every five of these in Germany's key export industries, mechanical engineering and chemicals (Kayser, 1971). Some 29 per cent of immigrant workers were engaged in vehicle manufacture (compared to 6 per cent of those native-born). Thus immigrant workers made a disproportionate contribution to Germany's spectacular export performance (Böhning and Maillat, 1974: 93). One of the more extreme examples of ethnic concentration occurred at Ford's Cologne plants, where 75 per cent of the workers were Turkish (54 per cent of Cologne's Turkish workers worked at Ford). The company sought to create a 'homogeneous' labour force in order to minimize management costs through the use of only two languages, German and Turkish.

In France, immigrants were concentrated in construction, metallurgy, chemicals manufacture, rubber and asbestos; one-fifth of foreign workers were employed as farm labourers. In time, as in Germany, immigrant workers followed the native-born, vacating the particular sectors in agriculture, mining and constructions that were their starting point, in favour of manufacturing, particularly the mass-assembly industries.

Knock-on effects were experienced in the immigrants' home countries. Malians and Senegalese went to work in Sicily as Sicilians moved north, and in Spain as Spaniards moved to France. Egyptians and Pakistanis migrated to Greece as Greeks went to work in Germany. Poles went to work in Germany, Scandinavia and Britain, while Russians and Ukrainians took jobs in Poland. Egyptians worked on Jordanian farms, and Jordan's Palestinians worked in the Gulf. Indonesians manned Malaysia's plantations, while Malays migrated to Singapore. This was not, of course, a process of simple substitution – the skilled emigrated (and became unskilled at their destination); others of lesser skill replaced them; and migrants took the unskilled jobs. Migration was very much more complex than simple flows in one direction.

The political turbulence in North America and Europe in the 1960s signalled a reconsideration of the process, and the onset of recession in 1973 marked the end of open movements of labour. The reuniting of families became the only ground for entry into another country, and even here much tighter control was exercised. In Britain, with one of the poorest rates of economic growth in Europe, regulations on immigration were introduced in 1962, tightened in 1968, and the door supposedly forever closed in 1971 (that is, well before the world recession). The French strengthened their immigration regulations in the 1960s. Germany, for its part, continued to expand its workforce up to 1973; even after that date there was much opposition to controls within the government and among employers. However, attempts to discourage immigration had occurred earlier – denying family members work permits, banning immigrants from settling in some areas, and so on. Indeed, the Federal Constitutional Court was obliged to rule in 1973 that it was unconstitutional to discourage immigrant workers from remaining in Germany. Yet the labour market was always more effective than governments in discouraging migration: in 1974, a year of slump, Europe's stock of foreign workers declined by a quarter of a million.

There had been sporadic opposition in most European countries to large-scale immigration, but this had been relatively marginal. Official reactions in the late 1960s for the first time focused public attention on immigration as an important issue, and as such were the prelude to the rise of anti-immigrant political movements in the 1970s. Governments now began to argue that immigration control was a primary means to combat racism against immigrants, rather than itself being an important source of racism.

To reduce the numbers entering was, in these circumstances, not enough. Governments needed to show a commitment to reducing the stock of migrant workers. An extraordinary panoply of measures was introduced at different times by European governments to induce people to leave or not to enter in the first place: from direct payments to persuade people to go, to endless bureaucratic delays, bullying, police harassment and deportations to create a climate of fear that would encourage departure. The sporadic, feverish, frequently deceitful and

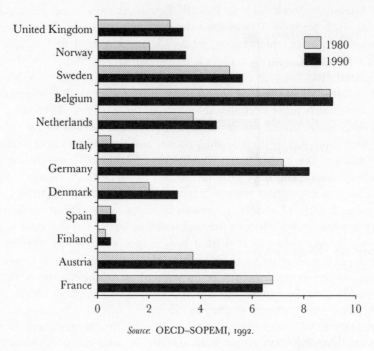

Source: OECD–SOPEMI, 1992.

Figure 1.2   Immigrants as a share of selected European populations, 1980 to 1990 (%)

expensive campaign to decrease the size of a particular group of inhabitants succeeded only in making immigrants a favoured political scapegoat. Only occasionally did liberal opinion rebel against this sordid and thoroughly dishonourable persecution – as when American churches organized clandestine networks to smuggle and protect illegal entrants to the United States, or when courts struck down the more grotesque executive orders.

Few established political leaders are willing to risk conceding the reality of the situation, especially when the anti-immigrant lobby bays for blood. It seems politically dangerous to admit that (as in Germany) half the miners and half the refuse collectors are immigrants; that it would be impossible to run the railways without them, and likewise most of the hotels, restaurants and cleaning services. In the mid-1980s, Stuttgart City Corporation estimated the impact of the loss of three-quarters of the city's 36,500 foreign workers, and concluded that it would be impossible to maintain public transport and services and the

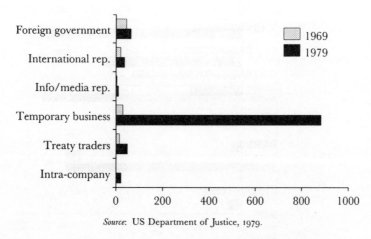

Source: US Department of Justice, 1979.

Figure 1.3 Short-term entrants to the United States, 1969 and 1979 (thousands)

construction industry; many other activities would be disastrously affected, including schools and nurseries; unemployment would rise sharply and the quality of life deteriorate markedly (*The Economist*, 4 February 1984).

The agitation to end immigration and reduce the existing numbers of immigrants was not susceptible to evidence. Yet throughout the 1980s the mobility of populations continued to increase despite confident declarations that the issue would be resolved. The reuniting of families, despite all the harassment, continued to increase the proportion of the foreign-born population in nearly all European countries (see Figure 1.2). Even in France, where there was supposedly a decline in numbers, naturalization policy was generous; the foreign-born population continued to increase (although many ethnically French people were included in the statistics). Yet many immigrants did return to their original homes, many permanently.

Other movements also continued to expand. Figure 1.3 shows the extraordinary growth of temporary business entrants to the United States: by 1989, the number had reached 2.5 million (and intra-company transfers of 160,000). Tourists, at least some of whom stayed on to work as illegal immigrants, increased in the 1980s from 7 to 16 million.

Worldwide there are increasing numbers of staff of transnational corporations living abroad – an estimate for 1986 puts the number at

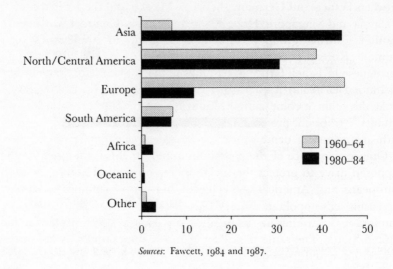

Sources: Fawcett, 1984 and 1987.

Figure 1.4 Immigrants to the United States, origins, 1960–64 compared to 1980–84 (%)

25 million of the 65 million staff employed by these institutions (65 per cent of them living in Europe and North America). The more recently developed countries are following suit (Skeldon, 1992). Business executives moving abroad for three- to four-year stints experience few of the impediments to crossing borders that other workers face – indeed, to most observers they seem 'invisible' (Gould and Findlay, 1994: 21).

Political contingencies also lead governments to ease restrictions for special groups of people – as when the German government permitted entries from Eastern Europe for particular jobs (construction, agriculture, hotels and restaurants). The legal entrants opened the way for the illegal – some claimed that in 1990 there were 2 million Poles working in Germany on three-month visitors' visas (Heyden, 1991). German demand for workers, whatever the macro-economic performance of the economy, seems insatiable. Blaschke (1994: 90) reports that in 1990–91 the German government gave permission for 800 Poles to enter for work; yet in October 1990, German employers applied to recruit 70,289 under various schemes, 98 per cent of the workers by name.

The volume of trans-border daily commuting is also increasing – from Poland, the Czech Republic, Slovakia and Austria to Germany;

between France and Germany; between Mexico and the United States, Malaysia and Singapore, Hong Kong and China. Contract workers are another growing group – 20 million of them in Appleyard's 1989 estimate. Korean construction workers were busy in Africa; Thais and Portuguese in Israeli farming; Filipinos in many places (for Canada, see Richmond et al., in Appleyard, 1989).

At the other income extreme from unskilled contract workers, consultants – 'transient professionals' (Domenach and Picoud, 1989) – grew with an increasing demand for specialized services internationally.

One consequence of these continuous movements is that, despite the supposed drive to protect the social, ethnic or cultural homogeneity of Europeans and Americans, the life of big cities continues to display increasing cosmopolitanization. The diversification of the sources of immigrants is striking in this respect – as Figure 1.4 illustrates for the United States. The same is true for Canada: for example, Asian immigration increased from 8.4 per cent of the total in the 1960s to 29.1 in the late 1970s. In Europe (including Scandinavia), comparing the 1970s and 1990s, the proportion of the foreign-born population in each country born in Europe declined almost everywhere, while the proportion born outside Europe increased (OECD–SOPEMI, 1992: 135, Appendix).

The growing diversity of sources is also remarkable, such that each major city appears increasingly like a microcosm of the world's peoples. Iranians work in Tokyo, Lebanese in Stockholm, Pakistanis in Oslo, Senegalese in Rome, Chinese in Budapest (Szoke, 1992). Filipinas are everywhere, a genuine global labour force – maids gossiping and smoking on their day off in downtown Hong Kong or Singapore, working Japanese farms, running the duty-free shops of Bahrain, cleaning most of the world's cities from London to São Paulo.

To summarize, then, the period of rapid postwar growth in Europe resumed processes not seen on the same scale since before the First World War. This was true not only in terms of increasing international trade and capital movements, but also in terms of the increasing movements of workers. However, after the first major world recession of 1973–75, the admission of primary immigration was suspended – while governments continued to seek economic growth as if this were consistent with a stagnating labour supply. The beneficial process of the earlier periods (for example, 1950–73), in which the native-born were able to improve their position in the labour market while immigrants raised their income by moving into the jobs of the native-born, came to a halt. It was replaced by a situation of declining real income for the unskilled workers of the United States, and long-term unemployment for those in Europe.

A New World Economy?

The increased movement of workers internationally is still very small as a proportion of the world's workforce, and even smaller relative to the extraordinary growth of traded goods, let alone the spectacular (by past standards) 1980s' growth in the movement of capital. These processes bear witness to the arrival of an integrated world economy, emerging out of its constituent national parts and imposing on the old national economic order new and unforeseeable processes of restructuring. In many developed countries such processes seem to be epitomized in the decline of manufacturing employment (and the matching rise in services). If these trends continue, the share of manufacturing in national employment in the United States, for example, will decline from 27 per cent in 1970 to 12 per cent by the year 2005 – at which stage manufacturing will be going the way of agriculture in terms of jobs.

Institutionally, the old socialized state, the embodiment of the social contract, is also being reordered. It had for so long been the dominant partner in the national alliance that its withdrawal in favour of private interests – those supposedly integrated into world markets – is continuing to cause social shocks. Furthermore, world markets seem to demand such a degree of flexibility on the part of national economies in response to external changes, that the old structures produced by the political will of the social contract are no longer defensible – the large public sectors directed along political rather than economic lines, welfare, health, education and housing programmes, and so on. Nowhere have the results of this reorganization been more dramatic than in the case of the most extreme forms of military-nationalist autarky in Eastern Europe and the former Soviet Union.

If the old command economies of the Eastern bloc could not resist the impact of world markets without reorganizing beyond recognition, the centralized transnational corporations were even less able to do so. Networks, federations, alliances, outsourcing, empowerment – the buzzwords of management studies in the early 1990s – may only muddily relate to reality, but they indicate the widespread reform being forced on companies. The dangers of not reforming quickly or radically enough – so painfully evident in the old Soviet Union – were also apparent in the afflictions of the largest corporations like IBM and General Motors.

As regards the labour force, the changes appear no less dramatic. In the old order, a relatively isolated national economy supposedly allowed the state to manage it, ensuring stable high employment in regulated conditions, with permanent lifetime work for the majority. The decline

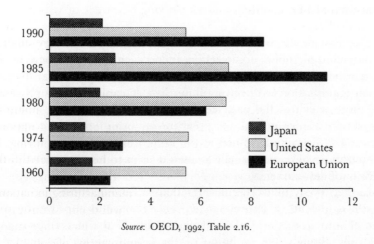

Source: OECD, 1992, Table 2.16.

Figure 1.5   Unemployment as a proportion of the total labour force (%)

of manufacturing industry – the decline in permanent full-time employment of mainly men – was an early sign of change here. Relatively high unemployment became an accepted feature of the labour market and, particularly in Europe, long-term unemployment became an established pattern (see Figure 1.5). However, 'non-employment' – that is, withdrawal from seeking work altogether – became even more important. In the late 1980s, unemployment and non-employment together accounted for something in the order of 10 per cent of male workers in the prime working age groups (25–54 years). In older age groups, early retirement and retirement on disability pension accounted for an even larger proportion of the age groups involved (Freeman, 1994).

For those employed, the nature of work seems to have changed ('seems' is the right word since the factual evidence is more ambiguous). Many more workers, especially those entering work for the first time, are concentrated in the temporary, casual, part-time, sub-contracted and self-employed categories – a development that has created many more opportunities for women workers. This change gives employers much greater flexibility of response to the apparently more capricious demand generated in world markets and the greater competitive pressure on profit margins. For many workers, the distinction between 'work' and 'non-work' (or unemployment) is becoming less clear than before, and the standard working day, week or year may well be in decline.

The change affects the possibility of stable collective bargaining and traditional trade-union organization. Indeed, the sectors of the economy most radically reduced by structural change are those where trade-union organization has been traditionally strongest. The growth sectors are those which in the past seemed the least promising for union organization. Hence one of the great institutions of the old corporatist society has been undermined at the same time as the largest business organizations have increasingly focused their energies upon global rather than national markets.

In the heyday of worker immigration to Europe, those who actively sought to defend or improve their rights aspired to improve the position of immigrants until it was equal to that of the native-born. Paradoxically, though, the evolution of the labour market has tended to push the native-born closer to the conditions of insecurity experienced by the immigrant. Indeed, immigrant workers – leaving aside the issue of skills – are in fact the most flexible of all, and thus best suited to the new pattern of labour demand. The first generation immigrant had few family or other resources to fall back on, was unfamiliar with local mores that governed work intensity, and was driven to earn as much as possible in a short space of time. Nevertheless, a residual commitment to defend, at least in principle, the social contract with the native-born inhibited governments from exploiting this matching of labour demand and immigrant supply.

Social Crisis

The social changes brought about by – or coinciding with – the opening up of national economies are, for many of those worst affected, an indictment of the social order. The poorest fifth of the population in many developed countries experienced declining real incomes in the 1970s and 1980s, and in Europe historically high levels of unemployment, particularly long-term unemployment. By the early 1990s, some 18 per cent of the 81 million full-time employed American workers earned less than the official poverty level (compared to 12 per cent in 1980); poverty was increasingly concentrated in households headed by single mothers (the references here are legion, but see McKinley et al., 1990; Office of Technology Assessment, 1991; Levy and Murnane, 1992; Mishel, 1992; Michie and Grieve Smith, 1994). An increase in inequality of income has also been apparent – a particularly critical factor for the

maintenance of the old social contract, within which none was supposed to gain disproportionately.

More damning still for the idea of a social contract, the worsening
in the condition of the poor is not simply attributable to changes in the
labour market. Changes in government policy have served to exagger-
ate the process. In the United States, while overall federal spending on
welfare increased three and a half times between 1965 and 1987, the
bulk of the increase went to the aged, whereas spending upon the rest
of poor households declined. While the picture in Europe is more
mixed, even in Germany, the number living below the official poverty
line doubled in the 1980s.

Some commentators (for example, UNDP, 1991: 2) see these changes
as undermining the cohesion of society. Certainly there seems to be a
higher level of insecurity and sense of dissatisfaction with existing
governments today, regardless of their political persuasion, even when
the statistical evidence shows no indication of a decline in average living
standards. On the other hand, campaigns to lower taxation and reduce
social-security programmes – as in the United States – do not suggest
a continuation of the sympathies which underpinned the old social-
democratic order. A new global economy seems only to have removed
national responsibility in favour of those who are able to make good
when allowed to do so.

Hearts are also hardened by the perception that there is rarely an
absolute shortage of jobs. In London or Washington, at times of peak
unemployment, there were still shortages of unskilled labour; but at pay
rates so low and in conditions so bad, it would have meant self-
destruction for the native-born worker to take them. In any case, it was
implicit in the popular morality implied by the social contract that no
one should be forced to take such jobs. In New York, in the two to three
thousand garment shops in the high-fashion garment industry, there are
perpetual vacancies – to work a ten-hour day at a furious, piece-rate-
governed pace, in dark and dangerous conditions for pay which was at
worst, in the 1980s, no more than $1 an hour (compared to a federal
minimum wage of $3.35). Single mothers with dependent children could
not take such jobs even if they lived close enough to avoid travel costs;
but illegal immigrants could.

People develop their own diagnosis of this social condition. The social
decline of the bottom fifth of the population is a result of the internationalization of the economy, and is to be compared with conditions
of relative prosperity in the 1950s and 1960s in much more closed economies. Internationalization, it is further said, occurs because governments
betray the trust vested in them by the people and sell out to foreign

interests. To many, the clearest sign of that abandonment of people by their traditional protectors lies not so much in the foreign-made shirt or the foreign-owned company (if it could any longer be identified as foreign-owned), but in the growing presence on the streets of the foreign worker, supposedly undercutting the native-born by doing work that all decent native-born workers would spurn.

Given this diagnosis, the fluctuating level of racist incidents and support for racist parties is surprisingly small. The poor have so far been immured in their private grief, lacking access to the politics of the broader society. Yet the Establishments of North America and Europe are, at least in theory, remarkably vulnerable to the charge of betrayal, particularly because their own position ultimately rests upon a nationalist commitment which also, implicitly or explicitly, targets the foreigner as the source of all problems. And they have clearly identified immigration as an important issue, the source of social problems.

There is never a solid argument for a robust and unsentimental internationalism, an acknowledgement that the material conditions of life of the native-born depend upon the work of foreigners. At best there is a plea not to be unpleasant. Those with a material concern with internationalism, the global businessmen and bankers, are not trusted to do more than advance their own narrow interests. Those who historically championed worker internationalism, the Marxists and socialists, have all too often retired into defending the old nationalism as the only way to defend the poor.

In the end, the issue is not about immigration at all. It is about the integrity of the state – its supposed omnipotence eroded by the new global economy, its responsibilities to the poorest citizens abandoned. Thus, on the back of the lowly immigrant, a new world order is being created.

2

The Sweated Trades in the Developed Countries

Introduction

There is, in theory, a degree of substitutability between worker migration, capital flows and trade. In principle, depending on the relative prices involved, capital can employ workers either as migrants in a developed country, supplying the local market with goods, or as non-migrants in their country of origin, making goods which are then imported by the developed country. On this simple theorem, immigration controls in a developed country would, if capital movement is unrestricted, produce an increase in both the export of capital and the import of goods. The price of immigration controls would then be a deterioration in the balance of payments (both on trade and capital accounts) and a reduction in employment (the loss of the jobs which would have been created by the capital that has 'migrated').

In practice, there are many more complicating factors involved. Even if the theory were valid in this simple form, it only holds in the case of 'movable' jobs – pre-eminently manufacturing, but also now, with improved telecommunications, some important services (for example, software programming and data processing). The boundaries between movable and immovable jobs are not stable; technical innovations shift them. Nevertheless it is still true that a mass of services for the population of the developed countries cannot be moved – or at least, the consumers must be moved to the service (as happens, for example, with international tourism).

There is a peculiarity in pricing many of these services. Theoretically, the average level of pay in society relates to the average level of productivity in the economy at large – expanding sectors getting above the average, declining below. However, the average is pulled up by the sectors where productivity can be most easily identified and, usually, increased most rapidly. In the past, the bench-mark has been manufacturing, and this has pulled up remuneration in all other sectors, including those which have experienced no increases in productivity – or where the concept makes little sense. For example, actors playing *Hamlet* cannot play it twice as fast; teachers cannot teach at double the speed; doctors cannot examine in half the time. Of course, productivity gains can be made in the organization of theatres; teachers, with the use of film, video and other technical innovations, can help children to learn more thoroughly and perhaps more quickly; and doctors with access to computerized records can increase the speed and accuracy of diagnosis. But the general point remains: there is a great difference between activities in terms of the potential to increase productivity. From this it follows that, if the average is pulled up by the leading sectors, the income of society must shift towards those activities with the poorest potential to increase productivity. Low-productivity labour-intensive activities would become increasingly and disproportionately expensive, which in turn would produce a decline in demand.

In a closed economy, people might decide that this was perfectly reasonable – some consumers would find substitutes; some sectors would move to full automation, with the highest levels of labour productivity; while the bulk of the labour force would become concentrated in the most labour-intensive sectors, which in turn would become increasingly expensive. However, national economies and companies are not isolated; they are increasingly competing in a global system (and the global system is increasingly competing in their domestic market), where the levels of pay and average productivity are very different. The more that is paid to the low-productivity sectors, the greater is the competition to supply cheaper services – either through cheaper workers moving to the country concerned or the services (or consumers) moving. There are already many examples – such as Americans travelling to Mexico to use the cheaper medical services there. In sum, the logic of a closed economy conflicts directly with that of an open one in terms of the pricing of labour power.

Furthermore, the overpricing (by world standards) of particular services can damage the competitive capacity of a whole national economy. High medical or teaching costs can raise the cost of current output and, unless offset by disproportionately large increases in pro-ductivity, damage the tradable-goods sectors. The logic of income-pro-ductivity imbalances, along with innovations, rising expectations and changing demography, is the general source of the apparently universal phenomenon in developed countries of rising medical, educational and other public and social-service costs. Equally universal is the struggle on the part of governments to find means to contain these costs – or to escape responsibility through privatization (or quasi-privatization by establishing competitive cost centres within public ownership).

The competitive international context sets limits to the decisions which can be taken concerning domestic pay rates. The decline of economic boundaries between countries vastly extends the potential combinations of capital and labour that are possible, and the opportunities facing employers. This may not express itself simply in terms of levels of pay, but rather in the quality of labour at a given level of pay. Employers can gain access to young educated workers (often women) abroad or as immigrants at rates of pay which would otherwise attract only native workers capable of the lowest productivity – the aged, disabled or handicapped (and, depending upon the social-security system and alternative opportunities in the black economy, they may not attract even them).

The movement of labour and capital, then, may be partial alternatives. However, in a world economy with free movement, this may not simply mean the movement of skilled or energetic young workers from developing countries to become unskilled workers in developed countries. The reverse movement could also occur. Many rated as unskilled in developed countries may qualify as skilled in a developing country because they possess competencies taken for granted in the one but scarce in the other – the ability to read and write, to drive a vehicle, to undertake elementary calculations. Of course, in real wage terms, let alone relative to different systems of social security, this would not be a sensible move.

The gap between average pay levels in developed and developing countries has also been exaggerated by the fact that real wages in the statistically recorded sectors of the latter have been in decline throughout the 1980s (Riveros, 1989). This relative decline has gone with a continued upgrading of the quality of infrastructure and facilitating services, as well as a liberalization of the conditions for the import of capital and for trade. Thus, despite often lower levels of productivity, the pressures to relocate sectors of manufacturing away from the developed countries are almost irresistible.

This growing comparative advantage of developing countries is reflected in the growing dependence of developed countries upon imports of manufacturing from developing countries. Thus, in the 1980s the developed countries experienced the lowest rate of growth for the decade since the interwar Great Depression, yet imports from developing countries continued to grow. For the countries of the European Union, when the value of manufacturing production increased by under

60 per cent, the dollar value of imports increased 155 per cent (and intra European Union trade increased 139 per cent). The developing country share of these imports increased from 20 to 24 per cent. For the United States, while the gross domestic product in dollar terms doubled in the decade and manufacturing value-added increased 43 per cent, imports of manufacturing increased threefold.

There was a greater diversification in the source of imports: the four 'Little Tigers' (South Korea, Taiwan, Hong Kong, Singapore) were joined by other countries of Southeast Asia and China (manufactured exports to the European Union increased fourfold), and some important Latin American countries, particularly Mexico and Brazil (Baneth, 1993). Only the two major manufacturing powers among the developed countries, Japan and Germany (followed by Italy), partly escaped these trends in the 1980s, but it was not clear that they would not follow suit in the severe recession of the early 1990s. Furthermore, for the developed countries as a whole, the trend was increasing: for each 1 per cent growth of gross domestic product between 1963 and 1973, the developed countries increased their imports of manufactured goods from developing countries by 3.6 per cent; and between 1973 and 1987 by 4.0 per cent (Balassa, 1989). Despite much talk and sporadic incidents of protectionism, it was not clear that the developed countries could any longer control their borders at an acceptable financial and political cost.

In sum, the tendency for increasing capital exports from the developed countries and increasing manufactured imports seems to be gathering strength and diversity (both of goods and sources), and to be beyond the point at which it can be checked. If attention is restricted to the labour-intensive component of world trade, the longer-term trend is unmistakable: between 1965 and 1986 imports to the developed countries increased sixteenfold, and the share of developing countries in labour-intensive imports to the European Union increased from 8 to 12 per cent; to Japan from 10 to 44 per cent; and to the United States from 18 to 44 per cent. Note that the expansion is precisely in those sectors which the developed countries protect most – especially garments and textiles, footwear, and so on, suggesting limits to the capacity of governments in developed countries to frustrate the trend.

Nevertheless, the composition of this trade has shifted from the traditional concentration on items such as garments, textiles and footwear, and has come to include goods such as industrial transistors and valves, telecommunications equipment, statistical machines, office equipment, radio broadcasting receivers, electrical power machines, sound recorders (Balassa, 1989: 13, Table 3), or what the World Bank defines as 'technologically intensive goods' (World Bank, 1992: Appendix B): Malaysia, for example, expanded production of this class of good from US$3 million in 1968 to $1.4 billion in 1988 (at constant prices).

The shift of labour-intensive activities (manufacturing and services) to developing countries is an element in the emerging division of labour of the global economy. But it does not mean that the developed countries can therefore restrict their labour force to the highly skilled – the simple-minded picture presented by many governments in the developed countries. The point is not just that the whole workforce is unlikely ever to be highly skilled, but that an economy, operating in an open global system, could never survive simply on the basis of the highly skilled. As we have seen, highly productive workers who are also parents require intensive child-care services in order to work. Advanced scientists might rely on imported clothing from developing countries, but not imported street-cleaning services, highway-building, restaurants and hotels. The highest skilled hospital physicians depend for their effectiveness on a legion of unskilled workers supporting them – cleaning, laundering, bed-making, cooking and serving, carrying and portering, manning telephones and security services. An army composed only of staff officers cannot fight wars. Indeed, the more highly skilled the labour force of the developed countries becomes, the greater is the need for unskilled support workers; and, in an open economy, many of these will come from developing countries, legally or illegally.

When all the workers of the world are employed, automation may become generally viable. As it is, robots are substituted in manufacturing for only some unskilled and semi-skilled workers. The degree to which this is generally feasible is limited even in manufacturing by the relative pricing of robot-time (its capital and running costs) and labour costs. Given the enormous range of variation in labour costs, robot substitutes could make import-competing production more expensive. More likely is the combination of robots or automation and cheap labour. Furthermore, in a wide range of services there is a limited role for automation, and, as we will discuss later, it is these sorts of services which are scheduled to expand.

However, even though there is inevitably a need for unskilled workers in the developed countries, many factors determine whether or not they are fully employed. There is also a particular problem: unskilled workers, legitimately geared to expectations of average income which relate to the local average level of productivity, cannot seriously consider the low-paid jobs on offer, particularly if compared to the income that can be earned outside the official economy (especially if it is supplemented by social-security payments). Although the educational background of young workers in these societies may in many cases be relatively poor by the average standards of developed countries, it nevertheless entitles them to considerably more than is on offer in the market for unskilled labour – a situation exacerbated by the much higher incomes they can observe being paid to other people without much claim on high skills or to valuable social function. It would seem more sensible to contract out of unskilled employment than be driven to work for a lifetime at a pay level inadequate to meet the minimum standards of the society. Thus the stage is set for considerable scarcities of unskilled labour to coexist with high levels of unemployment.

Some governments have disastrously misinterpreted this problem, injecting into the discussion a tone of moral self-righteousness. The popular argument is that unemployment is high because the wage levels for unskilled work are too high, thus discouraging employers from hiring – wages are downwardly 'inflexible'. And the unemployed, it is suggested, and particularly the young (where unemployment rates are highest), are lazy, or are allowed to be lazy by the 'lavish' character of unemployment benefits. On this reading, unskilled wages need to be forced down to 'market clearing' levels, and unemployment benefits cut to drive workers to work.

The British government has been particularly addicted to part of this diagnosis and remedy. During the 1980s some unemployed families in Britain are estimated to have experienced a 40 per cent cut in the real value of social-security benefits, and the annual income support for the single unemployed adult has declined by nearly 10 per cent. Furthermore, for the lowest paid, who in the past received incomes supposedly set by Wages Councils, the government endeavoured first to push down the income levels set by the Councils and then finally abolished them. By the mid-1980s, British labour costs had declined to among the lowest in the European Community (exceeded only by Spain, Portugal and Ireland), with social contributions taking among the lowest shares of hourly pay (41 per cent, compared to 81 per cent in France, 94 per cent in Italy; but 38 per cent in the United States and 36 per cent in Canada). Indeed, the poorest 10 per cent of male workers in the United Kingdom received in 1993 lower pay as a proportion of the average wage than at any time since records began in 1886.

Yet, although wages declined in Britain, there is no evidence that this served to increase levels of employment (or – a different matter – lower unemployment). If the decision to work is related to income expectations, linked to the average productivity of labour in Britain (rather than the world at large), and reflected in the norms of standard of living, then lowering wages would tend to increase official unemployment rather than lower it. The obverse would be an increase in the size of the black economy. In economic terms this would imply what is known as a 'backward bending' supply curve – lowering the wage reduces the numbers willing to work.

What kinds of activities demonstrate the continued vigour of labour demand for unskilled workers?

Women Workers and Paid Employment

The growth in the paid employment of women, particularly married women and those in the reproductive age groups, has been one of the most remarkable transformations of the labour force in developed countries, and, in terms of scale, far larger than anything related to immigration. In a quite short space of time, the transition has been made from women constituting a 'reproducing' section of the work-force, primarily concerned with the maintenance of the household and the reproduction of the population with occasional periods of employ-ment, to their being a standard part of the labour force with occasional – but now relatively rare and brief – periods out of employment. In theory, household maintenance – like the earning of the family income – has become shared, albeit notoriously unequally. The changes were long in the making, but the final outcome has been sufficiently power-ful to change the perception of women and men of themselves and their roles in society.

Consider the figures for the 1960s and 1970s. While the participation rate of single women in the labour force has always been fairly high (and pay rates are now not very different for comparable jobs), the more dramatic changes have affected married women. In the United States the participation rate for women increased from 30 to 47 per cent in the fourteen years to 1974; and for women in what were then the peak child-bearing years, 20–24, from 45 to 63 per cent. For women with pre-school children, participation has increased in virtually all developed countries: in Sweden from 37 (1965) to 57 (1974) to 66 per cent (1977); in the United States from 19 (1960) to 30 per cent (1974); in Canada to 47 per cent, and Italy, 40 per cent (1975). In every gen-eration, the number of years women spend in paid employment has increased, with a declining period of time off work for child-bearing (seven and a half years between the birth of the last child and return to work in the 1950s; three and a half years in the second half of the 1970s [Martin and Roberts, 1984]). In Britain by the end of 1992, the number of employed women (10.1 million) was almost equal to the number of men with jobs (10.7 million); and while the number of women in the labour force had increased from 9.4 million thirteen years previously, the number of men had declined from 13.1 million.

However, the type of work women do remains substantially different, and the degree of competition between men and women for the same work is restricted. Women's employment is concentrated in services, in part-time work, and in a handful of sectors – in 1975 in community, social and personal services (41 per cent of all employed women in the developed countries), in wholesale and retail trades, hotels and restaurants (21 per cent), manufacturing (25 per cent). Indeed, in some occupations, women are sufficiently segregated to form a near-monopoly (as have men also in some occupations) – as with the bulk of clerical staff and typists, nurses, health-care workers, teachers, child-care and social workers, cleaning and household service workers, sales clerks, the basic production workers in garments and textiles. Furthermore, there is strikingly little variation between countries. For example, in Japan in 1975, women accounted for 97 per cent of nurses, 97 per cent of typists, 98 per cent of household workers, 72 per cent of textile workers, and 64 per cent of all service workers; in Germany in 1976, women constituted 99 per cent of all health workers, 97 per cent of secretaries, 60 per cent of trade workers, 75 per cent of textile workers (but only 2 per cent of carpenters, 6 per cent of electricians, 5 per cent of chemists, physicians and mathematicians). The sectoral differences in activity underpin the brute persistence of differentials in income.

Even in manufacturing, the particular types of jobs women do are often the most marginal – industries which are most likely to relocate to reduce costs, particularly to developing countries. However, impressions can be misleading: in Britain, some industries experiencing severe contraction in the 1960s and 1970s (for example, shipbuilding, dock work, mining) were overwhelmingly male-dominated, whereas the modern growth industry of electronic assembly is primarily staffed by women.

In the United States in 1980, over 90 per cent of production workers in both electronic assembly and garments were women, and these are sectors where competition from developing countries is strongest. The same is true of other key industries for the employment of women: leather and footwear; toys; sports goods; plastic products; miscellaneous light consumer goods; scientific and medical instruments; optical, video and photographic equipment. In addition, these industries are an important attraction for immigrant women. Thus, in 1980, 56 per cent of immigrant women in employment in West Germany were engaged in manufacturing: textiles and garments, footwear, food products, chemicals and plastics, metalworking and electronic products. In some of these sectors, conditions are notoriously bad. In 1973, one of the worst examples was that of a group of Filipina women discovered imprisoned in a clothing mill in Rochdale in Britain, confined to over-crowded rooms (eight per room), on very low pay, part of which was stopped by the employer to cover the air fares involved in bringing the workers to Rochdale (Maw, 1974).

There is no established explanation for the remarkable growth in women's employment. However, given that the past roles – and psycho-logical attitudes – of women (and of men) were defined by the totality of social relations, we would assume that the change in roles would be similarly accompanied by major structural changes in the developed countries. The changes would be spurred by the activity of women themselves, as well as by independent changes in the nature of the labour market. At this stage, the explanation is more speculative than proved, with empirical illustration rather than demonstration.

In terms of labour demand, the gross labour shortages which emerged in the great boom of the 1950s have already been discussed. They were overtaken in the 1970s by often violent structural adjust-ment, culminating in both much stronger competition (as a result of the growing liberalization of imports) and a disproportionate demand for 'flexible' workers as services expanded (in Britain and the United States, involving particularly part-time workers). As part of the traditionally male full-time labour force experienced increasing redundancy, the new part-time work in services went to newcomers to the labour market – married women. The precise situation varied between countries, depending upon such factors as the local structure of output and invest-ment levels, as well as tax structures and legal regimes – for example, the differing legal obligations of employers regarding fringe benefits. This last factor has been used to explain the disproportionate growth in Britain of part-time work:

> By replacing one full-time sales assistant with two or three part-timers, employers can save as much as eight man hours per week. (Robinson, 1985: 23)

Changes in the nature of the work process in the sectors concerned have reduced the incentive for employers to tie workers down to a longer-term commitment; and increased competition has obliged them to seek to reduce wage costs by not paying for time which is not fully worked, and by searching out cheaper labour – part-time women instead of full-time men, immigrant women rather than native women, and (in manufacturing) younger and better educated women in developing countries rather than older women in developed countries.

Changes in the nature of labour demand are difficult to disentangle from the no less dramatic changes in labour supply. On the one hand, there has been a very long-drawn-out process of decline in the size of the family (radically contracting the years involved in child-bearing); on the other hand, at the same time, the costs of reproduction and family maintenance as related to incomes have increased enormously. If we can return to the idea that the bench-mark for determining incomes is the average level of labour productivity in the economy as a whole, then this has improved remarkably, and requires a comparable increase in the preparation of the young for work. The expected future level of productivity requires parents to spend more on their children now – an increase in 'reproductive costs', in investment in 'human capital'. Changing standards of child-rearing – the appropriate diet and clothing, housing, holidays or recreation, toys, the notion of what constitutes an adequate education or desirable extra-curricular activities, and so on, may well function as a primary mechanism for the competitive upgrading of the future labour force to meet expected levels of productivity. 'Keeping up with the Joneses' may in this context be more than a response to fashion (or advertisers' manipulation of child viewers), but rather an important competitive mechanism to upgrade the productivity of the future worker.

Furthermore, the productivity of household labour has very much increased with extensive technical innovations, as on the factory floor. Tasks – the washing and ironing of clothes, the cooking of meals, carrying out house repairs and installing fixtures – which only 30 years earlier took days of labour can be accomplished now in a fraction of the time. This has had the effect of radically cutting the time needed for household maintenance, leaving women free for a much larger part of their active years to take paid employment.

On the other hand, the cost of household maintenance – because of the extensive use of machinery – is very much greater than before. The old bench-mark for household spending (assuming two adults and two children), the adult male wage, is no longer adequate. Households have become dependent upon two incomes rather than one. The single parent has become a major component of the poor. The earnings of women are no longer marginal (indeed, for poorer households, they were never marginal). Thus it was estimated for Britain in 1981 that, if all married women ceased paid employment, the number of families below the poverty line would increase threefold. Increased household costs may also have been a factor in producing the decline in the size of the family (rather than simply subjective preference or fashion) in order to concentrate higher per-capita expenditure on fewer offspring.

Finally, the change also increases the reserve price (or wage) which new workers expect to earn to attain the position in society which is seen as the natural right of all citizens – a wage rate capable of raising children at the average level of productivity. The modern kitchen and the modern nursery have come to be expected as the norm.

It would hardly be surprising if women, socialized in the old culture in which their central lifetime activity was the running of a household and raising children, should experience the changes in their role as painfully as the worker rendered redundant after a lifetime's devotion to what was seen as an essential craft for society. On the other hand, for men, raised with the expectation of bearing alone the responsibility of earning the income of the primary unit of society, the family, the immediate arena for male domination of society has weakened. The divorce rate and the rise in the single-woman-headed household is some reflection that the old family form has proved incapable of absorbing these violent and painful demands made upon it by the changing demand and supply of labour.

In sum, at both ends of the equation – the demand for workers and the supply – many forces have conspired to drive or draw women out of the household into the labour market. The change occurred when women were often ill-equipped for paid work, since they had been prepared for other tasks. They were thus obliged to accept what might have seemed to be marginal employment – but employment which, paradoxically, proved to be the growth sector in the demand for workers (while the traditional full-time jobs contracted).

On the other hand, the relative ease with which women secure work (even if it is part-time), while an increasing number of men remain stubbornly unemployed, shifts the terms of the former married relationship. Indeed, some have argued that women have been choosing to live alone (with or without children) rather than take on the obligation of maintaining a redundant man for his lifetime.

Part-time Work

The core of the growth in women's employment has been in part-time jobs. The growth in this sector accelerated in Britain (where it is defined as up to 30 hours work per week) with the onset of the first major postwar recession in the early 1970s, and thereafter slowed in relative terms. Over the three decades to 1981, part-time employment increased fivefold to just under 4 million (accounting for 39 per cent of employed women and 3 per cent of employed men). This was a period in which the number of full-time jobs declined by 2.3 million (1.9 million for men, 0.4 million for women) (Department of Employment, 1983). By 1993 the figure was 4.7 million (slightly down on the 5.1 million of the late 1980s) or a quarter of the employed labour force – 2.6 million earning less than the minimum threshold for income tax (£66.25 per week at that time), and 2.3 million earning less than the National Insurance threshold level (£56 per week). In the European Community as a whole, there were 11.8 million part-time workers by 1984, with particular concentrations in Scandinavia and the Netherlands as well as Britain.

The part-time sector has proved very resilient to fluctuations in the economy; as a result, women have experienced significantly lower rates of unemployment than men (in 1993 Britain, 5.6 per cent for women and 14.1 per cent for men). The reasons are perhaps not hard to fathom, since the cost of part-time workers has hitherto been relatively low. Employers avoid a major part of the costs of full-time workers – the work is often worse paid per hour, more routine and less regulated, without access to legal protection and to fringe benefits (holidays, regular hours, health and safety rules, medical services, crèches, sick and maternity pay etc.); there is usually no overtime or shift pay; often no meal breaks are allowed; and, in some cases, jobs are 'on call' – the worker works (and is paid) only when the employer demands it. The need for increased flexibility in many enterprises has also played a role. In the British retail trades, for example, full-time work is limited to 39 hours per week, while trading hours have expanded to 70 hours.

The growth in part-time work is related to the still ambiguous position of women relative to their old roles. Women still assume the primary role in the bringing up of children and the maintenance of the household, even though there is now no economic justification for this. In Britain, a 1986 Labour Force survey included a sample of part-time workers, and sought to identify how far part-time work was involuntary: 22 per cent of men, 17 per cent of unmarried women, and only 7 per cent of married women said they worked part-time because of the lack of full-time work. A survey carried out in 1980 also found a correlation between women's part-time work and the presence of children in the family (and the age of the youngest), a factor influenced by the poor availability in Britain of child-care facilities.

Part-time work blurs the distinction between work and non-work, between employment and unemployment, and this is exaggerated with casual employment where the hours may fluctuate between full- and part-time work. The more extreme forms of this occur in home-working (discussed below), cleaning and catering, child-minding, and so on (Huws et al., 1989).

Changes in technology have improved the capacity for managerial control and monitoring of many part-time workers, and, as we have seen, fluctuating demand has led to employers seeking to pay only for work done. Subcontracting for short-term supplies of manufactured goods to home-workers, small workshops or suppliers in developing countries reduces the financial commitment of the buyer to the minimum. In supermarkets, the close monitoring of stocks by computer allows multiple shift-working. And the workers themselves may have several part-time jobs, which taken together do not qualify for the legal status of full-time work (even though the weekly hours worked may be greater). Some of the jobs may be of very short duration. The proportion of part-time workers in Britain working eight hours or less per week doubled from under 4 per cent in 1975 to nearly 8 per cent in 1987 (and those working between eight and sixteen hours increased from 16 to 23 per cent).

Part-time work is not all unskilled, but the major part of it, particularly that held by women, frequently is. Men are particularly affected in the extremities of the age range – in 1981, 71 per cent of male part-time workers were under the age of 20 or over 65. For the young, the growth of part-time work has gone with high levels of unemployment (for the OECD group as a whole, unemployment for those aged below 20 rose, between 1966 and 1981, from 1.6 to 18.0 per cent of the age group). Some of the increase in youth part-time working may result from a decline in student funding, with those attending school or institutes of higher education having to make up for inadequate primary sources of income.

The Low-Paid

The persistence of low-paid jobs in developed countries is extraordinary, particularly because it is in such direct contradiction with the perceptions and preoccupations of official society, where the shortages of skilled and professional workers receive most attention. In Britain in 1990, it has been estimated that there were some 10 million 'low-paid workers' – as measured by the Council of Europe's 'decency threshold' (workers receiving 68 per cent or less of full-time mean earnings) – including 4.4 million part-time workers; 65 per cent of the workers concerned were women.

The position of low-paid workers has deteriorated in Britain and the

USA over the past 15 years. There are many explanations on offer for this decline: an increased supply of unskilled workers resulting from an earlier 'baby boom'; the major growth in women's employment; but also the changed structure of the US economy – as we noted earlier, the decline in manufacturing employment with relatively narrower income differentials than expanding services. However, the decline in incomes does not seem to have been sufficient to reverse the decline in labour-intensive industries in the USA, or the tendency to relocate to low-waged areas abroad. Thus, for example, in order to lower costs, San Francisco's Silicon Valley electronic assembly industries shifted recruitment successively to women and the foreign-born, to sub-contracted workers (to escape social security payments etc.), and then to Los Angeles. However, East and Southeast Asia were still more competitive and attracted US capacity out of America. Or, at the other end of the technological spectrum, the example of Los Angeles furniture-making can be cited. One firm in this industry sought to relocate its plant in separate places: the labour-intensive parts of its plant to Thailand (paying workers on average $40 per month), the capital-intensive sections to Taiwan, and the finishing to Mexico where it paid workers $520 per month (Mines, 1985). Not even illegal immigrants could keep the industry in California. In the end, the state's environmental regulations are said to have forced a major part of the industry to Mexico.

What types of activity command the lowest rates of pay in the developed countries? Let us take, for example, Britain in the early 1980s, accepting the poverty threshold of the Trades Union Congress (two-thirds of the mean manual earnings, divided by sex) as the bench-mark to assess how far below this level earnings stood (the figures in brackets are percentages):

For women: hairdressing (95.6); barmaids (89.5); shop check-out workers (96.9); shop assistants (91.3); waitresses (89.2); cleaners (87.6); sewing machinists (86.2); receptionists (83.3); chefs and cooks (81.7); packers and canners (79.3).

For men: general farm workers (88.0); barmen (74.4); hospital porters (73.9); caretakers (67.6); butchers (66.0); salesmen and shop assistants (65.5); goods porters (58.8); craftsmen's mates (57.8); general labourers (57.7); bakers (58.9) (Department of Employment, 1986).

Male average earnings were consistently higher than female – and the majority of low-paid workers were women – but the spread of low pay for men was much greater (so the bottom pay was not much over one-third of the mean male manual earnings).

Let us consider some of the sectoral characteristics of this mass of low-paid work, and how far immigrant workers have played a significant role.

1. *Hotels and restaurants*

This is a relatively labour-intensive sector related to a comparatively high-income population, often linked to mass tourism. In restaurants, for example, the supply of different types of food is relatively segmented (with little overlap) between fast-food outlets, intermediate service, full service and ethnic restaurants. Fast-food outlets, offering a standardized menu, have gone furthest in substituting capital for labour and employing standardized manufactured inputs; their workers receive the lowest levels of pay for strictly standardized operations. Often they are teenagers, without training and with a high rate of turnover; for example in 1982, in the United States, 70 per cent of the workers in this sector were under 22. In fiercely competitive conditions between food suppliers, labour supply is a constant problem and in the big cities there are persistent labour shortages. It was the fast-food sector in the United States that pressed the federal government to relax the ban on the employment of minors, and in 1982 the Labor Department helpfully proposed lifting the regulations for those aged 14 and 15.

Immigrants often play a very important role in the other types of restaurant, most notably in the establishment of their own ethnic restaurants (in the early 1980s, 60 per cent of the restaurants in New York's central borough were owned by immigrants). Working in the relatively protected environment of ethnic restaurants is also said to be an important entry point for illegal immigrant workers. Small-scale ethnic restaurants often provide food which is cheaper and tastier than that served in the standardized fast-food outlets; thus it is precisely the competitive strength of the fast-food providers (speed, not variety) that opens the way for competition. Ethnic restaurants often employ the native-born to wait at table, so the expansion of ethnic restaurants – as a San Diego study demonstrates – also expands native employment (US Department of Labor, 1989).

In Britain in 1971, 14 per cent of all hotel workers and 25 per cent of restaurant workers were born abroad, and in London the proportion was just under half for hotels. When the government stopped the issue of work permits to foreign nationals for unskilled and semi-skilled work, the measure was largely nullified by excluding hotels and catering, as well as hospitals and residential workers. Indeed, in 1971 hotels were granted 60 per cent of the unskilled male work permits. The concession was gradually reduced and finally ended in 1979. Initially, in the 1950s, the workers were mainly from Portugal and Italy; in the 1960s, the supply was predominantly from the Philippines and Spain; but later, workers came from Turkey, Egypt, Morocco, Colombia, and later still, from Poland. It is noticeable that few of the immigrants from South Asia, Africa or the Caribbean – the bulk of the settled immigrant population – were involved except as proprietors and staff of a relatively small number of hotels and ethnic restaurants (a sector of particular importance in Britain).

2. *Domestics*

Domestic labour has expanded very rapidly in recent decades. As household incomes have risen, inequality in income has increased and more skilled women have started paid work. Domestics have been a key component in migrant labour movements from East, Southeast and South Asia to the Middle East, Europe and North America; from Africa to Europe; from South and Central America to North America – and that is without considering the subsidiary movements of Colombian women to Venezuela; Filipinas and Chinese to Hong Kong, Taiwan, Japan and South Korea, and so on.

The movement is more international than ever before, but in part it resumes processes last seen on this relative scale in Europe and North America in the nineteenth century. In 1901, 40 per cent of employed women in Britain were in domestic service; in the United States in 1870, about half employed women were 'in service', and the numbers doubled up to 1900. However, whereas earlier urban families employed single rural women who lived in, today the great growth has come from the opening up of the labour supplies of developing countries. In general, there are now few domestic competitors as competent as immigrant workers.

The bulk of the supply to Europe and the Middle East comes from the Philippines (Catholic Institute, 1987), Indonesia, Bangladesh, Sri Lanka, Pakistan, and, closer to Europe, Portugal and Morocco (pre-eminently to France). The workers are generally younger, fitter and better educated than any native equivalents (in the case of Filipinas, over half the emigrants for domestic work had some tertiary education), so that the quality, apart from the wage cost, has been very favourable. It is not clear what numbers are involved, and even if there were a clearer picture of legal movement, illegal migration is an important component (as seen particularly in the United States). In Britain, work permits were officially abolished in 1979, but it seems the supply continues, with possibly 30–60,000 workers per year entering the country, mainly from the Philippines, Colombia, Nepal, India, Sri Lanka and, latterly, Poland.

Information on pay and conditions is also no more than anecdotal. Filipina maids in Australia are said to receive about $5000 per year, compared to the $15,000 earned by Australian domestic staff. However, the stability of income, in comparison with, say, unskilled construction workers, is much greater, as Rodrigo and Jayatissa report for Sri Lankan maids (1989). There are sporadic reports of bad treatment and the terrorizing of maids by their employers. In the Philippines, a bill was put forward to prevent women working abroad as maids because, the chairman of the Senate Foreign Relations Committee, Blas Ople, argued, such employment causes 90 per cent of the social and welfare problems. Under pressure from the women, the bill was dropped.

In many developed (and, for that matter, some developing) countries, governments appear as hostile to immigrant domestic workers as to others who are classed as unskilled, even though home help is a decisive factor in the productivity of women workers. In economic terms, domestics may contribute disproportionately to national productivity by enabling highly productive workers to work. The cost of refusing entry to foreign domestics is the exhaustion of women seeking to balance paid employment with child care and home maintenance. An obsession with excluding foreigners overrides economic good sense and hinders the advancement of women. Canada is among the few countries – in the 1981 Foreign Domestic Workers' Programme – to have taken steps to ease entry and settlement procedures and to have sought to regulate certain working conditions (Hong Kong also has a scheme of this kind for Filipinas).

3. *Agriculture*

Agriculture has been historically a prodigious consumer of workers, particularly on a seasonal basis, and there are ancient well-trodden paths beaten by the feet of generations of migrant workers crisscrossing the world's frontiers (indeed, many of the frontiers are far younger than the paths of migrant workers) – Portuguese and Andalusians to France, Poles to Germany, Irish to Britain, Mexicans to the United States, and so on. The difficulties and dangers of such movements have been enough without the added official persecution that comes with border migration controls.

Governments have usually tried to make special provisions for agricultural workers; for without immigrants, domestic production could not compete with imports (especially from lower-waged countries). However, in modern conditions, the movement of both workers and farm capital between countries can make it perplexing for governments to identify the national interest – as the chairman of a US Congressional Committee once found in listing the alternative supplies of tomatoes available to the government: those grown in Florida and picked by Caribbean migrant workers; those from California, picked by Mexican migrant workers; and those picked by Mexicans in Mexico. All three sets of farms were, legally or not, owned by farmers with United States nationality.

Given the importance of agriculture in the United States, the issue of labour supply has always loomed large. The 1917 Immigration Act permitted the Federal Secretary of Labour to waive the provisions of the Act to allow the temporary entry of Mexican farm workers. During the Second World War, bilateral agreements were signed with Jamaica and Barbados to admit fruit pickers for Florida and sugar-cane cutters for Louisiana – arrangements which continue to the present (covering some 11–12,000 workers annually; a similar scheme operates for Ontario in Canada). The Bracero programme, lasting from 1942 to 1964, allowed Mexican seasonal workers to enter the United States for agricultural work (some half a million workers were employed at the programme's peak in the late 1950s). Under the pressure of trade unions, church and civil-rights groups, the official programme was ended. Migrants were forced underground where they could no longer be seen. However, the government acknowledged the real state of affairs when, in the 1986 Immigration Control and Reform Act, the amnesty offered to illegal immigrants explicitly permitted the temporary entry of farm workers (under the Special Agricultural Workers and Replenishment of Agricultural Workers [RPA] provisions), and included in this proviso workers in industries processing and packaging fruit, vegetables and meat. The RPA was introduced in response to farmers' fears that the legalization of illegal immigrants would lead to their flight from farming; legalization was therefore made conditional upon the worker continuing to work in agriculture for three years (with two further years needed to qualify for citizenship). In practice, it seems that a measure of automation in agriculture is reducing the need for seasonal labour, and a shortage of workers is becoming more important in services, construction, light manufacturing and domestic work.

However, the American farm sector is very heterogeneous, and labour demands vary widely between farms of different size and prosperity. For smaller farmers on marginal lands, labour shortages sometimes lead to desperate measures. In April 1986, the press reported that the

Ellebrant family in Kerr County, Texas, had, over three years, kidnapped 75 'hitch-hikers and drifters' and forced them to work on the family farm. North Carolina experienced in 1981 ten convictions for 'involuntary servitude'; and in 1985, two farmers were convicted for holding and forcing to work 19 Mexicans who had been purchased for $50 each. These are anecdotal fragments of information which suggest, not that these conditions are standard for American farmers, but that a continuing scarcity of workers means that some farmers cannot hire and hold them through orthodox means, and foreigners are fair game for exploitation. The Europeans are perhaps more discreet.

4. *Food processing*

The food-processing industry in the United States, like agriculture, has an endemic problem in recruiting labour, so much so that the beef-packing sector made a special bid to recruit refugee workers through the US Refugee Resettlement Program (US Department of Labor, 1989). This is only the latest phase in the industry's historic tendency to search out the newest workers due to persistently high labour turnover. Thus, the Chicago industry set out to recruit black workers before the First World War – the proportion rose from 3 to 30 per cent between 1909 and 1928 – and Mexican workers in subsequent years. The industry is constantly being pressured by domestic competition to innovate and change location to reduce costs. In the 1970s the retail trade, which historically cut and prepared the meat for the buyer, relinquished this role to standardized manufacturing processes upstream so that meat was packaged and sealed before reaching the retail outlet. This change simultaneously involved a shift from a workforce of stable native-born permanent packers in trade unions to temporary foreign-born non-union packers. Even these changes did not protect the industry from crippling bankruptcies in a downturn – despite, for example, a fall in hourly wages in the 1970s from $11 to $5 for the same work. Conditions are said to be among the worst, and labour turnover is very high (80 per cent of meatpackers leave their jobs within the first year).

A not dissimilar process occurred in poultry farming, transforming the industry from a predominance of small farms, run by local women in the Midwest and northeast, to large-scale battery farms on the south Atlantic and south-center regions, often employing illegal immigrants.

In fruit farming, there is a much greater dispersal of capital and plant to other countries. By the 1970s, under half of the national output of canned fruit came from sources in the United States. The domestic labour force is predominantly Mexican, and they are crucial in the canneries, and subsequently in the production of frozen food.

In general, then, structural change in the different sectors of the food-processing industry, under the pressure of intense competition, part of it in foreign markets, shifted the labour force from native workers to immigrants, legal or illegal. It is employer initiatives that reshape the labour demand of the industry and make its survival dependent upon a continuing flow of foreign workers; for as one generation fled the conditions of the industry, another had to be recruited. There is no possibility of native workers in appreciable numbers working under such conditions and for the pay on offer, with little opportunity for improvement in a highly competitive world market.

5. *Medical services*

In general, the field of medical services is not well known for being badly paid because the foreground is occupied by the tiny minority of the more highly paid professionals, medical doctors. However, as with so many activities, the majority of workers, who make it possible for the physicians to practise, are among the low paid.

Since the Second World War the provision of medical services has been a major growth industry in the developed countries, and foreign workers have been of great and growing importance as doctors, nurses and support staff. Indeed, it seems that the desire for mass medical services increases in proportion to the unwillingness of the native-born to work in providing them.

The cosmopolitanization of physicians (particularly in the lower echelons of the hospital service) has been happening for a long time, especially in the United States and Britain. In the United States, more than one in five doctors is foreign-born, making the medical profession one of the most mixed in terms of nationality of all upper-income groups. At the same time, leaving aside the special issues relating to the insurance system, rapidly rising demand coupled with a shortage of services has raised the costs of medicine in the United States to renowned levels – and in so doing has rendered alternative suppliers abroad highly competitive. For example, as noted earlier, on the Mexican side of the border, medical services designed for use by American visitors are everywhere overdeveloped. Thus, as in other fields, the role played by immigrant workers in the United States is matched by the extension of US demand beyond the borders to workers abroad.

Shortages among nursing professionals are also notorious and have often seemed greater than for physicians. As with doctors, nurses have been exempt from much of the immigration-control system, and this situation has persisted regardless of the very severe pressures on hospitals to reduce staffing levels in the interests of economy.

Britain's persistent shortage of nurses is made worse by the fact that a significant proportion of native-born nurses choose to work abroad either permanently or on short contracts (Buchan et al., 1992). Under European Union rules, there has been free mobility of nurses within Europe since 1979, and Britain has to some extent benefited from this – although the differences in language and training qualifications offer some measure of protection for each national labour market. Britain, however, also has provision for 'working holidaymakers' – allowing entry to Commonwealth citizens, aged 17 to 27, or students (or the dependants of work-permit holders). This provision has permitted a continuous inflow of nurses from Nigeria, Australia, New Zealand, South Africa and Hong Kong. However, hospitals complain that regularizing this form of recruitment is cumbersome and time-wasting. Thus, some hospitals prefer to recruit abroad directly (particularly for the least-favoured types of nursing work). For example, the press reported in 1989 that a Surrey hospital was advertising in the West Indian press (particularly in Trinidad) for nursing staff to work in a geriatric hospital.

In the United States, nursing is characterized by the same persistent scarcity, particularly with the expansion of the medical system in the 1980s when the job vacancy rate doubled (especially in the cities of the East and West coasts, and in the lowest-income areas). There are fewer Americans in the relevant age groups, and fewer opting to train as nurses, particularly, it is said, because pay levels have failed to keep pace with national norms, let alone relative scarcity. The shortfall is filled by nurses from the Philippines and South Korea. Since controls on the acquisition of American nursing qualifications remain tight, many of the newcomers are employed in inferior conditions as temporary workers. In New York, where shortages are most severe, it is said that 20 to 30 per cent of nursing staff are foreign temporary workers (and the vacancy rate is still between 12 and 20 per cent). For other specialisms – for example, 'miscellaneous health technologists and technicians' – about one-third of those employed in the United States are foreign-born, and the proportion is said to increase as one descends the occupational hierarchy.

If the pay of nurses has failed to keep pace with average income, this is even more true of the army of unskilled and semi-skilled medical ancillary workers. In Britain in the early 1980s, for example, hospital porters were, according to official figures, the seventh worst-paid male occupational group in the country. Other groups – orderlies, attendants, cleaners, laundry and canteen workers, drivers and maintenance staff – are similarly poorly paid. Furthermore, hospitals depend upon a regular flow of unpaid voluntary workers and voluntary organizations to sustain their activities, and on relatives to support those under treatment.

It is remarkable, given the prodigious resources involved in such an institution as the US medical system, that it should be the employer of some of the worst-paid workers, most of them now foreign-born. The drive to achieve economies, in a situation where hospitals compete for the same patients, serves to prevent pay approaching the social norm, thus ensuring that the native-born opt decreasingly for these occupations and that the system is dependent upon recruiting either abroad (for nurses, doctors and other technical staff) or among immigrants at home.

Few of those opposed to immigration reflect on the fact that, if hospital pay levels are allowed to rise to the point where they might attract more native-born workers, the resulting price for medical services would rule out their use by a significant part of the population. An end to immigration cannot be reconciled with an open market in medical services.

6. *Other activities*

Hairdressing

The labour market has many peculiarities which do not allow simple deduction from supply and demand of workers. Hairdressing – at least in Britain – is peculiar in that it is simultaneously one of the lowest-paid occupations but attracts relatively few immigrants. There are in the region of 100,000 workers in hairdressing (turnover in the industry is so rapid that total numbers cannot be known). Over 80 per cent of them are women (between a quarter and one-third part-time), about half of whom are under the age of 22. The occupation thus combines three prototypical characteristics of low-paid workers: they are engaged in personal service, are women and are young. Yet the fourth characteristic, that of being foreign-born, does not apply.

A significant part of the workforce is classed as self-employed so that their quasi-employers escape statutory responsibility for fringe benefits and the normal employment-regulatory regime. In the second half of the 1980s, the level of pay (excluding overtime) was some 41 per cent of the national average – 60 per cent below the Council of Europe's 'decency threshold' (the Wages Council which then supposedly governed pay rates reported that 36 per cent of the workforce were underpaid in 1986); the starting pay for a first-year apprentice was about half this level (Low Pay Unit, 1987).

It would be worth exploring the 'anomalies' here, and indeed whether the British experience in the hairdressing trade was repeated in other developed countries. To what extent have native-born men, for example, who used to dominate the occupation in the USA, left it to women? How strong has been the tendency for white women to leave the trade? Given that the foreign-born had so often pretended to an aesthetic superiority (commercially reflected in the success of foreign restaurants), why has this factor failed to be extensively marketable in barbering?

Cleaning

Cleaning has always been a major activity of mankind, and the larger the employment sector, the larger has been the demand for cleaning services. In the past, such activity was usually internalized in firms, but as with so many such services, these are now increasingly 'spun off' into independent enterprises. The activity is intensely competitive, and one where labour costs account for a very high proportion of the total cost, so that cutting them is one of the few means to enhance competitive capacity. As discussed earlier, this has driven firms to an increasing reliance on subcontracted workers. Originally employing in the main full-time permanent employees, firms in the United States have switched to part-time and temporary workers, from older native-born women to younger and better educated foreign-born workers. Annual pay – and sometimes hourly pay – has declined.

However, in Britain up until quite recently, a major part of cleaning services (particularly rubbish collection and street cleaning) has been operated within the public sector. This has protected groups of native-born workers from open market competition, albeit at the price of increasing costs (and hence local taxes) and consequent successive campaigns by public employers to reduce costs. The conflict has sharpened, and in the 1980s, under continuing pressure from central government, local authorities were obliged to privatize services, or at least to open public services up to competitive bidding.

Public services are often protected from direct competition with foreign suppliers, and therefore with prices which reflect world scarcities rather than local ones. They are, therefore, often identified by economists as part of the 'non-tradable' sector. Even so, as we shall see, the 'protection' they enjoy in this respect is beginning to crumble.

Shipping

To escape high-cost local regulation of pay and conditions, shipowners in developed countries have, notoriously, 'denationalized' themselves by registering their ships under 'flags of convenience' (primarily Liberian,

Panamanian, Cypriot). Simultaneously, they have recruited foreign crews – in the same way that international construction firms have recruited foreign workers. By 1975, 5800 'non-domiciled seamen' – one-third of the crew of deep-sea-going ships – were employed on British-registered ships. On average, foreign-born staff on British ships were paid just over half what was earned by British-born seamen; however, a different estimate in 1983 suggested that, of the 4220 foreign seamen then employed, the 2010 Indians were paid a quarter of British rates (£78 per month, compared to £82 per week). The number of British-born crew employed fell from 99,000 in 1970 to 17,000 in 1993, and the number of officers from 45,600 to 12,080. The wage levels of British ratings were said to be the third lowest in the European Union – but even then they were significantly above Asian and East European levels; in the mid-1980s, the ILO estimated, for example, that Bangladeshi ratings were available at 44 per cent of the world average monthly minimum pay, and Chinese at 18 per cent.

In the British case, the National Union of Seamen presided over this decline in the role of native-born seamen by accepting the so-called 'Asian levy' – a payment by the shipowners to the union of some £30 annually per foreign worker employed (in total, the levy came to represent 10 per cent of the union's income). The shipowners are said to have saved some £50 million annually on this scheme until the union, embarrassed by pressure from its members and the decline of the industry, cancelled the arrangement in 1983. The union was not the only embarrassed party: the government was obliged to lift the application of the Race Relations Act to allow workers, distinguished only by nationality, to be paid differently for doing the same job. With the ending of the arrangement, it seemed likely that more British ship-owners would go offshore, thereby further damaging the position of British ratings. So far as these latter are concerned, the long-term options are equally bad.

Shipowners have in general shifted recruitment to the foreign-born. For example, in the mid-1980s it was reported that 200 Japanese ships were staffed by foreigners; both Japanese and Taiwanese fishing fleets recruited seamen from China. Particularly important for the world marine fleet in terms of supplying seamen were South Korea (143,000 in 1986), the Philippines, India and Bangladesh. The numbers of Filipino seamen supplied to foreign employers doubled in the decade before 1986 to 57,000, and they are said to be serving on ships from 69 countries (70 per cent of which, however, are sailing under flags of convenience). Many are above average in educational terms and trained as ships' officers.

In terms of native-born employment, the heart of the shipping industry in the developed countries has been eaten out since the early 1970s, and it seems unlikely that it can ever be restored. Shipping is in microcosm a vivid illustration of the larger trend in all relatively labour-intensive activities, exaggerated because shipping is intrinsically offshore and cannot escape the logic of world prices. Here the foreign-born might not 'immigrate', but their role as a quasi-extension of the labour force of the developed countries is wholly comparable to that of the immigrant.

Garments

Labour-intensive manufacturing – garments, footwear and leather goods, toys, plastic products, and so on – has been notoriously affected by low-waged competition through imports from developing countries, and, as a result, employs foreign-born workers on a large scale. It is also characterized by a third process: the relocation of production to low-waged regions or countries. These industries – particularly garments – are also those that benefit most from state protection in developed countries. However, 30 years of protection from the late 1950s seems to have done as little to deflect the inexorable decline in employment as it has done in agriculture. In each downturn, the industry tends once again to be hammered; for example, between 1972 and 1977 the European Union industry lost half a million jobs in garments and 400,000 in textiles.

In the case of the United States, the garment industry has historically long been associated with immigrants, and has often played the role of urban reception door for newcomers. In New York in 1900, 'Men's clothing was produced by Italian women, working out of home; other apparel came from factories owned and operated by Europeans (most of whom were Jewish)' (US Department of Labor, 1989: 115). Native-born but migrant black women from the South and Puerto Ricans ultimately replaced the European immigrants in the 1930s, and today they in turn have been replaced by Chinese, Koreans, Dominicans and Mexicans. There are still persistent labour shortages in the industry.

In fact, the picture differs by subsector. Menswear and jeans manufacture is the most stable, with a handful of unionized firms employing a relatively high proportion of full-time permanent workers. The most unstable is women's outerwear manufacture, in which high fashion dictates a high turnover of stock and style. The major part of the industry has a chronic shortage of labour, and is therefore obliged to employ whomever is available, adjusting the work process to accommodate special needs (allowing, for example, working mothers to bring their infant children to work). Some 80 per cent of the labour force are women, and the majority of the production staff foreign-born. However, despite – in the early 1980s – paying low wages (61 per cent of the national manufacturing average for the USA), the industry could still not compete in labour costs with South Korea (then 13 per cent of the US average), or Hong Kong (16 per cent); it continued to decline (New York City lost 80,000 jobs in garment manufacture between 1969 and 1975). The only success story in the United States industry in the 1980s was in Los Angeles, but there the industry was based on illegal Mexican workers.

The contest over wage costs can never ultimately be won. Indeed, the logic threatens to drive the industry into competitive barbarism. An example of this occurred in the Darwin Trade Development Zone in Australia where, in 1990, the Hengyang Company was indicted for importing women from China and putting them to forced labour in prison-like conditions for two years – using threats against the women's families in China to enforce this discipline (*Far Eastern Economic Review*, 19 April 1990).

Other forms of competition – and the development of a more elaborate division of specialization – might secure the survival of the industry in the developed countries on the basis of enhanced productivity. Alternatively, new divisions of labour with particular developing countries can offer a mode of survival. Combining automated fabric-cutting in the United States with hand-sewing in Southeast Asia is an example of this; the arrangement has restored to American sources a larger share of the value-added than in any other industry where part-processing abroad is important (for example, motor-vehicle manufacture).

Home-working

This discussion has so far covered sectors that – with the exception of domestics – are in principle open to some public inspection. But at the lower end of the labour market, work fades into a growing darkness where the evidence is often merely anecdotal. Home-working is part of this darkness.

Paid work at home is an ancient practice. It is a subterranean realm where the distinction between 'work' and 'non-work', between the economically active and inactive, is unclear, and where children and the aged participate. People enter into or leave activity for shorter or longer periods, do the work in parallel with other employment (for example, knitting while running a small shop), or sometimes 'lend a hand' to those engaged. Thus, assessing home-work as if it were simply another form of 'employment' is misleading, for there is no clear cut-off point between being employed and not.

As a consequence, estimating the numbers involved is hazardous. In the early 1980s, the British Department of Employment (1983) estimated the numbers 'working at or from home' – excluding those engaged in construction, haulage or family work – at 660,000, including some 251,000 working *at* home. The census of the same year, however, put the figures at 850,000 and 330,000 respectively. Others (Hakim, 1984) put the number of 'outworkers' at 1.68 million (or 7 per cent of the labour force). The sectors of activity at that time were, however, clearer: sewing, knitting, threading buttons on cards, packaging, assembling (for example, toys), filling (fireworks, envelopes, pillows), desk-bound work (copy-editing, proofreading, journalism, typing), glove-making. Since then, there must have been a considerable expansion in activities related to computers – from software programming to data inputting and processing.

It seems as if the numbers in home-working are tending to increase as labour demand extends to unexploited parts of the potential labour force and the substitution of casual for permanent labour proceeds in order to ensure flexibility of supply in relation to fluctuations in demand. Improved transport systems to supply parts (and the decline in the cost of moving parts) have facilitated the process. Immigrant women are often in the right age group for this; and some are unable to work successfully outside the home because of language problems, fears of an alien environment or religious seclusion. There is some suggestion that the greater number of home-workers are women in their 30s, the age group for whom participation rates in outside employment are lowest. Furthermore, as noted earlier in the discussion of part-time work, new technology in office work has enhanced the capacity of managers to monitor and control work at a distance and in many different locations.

The home-worker is at the mercy of the employer, without the possibility of collective organization to standardize pay rates and conditions. The employer (or rather, the buyer of the self-employed worker's output) avoids the statutory obligations and provision of fringe payments which are the normal entitlement of full-time workers in proper workplaces, as well as the costs of premises, heating and lighting, and so on, all of which are shifted to the worker. Furthermore, the buyer can vary purchases according to demand without any obligation to the outworker, who thus bears the risks of fluctuations in the market.

The gains in revenue terms must be considerable. Piece rates for manufactured output are often very low, and sometimes a competent worker can barely make half the legal minimum for normal factory workers in the trade. Illustrations occasionally surface in the press, although it is impossible to know how representative they are. For example, the *Guardian* (19 October 1979) reported the case of 6000 Asian women home-workers in Nelson, Lancashire, being paid piece rates for sewing ribbons, bows and rosettes: a competent worker could produce enough to earn about 10 pence per hour. With dexterity and with all family members at work, this might yield 2–3000 small satin bows per week, and an income of between £11.00 and £16.50 (in the same year, it was estimated that £61.75 was required to support a family of four, and the government's supplementary-benefit entitlement was set at £55.90).

Child Workers

The stubborn persistence in demand for a workforce paid at well below the existing social norms is most strikingly exemplified in the employment of under-age workers. The evidence is impressionistic and there is too little to suggest trends. In the early 1980s in Britain, it was estimated (LPU, 1985) that 40 per cent of those aged between 11 and 16 worked and did so illegally, either through working at an age not permitted (below the age of 13), hours not permitted, or in jobs that were not permitted. For example, as a BBC documentary (*Brass Tacks*) showed in 1985, children from the age of nine were employed in East Anglia to top carrots between 5.0 and 8.0 p.m. – it being illegal for those under 16 to work after 7.0 p.m. or for more than two hours on school days.

The activities of child workers range from the marginal, such as newspaper delivery, to working in shops and restaurants, farm work, hotels, painting and decorating, cleaning, modelling, clerical work, running street stalls, serving in public houses or engaging in construction work. A 1982/83 survey (LPU, 1985) suggested that perhaps one-third of school truancies were related to work demands.

Italy has provided some of the more striking examples of child labour in the postwar period. From the 1950s, occasional surveys showed the scale of illegal employment of those aged between 10 and 13, particularly in textiles, metallurgy, machinery and shoe-making. Some 62 per cent of child workers did not attend school in the late 1960s (from a government survey, cited in Valcarenghi, 1981), and another 36 per cent attended for only five of the compulsory eight years of education. In fact, these figures are thought to have been an underestimate, particularly for the south of the country – in Naples, it was said, the 55,000 small enterprises in 1980 employed at least one child each, and there were said to be a total of 200,000 engaged in cottage industries in Sicily. Pay for those aged 10 to 15 (on a 36-hour week) was said to be roughly 3 per cent of the unskilled basic rate.

Below even the illegal section of the labour market, there are other activities involving children and women which are, usually, criminal. A 1988 report for the Norwegian Ministry of Justice alleged that annually worldwide up to 1 million children were purchased or kidnapped for distribution through a network of sex markets; most of these minors were shipped from developing to developed countries for the tourist trade and video pornography. Similar anecdotal evidence exists on the forced international movement of women for prostitution.

Illegal Migration

Low-paid employment is not the sole source of work available for legal or illegal migrants, but it is one of the largest sources, and migration is the evidence that unsatisfied demand for workers exists in the developed countries. The more advanced these countries become, the greater is their dependence on production by low-paid labour whether at home or in developing countries. The illegal immigrant is the most striking illustration of the growth in the demand for the services or output of the low-paid.

The subject is most actively explored in the United States, where, it seems, there is scarcely a year in which a congressional inquiry is not set up to examine it. However, it is almost impossible to calculate the number of illegal immigrants accurately, a fact that licenses all kinds of wild guesses, ranging as high as 12 million illegal aliens. Even the federal government's Immigration and Naturalization Service gave credence – and a spurious precision – to the figure of between 5.5 and 6 million in the mid-1970s (US Senate, 1976). More sober estimates in the 1970s suggested that the annual gross inflow of Mexicans alone was possibly of the order of 1.5 million, and the net balance after departures some 116,000 (Heer, 1979). Borjas, Freeman and Lang (1991: 78) suggest that by 1980 the number of illegal Mexicans in the United States was in the order of 1.8 million (the census of that year enumerated 1.2 million), and this had probably grown to between 2 and 2.3 million by 1984.

The bulk of illegal immigrants were traditionally temporary workers in agriculture. Contrary to popular opinion, they arrived seasonally and left afterwards. A sample examined by Wayne Cornelius (1978) found that less than one-fifth expressed any interest in staying in the country even if it proved legally feasible. However, over the past two decades, labour demand for illegal immigrants has tended to grow more quickly in the urban areas, in construction, manufacturing and some urban services. Unlike legal Mexican migrants – of which 46 per cent were women according to the 1980 census – 80 to 85 per cent of the illegals were men.

Under a 1986 Act, the federal government offered an amnesty to illegal immigrants, and some 1.8 million took advantage of this (a further 1.3 million registered under the special schemes for agricultural workers [Papademetriou, 1993]). By 1989, some 480,000 of them had secured permanent residence. However, there is no evidence that what was intended as a once-and-for-all settlement of the issue of illegal migration did indeed end, or even reduce, the flow. Nor, for that matter, is there evidence that, when the US government maintained the old Bracero scheme (to allow the entry of agricultural workers during and after the Second World War), this reduced illegal flows; indeed, a public wages board estimated that in 1951 some 60 per cent of the workforce picking the tomato harvest was illegal (Kushner, 1975).

The Immigration and Naturalization Service (INS) has frequently tried to suggest that the number of illegal aliens is rising. The evidence here is that the rate of arrests has risen – from 100,000 in 1967 to 750,000 in the 1970s, and nearly 1 million in the first half of the 1980s. The arrests were in the main on the southern border of the United States, where, notoriously, apprehended immigrants, once returned to Mexico, try again to cross, and may be arrested three or four times before they succeed. In addition, the arrest rate is closely related to expenditure on the INS (1986 represented in real terms a 140 per cent increase in expenditure on 1967) – indeed, increased spending explains about half the increase in arrests. The INS figures are, therefore, a suspect indicator of trends.

However, what does seem to be the case is that labour supply is increasingly sensitive to changes in US labour demand, regardless of the legal impediments to mobility. This in turn suggests the development of long-distance facilitating networks, recruiting workers at one end and then feeding them through the successive barriers of inter-mediate countries to their final destination. This has long seemed to be the case in Europe, with recruitment networks stretching deep into Africa and the Middle East, carrying workers through many countries, securing the necessary documentation, bribing officials, providing safe houses, food and transport by road and sea, to their ultimate employment. These are sophisticated arrangements which imply large criminal organizations rather than solitary migrants driven by hunger.

The same method seems to have been behind one of the stories in the American press in 1993: the arrival of shiploads of intending immigrants without papers off New York from Fujian province in China. According to the reports, one ship had been travelling for 18 months. The passengers had paid $25–30,000 each for the trip, and remained indebted to the organizers, the *shetou* or snakeheads, until they had worked enough in the United States to pay off the obligation (failure to pay could lead to family members in China being threatened). The first boat was apprehended in May 1991; the largest held 524 passengers (a further 661 people are said to have been caught off the Mexican coast and repatriated). Press interviews in the town of Changle in Fujian province (*Far Eastern Economic Review*, 8 April 1993: 17–18) confirm some of these details – and suggest that 100,000 Chinese entered the United States illegally in 1992, 85 per cent through this town. Some estimates suggest that between 17 and 20 ships are involved, and put the value of the trade at some $3 billion annually. The destination is New York because one of the largest colonies of Fujianese in the United States lives there.

In Japan, too, the Yakuza (Japan's mafia) have clearly been a key force – in collaboration with gangsters in the sending country – in bringing illegals to the country, often to work in gangster-run enterprises. Estimates of the size and composition of the illegal workforce in Japan are, as in the United States, based upon the arrest rates; officially, these range from 70,000 to 320,000 (Spencer, 1992) – with women predominating in the early 1980s (some 93 per cent of all arrests) and men in the late 1980s (71 per cent of the arrests in 1989). The process of drawing in foreign workers began in those sectors which Japanese workers vacated first (but which, as incomes rose, expanded more rapidly): bars, brothels, hotels and restaurants, construction and farming. In 1983, some 68 per cent of those arrested were hostesses. From these sectors, scarcities moved on to the mass of small-scale manufacturing and services. The nationality of the workers was Filipino (especially in the case of women), Pakistanis, Bangladeshis, Koreans, Malaysians (especially in the case of men), and later on Iranians. Gangster control of the bars, brothels and patinko parlours ensures that illegal immigrants become one of the preoccupations of criminal groups, labour recruiters and brokers for companies in need of workers (the physical power wielded by the gangsters also ensures the discipline of the workers and the repayment of their debts). The Yakuza are said to take half of the daily pay of the illegal workers under their control (*Financial Times*, 10 July 1989).

What made the slow erosion of Japanese migration controls accelerate was the spectacular boom in the second half of the 1980s. Bankruptcies of small firms at the height of the preceding boom were attributed to a scarcity of labour, and this phenomenon was exaggerated in the late 1980s. A Labour Ministry survey of 15,000 firms in the autumn of 1989 indicated that 60 per cent had been obliged to change plans and practices because they had too few workers. The worst-affected industries were oil, paper and pulp, electrical and electronic machinery, vehicles, shipbuilding, construction, transport, shipping, hotels and restaurants.

The labour effects of the boom can be seen not only in illegal immigration but also in the arrivals of those of Japanese descent from Latin America who had the right to work. There were officially in January 1991 some 150,000 *nikkei*, (ethnic Japanese), mainly from Peru and Brazil.

For the larger companies, the shortage of labour, reflected in increasing mobility of workers between firms and strong wage pressure, is a powerful factor impelling them to export production capacity to Southeast Asia and to invest in labour-saving equipment (Japan, with two-thirds of the world's robots, doubled the number between 1986 and 1992 and, it is projected, will double them again by 1995). To ease its labour-supply problems, Nissan tried to push back the retirement age of its workers from 60 to 65. Other Japanese companies have become increasingly dependent upon imports from their subsidiaries or other sources abroad. But the smaller – and more labour-intensive operations – are reduced to stealing workers from each other or turning to the Yakuza for illegal immigrants.

At the height of the boom, for example, the trucking industry – with a labour force of 750,000 – estimated its labour shortage at 100,000 workers. Construction likewise claimed 100,000 vacancies, some 34 per cent of the total number of workers required. By November 1989, in the labour market as a whole there were two vacancies for every applicant. The government estimated the national labour shortage at 2.06 million, and the Ministry of Labour projected the trend to a national labour shortage of 9.1 million workers by the year 2010.

However, the government remains paralysed on the issue of the legal importation of workers. Employers, especially in the sectors most threatened, press hard for expanded immigration, and for the use of Japanese aid to Southeast Asia to train potential immigrants. MITI (Ministry of International Trade and Industry) might speculate that 1 million foreign workers would be needed by the year 2001, but the most that the Ministry of Justice would concede was an expansion in the number of trainees coming to Japan for educational purposes – ten thousand were to be admitted initially, and the Ministry of Foreign Affairs eased restrictions to allow pay at the level of minimum wages, rather than the very low 'training allowance'. With admirable sensitivity, the crime syndicates started opening language schools for foreign students to learn Japanese while working (they were said to own one-third of the schools in the late 1980s). By 1991, there were officially some 30,000 foreign 'students', with up to half a million illegal immigrants (Kowahara, 1992). Schools usually arranged employment at the same time – working in factories or on construction sites. The government finally recognized what was happening and sharply reduced the number of visas permitted and imposed stricter controls on the schools.

Neither the United States nor Japan can be seen as representative of the developed countries on the question of illegal immigration. In the illegal movement the underworld is in control, and there is as little public knowledge of the patterns of activity as there is of, say, the $200 billion illegal narcotics trade. Nonetheless, as we discuss later, the labour brokers, like termites, bore their way through the fortifications of the state to connect demand and supply. They have created facts to which governments are obliged to respond.

The more disaggregated the data, the more restless and changeable seem the continuing efforts to breach government barriers. Let us consider one area: Eastern Europe. In the first half of 1991, some 1.4 million Ukrainians left their country 'for personal reasons' (the majority, over 800,000, went to Poland, as thousands of Poles streamed westwards). Most engaged in cross-border trading (Shamshur, 1992). In the spring of the same year, 317,000 Russian tourists travelled to Poland, 46,000 of whom did not return within the time allowed and are thought to have taken work in Polish farming and construction. In 1988, 7 million Poles are estimated to have travelled abroad, of whom 280,000 had not returned within one year. The Hungarian government estimated in 1991 that the country was host to a quarter of a million illegal immigrants, compared to the official figures for legal foreigners of 120,000 – 3000 refugees, 20,000 seeking refugee status, 80,000 resident foreigners, and 20,000 'guest workers' (Szoke, 1992). On the other side of the world, in Guam in the South Pacific, the government was accused of conniving in the exploitation of illegal immigrants from Korea and the Philippines (IUF, 1978).

Conclusion

Workers were moving to work, despite the obstacles that governments and others placed in their way. Indeed, for the many governments that claimed to believe in capitalism and free markets, it might have seemed a strong tribute to the efficacy of the system that, despite public resistance, the workers did move. If the theory was correct, world output grew as a result. Yet everywhere the poor, the victims, were converted into the enemy. Not only was the poorly paid worker generally ignored, even though the developed world continued to depend heavily upon his or her labour, but the illegal immigrant was identified as an enemy of civilization, the agent of destruction.

Unskilled labour, if also poor, has everywhere been historically abused. The labour of such workers, like that of the common infantrymen in war, achieved spectacular results for those who directed it; it was the precondition for any advance. Yet everywhere the unskilled worker was seen as a failure – despised, denigrated, and frequently denied even the minimum conditions of human decency. The rich man treated his horse or his dog with greater favour in the long harsh winters of northern Europe. The large-scale entry of women into the unskilled labour force created no new conditions, but rather reinforced ancient oppressions. Below the surface, the home-worker was hardly seen as a worker at all, even though her earnings supported vast numbers of others.

Immigrants, legal or not, made only a very small addition to this total labour supply; but, as with women in paid work, they were often physically marked with the stigmata of inferiority, a black or brown skin or a foreign accent. Although only relatively few in number, they evoked extraordinary attention, as if their very illegality could overthrow the legal whole. Only an extraordinary expansion in the economic system could begin to wash away some of the inferiority of being an unskilled worker, a woman or a foreigner.

The illegal worker – whether a native adult working in illegal activities, a working child, or an immigrant – extends the labour force beyond both statistical reach and public consciousness. As among the low paid, many who work in this sector are particularly vulnerable to economic change; their lives are frequently the anvil on which the world works out its purposes in more personal and painful ways than it does on those with material defences. Yet migrant workers are not simply victims. On the contrary, they often shape their lives more decisively than the majority who stay at home; they risk themselves in a world unknown and dangerous. Furthermore, they unknowingly slip through the contrary perspectives of national states and, in doing so, subvert their power.

Even the impoverished worker shapes his or her environment. Given the opportunity of mass leverage, immigrants join trade unions in disproportionate numbers and are active in resisting their downgrading. From the great strikes in the motor industry in France to the multitude of local disputes in small factories, immigrant workers have reacted in ways identical to those of the natives. Official unions are in general supportive, although as with all disputes they keep one eye firmly fixed on their reputation in established society. The erosion of union power in the 1980s to some extent makes them more dependent upon the energies of immigrants.

3

The Sweated Trades in the Developing Countries

Introduction

The migration of workers from developing to developed countries is only a fragment of the wider picture – the search for cheap labour at given levels of productivity (which, in turn, implies a host of supportive services, infrastructure, and so on). The integration of the world economy opens up to each national business class the possibility of buying goods from, or investing in, places where educated labour is cheap, as an alternative to bringing labour to a developed country. Indeed, competition between firms in the developed countries forces them to seek out new sources of supply of goods in order to survive. This may be the purchasing of labour-intensive output at 'arm's length', or subcontracting for an output, produced under the supervision of the buyer to ensure it meets the right specifications of quality and price, or setting up a joint venture or a subsidiary. But the subsidiary of a company in a developed country is only one form of this process of 'capturing' a foreign workforce (a no less misleading formulation would be to say the workforce had 'captured' a share of foreign capital). Through whatever complex forms, over several decades, elaborate manufacturing networks have been created so that single production processes straddle locations in many countries and involve many different types of collaboration, much of it hardly known outside the office of the purchasing manager.

Where regulations permit, the dynamic effects of this process are especially visible in border regions or where developed markets and developing suppliers are close together – for example, on the US–Mexico frontier and, later, on the Hong Kong–Guangdong border region of south China. They are, depending upon the context, often boom areas for manufacturing. Thus, in the 1980s, when the world economy grew relatively slowly and that in Mexico hardly at all, off-

56

shore manufacturing employment on the Mexican border grew by some half a million, and by between 3 and 6 million in Guangdong province, next to Hong Kong.

The system appears to change continuously, with new products and locations endlessly replacing old as new demands and new advantages emerge. The manufacturing location – as opposed to particular companies (which are created and destroyed as relocation occurs) – might start in Hong Kong in the 1950s, move on to Taiwan and Korea in the early and mid-1960s, to parts of Latin America, to Israel and Portugal, and to Singapore in the late 1960s, to Malaysia and Thailand in the 1970s, to China, Bangladesh, Sri Lanka, Mauritius in the 1980s. In the 1980s particularly, the geography became even more scrambled, as Hong Kong firms moved manufacturing capacity into southern China; Japanese, Korean and Taiwanese capital opened capacity in both China and Southeast Asia, in Sri Lanka, the Caribbean and the United States (in search of technology and markets). Activities which began on the Mexican border moved on to the interior, to the Caribbean and to East and Southeast Asia – and might easily return if the conditions are favourable. Once location has become an element in the competitive struggle of firms, it is difficult for a single stable division of labour to last long.

The boom in Europe in the 1950s had been the first force to precipitate this change in location, but by the 1980s the suppliers no longer depended so completely on the markets of the developed countries. The growing markets of Asia themselves partly fuelled Asian growth (Kwan, 1994). Increased competition in the developed markets, the product of recession and slump, was also a force pushing production capacity out of the developed countries (or bankrupting the former producers, with alternative supplies coming from imports produced by new foreign companies). Shifts in capacity seem impervious to boom and slump, but rather accelerate over time, and increasingly back and forth; innovations in a developed country might claw back an activity thought to be entirely lost, even while activities thought to be incapable of relocation disappear. The process presupposes an enormous apparatus that makes possible the rapid and cheap movement of capital, labour and goods.

Governments in the developed countries are torn between the contrary imperatives of trying to protect what they already hold – which, in terms of jobs, has an important bearing on their own political survival – and helping domestic firms compete against manufactured imports by allowing them to import cheap components or relocate part or all of their manufacturing capacity to cheaper locations. The first tends to dominate the political scene, but the second has always been important; for example, a number of European governments made provision in the garment industry for 'outsourcing' – part processing abroad (Fröbel et al., 1980) – and in the United States, special tariffs (formerly 806 and 807) encourage American firms to relocate labour-intensive segments of production abroad. Indeed, as we have seen, it is precisely where protection is greatest in the developed countries, in labour-intensive activities (most notably in garments and textiles, regulated under the Multi-Fibre Arrangement), that imports from developing countries have expanded most strongly. Of course, a proportion of those imports are the output of international companies that had relocated plants to the exporting country. As employment – and thus voting power – in these industries declines, the pressure for protection weakens, and the counterpressure of importers to keep open national frontiers increases.

However, integration is not a smooth process; it is very uneven, producing rapid growth in some places alongside notorious backwardness and poverty (and sometimes both occur in the same place). One of the most striking examples of growth – with ramifications in terms of labour migration extending as far as East Asia and the Americas – came in the Middle East.

The Oil-Producing Middle East: An Instant Cosmopolitan Labour Force

Even while the Europeans were trying in the early 1970s to construct or perfect the barricades to exclude immigrants, a major new destination for migrant workers emerged. The extraordinary increase in oil prices in the early 1970s vastly expanded the revenues received by the governments of the oil-producing Middle East (and North Africa) and created for a time an unprecedented boom in investment (something similar happened in a number of other oil-producing countries – for example, Nigeria, Venezuela, Indonesia, Brunei and later Mexico). In the Middle East, the Arab countries had very small labour forces, and the development strategy chosen entailed a major importation of labour, its scale and its social and skill composition (and therefore its ethnic, national and religious composition, as well as its gender) changing with the pattern of expansion.

By 1975, some 2 million workers had moved to work in the oil-producing states of the Middle East. At this stage, nearly 60 per cent were of Arab origin, the bulk of them drawn from Egypt, Jordan and what was then North Yemen (although even then 18 per cent were drawn from the Indian subcontinent); another 6 per cent came from

Europe and North America. There were about 1.5 million dependants. Relative to the local population, these were large numbers: 89 per cent of the total employment in the United Arab Emirates, 83 per cent in Qatar, 71 per cent in Kuwait, and nearly 40 per cent in Saudi Arabia and in Oman. In time, labour demand spread further afield: to much of North Africa (Algeria, as an important oil producer, imported workers – 21,400 by 1975 – while it continued to send Algerians to France), to Sudan and Turkey, to West Africa.

The investment boom initially increased the demand for building workers: 36 per cent of workers in the first years of immigration went into construction. Some 22 per cent were engaged in services, 16 per cent commerce and finance, 9 per cent agriculture, and 6 per cent manufacturing (agricultural employment was more important in Libya and Saudi Arabia, manufacturing in Kuwait and Bahrain).

Surprisingly quickly, different nationalities (and possibly, if the figures were available, subnational regions and cities) became associated with particular occupations, with Jordanians and Egyptians spreading the most widely between occupations. Take, for example, Kuwait in 1975, excluding Americans and Europeans. In the highest category of jobs ('professional jobs usually requiring a science or mathematics-based university degree'), Egyptians (with 13 per cent of total employment) accounted for 27 per cent of the jobs – contributing 39 per cent of physicians and dentists, 39 per cent of statisticians, 29 per cent of economists. Jordanians (most of whom were Palestinians) – also with 13 per cent of total immigrant employment – accounted for a quarter of the total number of jobs – contributing 30 per cent of physical scientists, 28 per cent of physicians and dentists, 29 per cent of economists. Indians (with 7.2 per cent of total employment) accounted for 26 per cent of the professional nurses; and Jordanians and Egyptians for another 38 per cent.

Coming down the occupational hierarchy, curious niches of specialization are revealed. In skilled jobs, 38 per cent of those employed in food and beverage preparation were Iranians; 49 per cent of tailors and dressmakers were Pakistani (with 3.7 per cent of total employment); and 54 per cent of shoemakers were Iranian, the other 46 per cent being Syrian (with 5.6 per cent of total employment). One-fifth of cabinet-makers were Iranian (and two-thirds were Iranian, Jordanian, Egyptian or Pakistani); nearly 30 per cent of stonecutters were Syrian; 44 per cent of jewellery and precision metal workers were Pakistani; 70 per cent of those making rubber and plastic products were Syrian; over one-third of the painters were Iranian; and nearly two-thirds of the bricklayers and skilled construction workers were Egyptian or Jordanian.

For the unskilled or semi-skilled something similar occurred: 38 per cent of cooks, housekeepers and waiters were Indian, as were 43 per cent of laundry workers, dry-cleaners and pressers; nearly half the hair-dressers and related workers were Pakistani or Jordanian; yet 97 per cent of policemen, detectives and fireman were Kuwaiti (figures calculated from Birks and Sinclair, 1978a: 47–9, Table 29).

If the figures could be refined, they would show much narrower recruitment patterns – from particular localities, cities or districts, ethnic, religious and, for Indians, caste backgrounds. Nor can we assume that these patterns of specialization are uniform in all countries where migrants worked – for example, there is no reason to assume Libyan employers attributed to Syrians the same occupational specializations as, say, did the Saudis.

Working and living conditions were notoriously bad. When immigration was relatively unrestricted, would-be workers often paid contractors to arrange jobs, tickets and visas, but were sometimes left with nothing by unscrupulous dealers. On arrival, local living costs frequently proved much higher than expected, and for the immigrant to meet his target savings he had to live in a slum or shanty town with minimum services. In Saudi Arabia, workers earning below a specified amount were not permitted to bring dependants. A labour importer would obtain a visa for the worker, and then held his passport, return ticket and part of what was earned as a forfeit to ensure good behaviour. There was no means of redress for fraud and few rights. Immigrants had no right to change jobs without permission, although many slipped into an illegal labour market to escape unscrupulous employers (the government published a blacklist of workers who had left their employers).

There are scattered accounts of resistance – strikes and protest demonstrations; these were often put down with force and the participants deported. Some governments – for example, the Indian and Filipino – tried to strengthen the position of their respective labour attachés to cope with the complaints of their nationals, but they had little or no power to influence host governments. As immigrant remittances became an increasingly important source of foreign exchange for the governments of the countries from which the immigrants came, circumspection in responding to complaints became more important. As labour brokers diversified the countries from which they recruited, sending governments found themselves in competition with each other, and as a result were even less inclined to pick a quarrel with the employers of their nationals.

The controls on workers tended to become stricter, and the enforcement of this regulatory regime in the construction industry increasingly tended to favour the Korean system of organization. Korean companies brought their own labour force (so the client avoided the costs of recruitment) – which usually consisted of single men without dependants; the company supervised their work, housed them in work-camps, provided them with services and foodstuffs, and repatriated them at the end of the contract. Thus, the client had virtually no contact with the workforce, only with the contracted company. Furthermore, from the Korean government's point of view, the system ensured that much less of the workers' incomes leaked into the local economy rather than returning to Korea. Indeed, the Korean government instituted a regime whereby companies were obliged to remit to Korea 80 per cent of the income earned – for payment to the worker after his return.

Companies from other countries emulated the scheme. For example, in the 1980s China offered companies self-administering work gangs under close home supervision (for instance, the system involved in the joint Brazilian–Chinese consortium which in 1985 won the contract to build the Iraqi Bekhme dam). In turn, as the income of Korean workers rose, Korean contractors moved to replace them with non-Korean workers; an official ruling supposedly permitted only 30 per cent of the workforce to be non-Korean, but in practice there was no way of enforcing this in a foreign country.

By 1980, there were some 4 million foreign workers employed in the oil-producing countries of the Arab Middle East. However, the great boom in construction work was declining, so that the types of skill required – and thus the countries from which workers were drawn – were changing. By the mid-1980s, in the countries of the Gulf Co-operation Council, while just under 29 per cent of foreign workers were employed in construction, 30 per cent were engaged in financial, personal and community services, and 14 per cent in trade. Generally, the main vacancies were in services, manufacturing, public utilities and agriculture. An increasing number of women were now recruited as domestics – the total rose from 8000 in 1979 to over 50,000 ten years later (when 76 per cent of women immigrants were domestics). The sources also changed – to Sri Lanka (where 65 per cent of emigrants were women), Bangladesh, Indonesia and the Philippines. A demand for better-educated domestics emerged and the proportion of Filipina migrant domestics to the Middle East with professional and technical qualifications consequently rose from 17 to 26 per cent between 1980 and 1987.

For migrants as a whole, there was a similar diversification of sources: in 1970, of all immigrants to the Gulf, 12 per cent were non-Arab; by

1980 the figure was 41 per cent, and by 1985 it was 83 per cent. Most came from South and Southeast Asia; by the late 1980s, for example, there were 140,000 Thai workers in the Middle East, most from the poor northeast of the country (as most Indians were from Kerala).

However, the oil price was not as buoyant in the 1980s as it had been in the early and the late 1970s, and the fluctuations in oil revenue squeezed and expanded the recruitment of foreign workers. The oil price decline in the early 1980s, for example, is said to have led to 700,000 leaving the Gulf area in 1984 (in 1985, the ILO calculated that if the price of oil stagnated at $15 per barrel, the number of Pakistani workers would decline by a third up to 1990).

The presence of foreign workers allowed them to be used as instruments of foreign policy. Thus Libya on occasions expelled its Tunisian and other workers to punish their respective governments. In 1991, when Iraq invaded Kuwait, there were 5 million foreign workers in the Gulf. Some 1.9 million Asians working in Iraq and Kuwait were obliged to flee, in many cases without their pay, savings or assets. For a period, half a million Asian workers were trapped in refugee camps in Iraq, Kuwait and Jordan. There were accusations that Baghdad had forced Bangladeshi workers to dig defensive trenches for its army. Some 60,000 Bangladeshi and Sri Lankan house servants were abandoned in Kuwait as their employers fled. On the other side, Saudi employers were accused of preventing their foreign workers fleeing the war zone by withholding their passports and return tickets. The Saudi Arabian government decided to expel those among its immigrant workers who hailed from countries which had supported Iraq (Yemen and Sudan) or, like Jordan, equivocated. At the same time, since the Palestine Liberation Organization had publicly favoured Iraq, Palestinians were also driven out of Kuwait and Saudi Arabia regardless of whether they personally supported or rejected the Iraqi position.

The Middle Eastern oil boom showed how an elaborately stratified multinational labour force could be recruited swiftly and put to work – an instant cosmopolitan workforce. It offered a model for the future, as well as giving a host of companies experience in putting together a multinational labour force. All over Asia and the Middle East, and in parts of Africa, fortunes were made and poor local economies lifted, all on the basis of work in the oil-producing countries.

Internationalization

Demand in developed countries gained access to the labour forces in developing countries in a growing variety of forms. One initially important form was the export processing zone, but the significance of this tended to decline as general liberalization took place. Subcontracting to producers in developing countries was of greater importance, blurring the differences between major multinational corporations and elaborate networks of small producers. A giant US shoe company ordered parts from Puerto Rico, and the Puerto Rican firms subcontracted the shoe-making to interdependent networks of small firms in Haiti, Dominican Republic, Antigua, Barbados and Jamaica. Nike and Reebok purchased shoes from companies in Taiwan and South Korea; the Koreans, in search of lower-cost production facilities, opened four factories in Indo-nesia (and subcontracted orders to two other Indonesian companies), employing in sum 24,000 workers in 1990 to produce 6 million pairs of shoes, or 8 per cent of world production (the Indonesian unit cost was said to be US$12; the selling price in the United States, $65). When American newspapers criticized Nike for tolerating bad working condi-tions, pay below the legal minimum, and the employment of children, the company countered that the plants were owned and run by South Korean and Indonesian firms. Popular perception – and governments – identified commodities with clearly distinct firms and straightforward patterns of nationality, location and employment. But in this case, it seemed, no one was ultimately responsible; and, indeed, the complexity of relationships meant that the source of output could not easily be identified, even by nationality (that is, related to a clearcut political authority). Networks, like cobwebs, festooned and blurred the lines of moral responsibility.

However, manufacturing at least deals with tangible objects. The rapidly emerging sectors of world trade in services are much more difficult to grasp, ranging from some of the most sophisticated activi-ties in Research and Development to some of the least, from activities dispatched by fax or e-mail to those parts moved in containers. The data on such activities are particularly unreliable, and much of the discussion is reduced to anecdote – for example, the translation of the 3 million criminal records for England and Wales into computer format by 200 touch typists in the Philippines (organized for the British police by an Australian company, Saztec); or the transfer of the processing of Canadian medical records and American airline tickets to the Caribbean, of Swiss Air's accounts to Bombay, and of the largest Japanese real-estate company's land transactions to south China. In the last chapter, we noted the phenomenal growth in the supply of domestics, where the person carries his or her services to the destination country.

China

As a relative newcomer to significant world trade, China offers a good example of expansion into areas other than manufactured goods. Shenzhen, on the borders of Hong Kong, presents striking examples here, offering to Hong Kong citizens in 1980 nurseries for their children and grave sites for their dead, language services, driving lessons and medical checkups. As Hong Kong's population ages, it will become increasingly dependent upon labour-intensive services; these links are therefore likely to grow even without the results of the political re-unification of the city and China.

As was the case with many other sectors in developing countries, the Middle Eastern construction boom offered an important training programme for China. It allowed the companies of many countries to spread out to other locations: for example, Turkish companies to what was then the Soviet Union; Korean companies to sub-Saharan Africa and Latin America. International construction companies operating out of developed countries tended to adopt the same strategy, becoming increasingly dependent on labour forces recruited in developing countries.

In construction abroad, China had a history that predated the Middle Eastern boom (as, for example, with the Tanzam railway). It had also supplied the Soviet Union with labour in the Russian far east to offset debts, as had Vietnam to all of the former Eastern bloc countries. In Russia's case, the practice continued into the 1990s. As late as 1992, there were reported to be 20,000 Chinese workers in Hungary, many of them employed in the textile industry.

The reforms of the late 1970s allowed Chinese companies and ministries to spread their interests much more widely, and particularly to the Middle East. The leading company, CCECC (the China Civil Engineering and Construction Company, established by the China Construction and Machine Corporation in 1979), claimed within a year of its foundation to have supplied 3000 workers to German, Italian and Japanese contractors working in the Middle East, while the CCECC was itself building factories in what was then North Yemen. A year later, *China Daily* (4 November 1981) claimed that 13,000 workers were on contract to companies in the Middle East and North Africa. In Jordan, the CCECC won in open tender against 39 companies (including Wimpey and other large international operators) the contract to build 2600 houses; with an Egyptian collaborator, it built part of the new town, '20th October', outside Cairo, 350 apartments in North Yemen, and a bridge in Iraq.

Other Chinese companies and ministries followed suit. For example, the Guangdong provincial government created Guangdong Manpower Services Corporation to supply labour on foreign contracts; Fujian province did the same, as did the national Ministry of Metallurgy (*Chinese Business Review*, July–August 1979: 48). Hong Kong firms recruited workers in China for contracts in the Middle East. In the far northern province of Heilongjiang, labour was supplied to Russia's far east (North Korea was at the same time supplying labour to cut timber in Russia).

By 1984, reputedly 40,000 contract workers were working abroad; and by 1992 the figure was 90,000. The countries now included those of Southeast Asia and sub-Saharan Africa, and the claimed value of the contracts was US$12.5 billion. Most workers were employed in construction, but some worked as ship crews (and there were even 24 cooks in the overseas workforce, supplied by the Beijing City Catering Services General Corporation). Working conditions could be bad. When the *South China Morning Post* (24 January 1982) investigated the working conditions of 50 Chinese contract workers in Hong Kong's Electric Lamma Power Station, it found inadequate sleeping areas, poor food, and what it alleged was systematic underpayment (the company supplying the workers expropriated 20 per cent of their earnings). The Chinese government, like the Korean, regulates labour exports to ensure that the major part of earnings is repatriated – the workers are, as it were, rented out. In the mid-1980s the government was said to have appropriated 70 per cent of earnings in the form of management, recruitment and placement fees, along with taxes and the workers' cost of living.

Inside China itself, something not dissimilar occurs. Thus, villages in advanced areas subcontract land to groups of migrant workers from poorer areas. In 1988 in the Beijing suburbs, 70,000 non-Beijing peasants grew vegetables under contract in this way. Contract workers are also supplied to factories to work alongside, or to replace, the normal permanent employees (Nolan, 1993). Thus, just as countries become simultaneously importers and exporters of workers, so domestic localities follow suit, in this case, both under contract.

The Philippines

The Philippines is a much older and larger exporter of labour. Indeed, by the early 1990s, it was – after Mexico – probably the second largest source in the world, with some 600,000 leaving annually (Martin, 1993). Of those abroad, 93 per cent are in the USA, Canada and Australia. They are an especially important source, as we have seen, for seamen

(230,000), nurses and domestics. Their particular advantage is a command of the English language and relatively high levels of education.

The Philippines' export of labour has been much influenced by the role of the government. The movement started spontaneously; but in 1975, under President Marcos, the government tried to establish control and pursue a deliberate policy of promoting work abroad. Workers were permitted to go abroad to work only if, one, the proposed rate of pay had been approved (and was double the comparable local rate); two, an affidavit had been signed to remit to the Philippines at least 30 per cent of the income (70 per cent in the case of seamen); and, three, a bank account was opened to ensure the remittances could be monitored. Remittances were required to be paid in foreign currencies, but withdrawals could only be made in Philippine pesos at the official exchange rate. The penalty for non-compliance was a refusal to renew the worker's passport and travel documents. Under international pressure, this penalty was subsequently withdrawn. Filipino employers abroad were required to deduct the minimum remittance at source and pay it directly to Manila. To promote Filipino workers, the Government's Overseas Employment Board (subsequently Administration) promises employers abroad that it will 'package and deliver workers to various sites around the world'. Labour-supply agreements are signed with 25 governments. The Administration aims to respond swiftly and accurately (in terms of skills) to all requests.

In 1983, the government published new regulations on remittances. Now 80 per cent of the earnings of sailors was to be remitted, 70 per cent of the earnings of employees working for Filipino companies abroad, and 50 per cent for all other workers (excluding those accompanied by their families, which tended to be the highly skilled, professional and better-paid workers; as always, the class system reasserted itself through the regulations). The greed of the government, however, was self-defeating. World labour demand for educated and English-speaking workers went well beyond the capacities of the government to control. A mass of illegal recruitment agencies developed – even though President Marcos at one stage decreed the death penalty for those running them. The costs of obeying the law were high. The illegal brokers easily supplied forged documents. The sheer scale of demand, the opportunities to earn, and the limited reach of the government beyond its shores ensured that Filipino workers had a powerful incentive and opportunity to escape official regulation.

Fighting the Labour Market

The Middle Eastern market for labour slackened in the 1980s. Yet, as it did, East and Southeast Asia emerged. The movement of workers between countries seems to be substantial, though much of it goes unrecorded in the official migration statistics, being caught only in occasional incidents. The worker flows in the Asian labour market come to resemble a night sky continually marked by summer lightning, as labour demand (and the arrival of agents selling labour) suddenly emerges in new areas, and new paths of movement are marked across borders. The Middle East made international migration a new way of life, a new culture, for thousands of households without experience of working abroad. When new opportunities for work opened in East and South Asia, there were workers ready and eager to move to them.

As the Middle East construction boom declined, workers – now freed from their own national labour market – moved on: in 1985, 91 per cent of Thai contract workers worked in the Middle East; by 1988, 77 per cent worked there, and rising numbers worked in Brunei (another oil boom area, but within Southeast Asia), Japan, Hong Kong and Singapore. Simultaneously, Cambodians and Burmese (some 200,000 of them) migrated to Thailand for work. In Indonesia, where rapid expansion in the oil industry was followed by a boom in manufacturing, workers emigrated to Sabah (one informed guess put the numbers at 40,000), and to Sarawak (10,000) in eastern Malaysia, as well as to the Middle East and western Malaysia.

Korea

South Koreans had moved to the Middle East during the boom (usually as the employees of Korean companies working there), while others migrated to the United States, to Chile and to Japan. By 1990, there were fewer than 20,000 Koreans employed in the Middle East; yet at the same time, an increasing number of foreigners were working illegally in Korea – 42,000 was the estimate for 1990, including 18,000 Chinese of Korean descent ('ethnic Koreans'), 16,000 Filipinos, and 1800 Nepalese, generally filling jobs in what the Japanese called the '3-Ds' category – dirty, difficult and dangerous. The government has for some time permitted immigrant labour in the coal mines (it did not stop the decline of the industry). By 1994, there were said to be 100,000 illegal immigrant workers in Korea. The government reacted, after much discussion, by permitting the legal entry of 20,000 foreign workers to relieve the labour shortage in small companies and to prepare for the expulsion of the illegal workers.

Parallel to the movement of different kinds of workers out of and into Korea was a diaspora of Korean capital. In the 1980s this was undertaken in the main by the large Korean companies, particularly to Indonesia and other parts of Southeast Asia. But the simultaneous pressures of high wages (particularly after the great worker rebellion of 1987), high land prices and the high cost of capital impelled smaller companies, particularly in light industry (garments, toys, footwear) to relocate, especially to China's northeast. In 1993, some 82 per cent of Korean overseas investment was by small and medium-sized companies, with an average value of only US$2 million. Korea was entering a familiar conjuncture, common to the Four Little Dragons of East and Southeast Asia: emigration, illegal immigration and a rapidly increasing export of capital. It did so at almost exactly the same time as the other three and Japan, a coincidence too striking to be spontaneous. Presumably the broker networks moved into action together to compensate for the decline of the Middle East market.

Malaysia

Malaysian workers, both skilled professionals and unskilled, migrated to Singapore (where they constituted 60 per cent of the foreign workforce), while perhaps as many as 1 million Indonesian workers worked in western Malaysia. The latter figure is something of a guess without much in the way of empirical foundation, since this was an illegal flow; other estimates suggested the total number of Indonesians abroad to be in the order of 300,000. Numerous shipwrecks in Indonesian coastal waters revealed the strength of the desire to work abroad – the clandestine flow of workers heading to Brunei, to Saudi Arabia (where the official movement of Indonesian domestics was also important), to logging camps and palm-oil plantations in west Malaysia's Trengganu, Pahang and Johore (Indonesians constituted about one-fifth of the plantation workforce), and to construction sites in Kuala Lumpur. The 1984 bilateral agreement between the governments of Malaysia and Indonesia to regularize legal flows was rapidly superseded by the mass of boats willing to ship people across the straits separating the countries: agents organized trips from east Java, Madura and Lombok, and the reverse flow of remittances through the State Bank was said to be of the order of 200 million rupiahs in 1990.

In 1989, the Malaysian government again endeavoured to put some order into the flow. Indonesians, the government said, were to blame for the escalating crime rate, displacing local traders, buying up land and working too hard. A monitoring committee of the Labour and

Home Ministries, the United Planters' Association and the National Union of Plantation Workers, established that 27,000 workers would be recruited annually, on three-year non-renewable contracts (with the employers lodging a per-capita deposit with the Immigration Department to finance the return fare). At the same time, the Indonesian government introduced an exit tax on departures. Both measures significantly raised the cost of legal migration, and thus increased the incentive to migrate illegally. In 1992, Kuala Lumpur instituted a registration drive to identify illegal workers, and found some 320,000 before the deadline expired. It was estimated that another 100,000 were not caught in the net; of these, it was thought that some 50,000 had returned to Indonesia because of the registration drive, and many others had fled to the countryside.

The battle by the Malaysian government to control the labour effects of the high rate of growth in the economy was only one example of numerous cases in the region. All high-growth economies, except the largest (such as China and Indonesia), decided sooner or later that immigration was a problem. In the 1980s, this particularly afflicted Hong Kong, Taiwan and Singapore.

Hong Kong

The city of Hong Kong has been largely created by migrants from China and the rest of the world, and immigrant workers have been an important factor in the extraordinary growth of the city's economy since the Second World War, propelling it into the position of a developed country. In the 1970s, for example, some 600,000 legal and illegal migrants joined the city's population. In 1979, at a high point in the city's frenetic economic growth (11 per cent in that year), some half a million people tried to leave the adjacent Chinese province of Guangdong; just over half were stopped by the Chinese authorities, and 90,000 were caught and expelled from Hong Kong, leaving possibly 140,000 who got through. Those who were successful relied on the collaboration of corrupt officials and police in China as well as the gangster networks that link Hong Kong and the mainland and which include the notorious 'Snakeheads', who – like Mexico's 'Coyotes' – for a price, organize the clandestine movement across boundaries.

Under an unofficial agreement with Beijing, Hong Kong operated up to 1980 what was known as a 'touch base' system. The Chinese government agreed to take back those who were expelled by Hong Kong, and Hong Kong agreed to accept those who successfully found a dwelling in the urban area without apprehension – and thus became entitled to a Hong Kong identity card. The system was acceptable, the Hong Kong government argued, as a means to prevent the growth of a stock of illegal immigrants, their being a prey to blackmail and to being forced into criminal activity.

However, in 1980, supposedly in response to rising numbers of arrivals, the government began to argue that immigration damaged the position of Hong Kong's existing citizens. Legislation was introduced to end the 'touch base' system and to penalize employers for hiring people without identity cards (up to HK$50,000 or £4200 sterling and one year's imprisonment). Existing immigrants without identity cards were offered an amnesty and the opportunity to regularize their status (6952 volunteered to do so), and Hong Kong agreed to admit 150 people daily from China as legal immigrants. At the same time, the administration began construction of an 18-foot-high barbed-wire fence along the border (complete with heat sensors, sound alarms and floodlighting). Simultaneously, Vietnamese refugees were arriving in substantial numbers – 79,000 in 1979 – and being interned. The cost of the new system of control was conservatively put at US$400 million for the two-year period 1979–81.

The new system was presented as an essential means to protect the existing citizens of Hong Kong. The plentiful supply of cheap labour which had for so long sustained Hong Kong's growth – and hence the remarkable growth in the employment and incomes of its citizens – had suddenly become, it seemed, a threat to their livelihoods. The 1980/81 Budget report thus noted that immigration 'affected the recovery of the labour force in that it is not being given the opportunity to enjoy the full benefits of economic growth' (*Far Eastern Economic Review*, 21 March 1980: 22). Government statements now reiterated that the supply of social services, hospital beds, public housing and schooling would be much reduced in quantity and quality if the flow of illegal immigrants were not stemmed; but nothing was said about the loss in these fields due to a lower growth in the output of the colony. Sir Murray MacLehose, the governor at the time, had observed in the same vein in the autumn that,

> Immigration reduced the extreme tension in the labour market ... but it also had a depressing effect on the real incomes of our workers.... Although the long term prospects for the growth of our economy remain good, immigration removes the incentive for higher productivity and movement into more sophisticated and capital intensive industries. (ibid., 31 October 1980)

No evidence was produced to support this proposition, nor that constraining the supply of workers might improve productivity – as opposed to what actually happened, the movement of Hong Kong firms producing labour-intensive goods out of Hong Kong to the mainland and to Southeast Asia. The number of workers in manufacturing in the city declined by over 30 per cent from its peak in 1981 (870,000) to mid-1992 (587,000), and the proportion of the gross domestic product generated by manufacturing declined from 24 to 16 per cent between 1984–86 and 1991. If the government had intended to placate trade-union opinion with this measure, the real effect of its decisions might have been to reduce, rather than enhance, the potential for employing Hong Kong's citizens.

In practice, however, the government bent its new rules on immigration when it suited its purposes, regardless of trade-union opinion. In the early 1970s, English-speaking families had been accorded the right to hire foreign domestic workers (a right subsequently extended to Chinese families). By 1976, 1917 contracts had been issued under this heading, but by 1989 the numbers had increased to 44,111. By the end of 1989, there were nearly 60,000 foreign domestics in Hong Kong, 91 per cent of them Filipino and the rest Thai.

The 1980s transformed the Hong Kong economy. On the one hand, government policy was committed to preventing immigration from mainland China, and, ultimately, to the forced repatriation of the estimated 51,000 Vietnamese refugees interned in Hong Kong (in the face of initial opposition from Washington but strong support from London). On the other hand, continued growth produced severe labour shortages, impelling both the export of capital and the import of 'guest workers' on restricted contracts. It seemed to be the economics of bedlam.

From the second half of the 1980s up to 1993, the numbers of official foreign passport holders (excluding those holding British passports) increased remarkably, doubling to 320,700: Filipinos by 310 per cent (to 99,200); Americans by 73 per cent (to 26,100); Thais by 245 per cent (to 23,500); Australians by 209 per cent (to 16,700); Japanese by 189 per cent (to 14,000); and Canadians by 287 per cent (to 20,400) (Skeldon, 1993). Professional workers were not restricted in their terms of entry. The inflow did not end the scarcity of labour, particularly of unskilled workers. The locally born labour force was not growing, the native-born population was tending to fall, and increased numbers were continuing in education or emigrating (42,000 in 1989). Furthermore, the extraordinary boom in China's neighbouring province of Guangdong was leading to increasing numbers of Hong Kong workers commuting to work on the mainland. The tight labour market led to increased turnover and delays in construction – as well as, according to employers, declining standards of workmanship.

Pressure from a broad range of businesses – via the Hong Kong General Chamber of Commerce and other important business associations – was directed toward trying to persuade the government that the city's competitiveness depended upon easing immigration controls. Service industries – particularly those involved in the vital tourist trade – stressed that there was no easy way to follow the government's advice and substitute capital for labour or find other ways to raise productivity; costs, they argued, would escalate rapidly without more workers.

The government ultimately agreed that a shortage of labour was indeed restricting economic growth, but its response was limited: 1500 blue-collar workers from China were admitted in October 1989, and a further 6266 skilled workers and 2720 supervisory and technical staff from all sources. In May of the following year, the government allowed firms to bring in 15,000 skilled and semi-skilled workers for government-approved projects, including work on the new airport (although there were estimates that 20,000 more workers were needed for the airport alone). The Hong Kong Chamber of Commerce welcomed the concession while complaining that the numbers were far too small (and the status of those admitted, as temporary workers without the right to change their work, too restrictive). The Chamber estimated that vacancies were of the order of 165,000 (the government's estimate suggested that in the third quarter of 1989 the number of vacancies was 88,000). The trade unions were strongly opposed to the relaxation.

In 1991 the government announced it would approve entry and work permits for 13,888 people, but in January of the following year this was increased to 25,000. In response, 452 trade unions of diverse political persuasions demonstrated their opposition to the proposal outside the Legislative Council Chamber during the debate. The new scheme permitted two-year contracts, renewable twice (the total time period allowed thus being one year less than that required to qualify for a residence permit).

While entry was eased, existing sanctions were tightened. The penalties for those employing illegal immigrants were raised in 1990 (up to three years imprisonment and a fine of HK$200,000 [about US$25,500], subsequently increased to HK$1 million, with additional fines for those persistently offending). The worker concerned was liable to a mandatory prison sentence of up to 15 months before being expelled. In 1990 it was said that about one-third of the city's prison population were illegal immigrants. Simultaneously, there was an increase in unannounced expulsions from the colony (in 1989, some 13,000 were expelled, most of them passed to the Chinese police).

The Hong Kong story illustrates the curious conjuncture of painful labour shortages with the expulsion of workers. In the case of those seeking asylum or entering illegally, deportation was justified by the government in terms of reducing the burden of support by the public exchequer. Yet this is only a burden if the people concerned are interned; if they are allowed to work – and the Hong Kong labour market clearly needed workers – there is no burden. Thus did the state invent the very pretext it requires to justify exclusion. The economics and the politics of immigration control apparently part company. The preoccupation with public-spending economies was accompanied by a remarkable laxity in terms of the costs of the machinery of control and the imprisonment of illegal immigrants, let alone the opportunity costs of depriving the Hong Kong economy of urgently needed workers.

Taiwan

Something not dissimilar occurred in the much larger high-growth economy of Taiwan. After 35 years of frenetic growth, by 1985 Taiwan was emerging as a developed economy of considerable wealth (with the world's largest foreign-exchange reserves). With only 23 million population, the island was the twelfth largest exporter in the world. However, in the second half of the 1980s the familiar squeeze on the labour market developed with great speed. The strength of the economy was reflected in a radical appreciation of the currency (by 40 per cent in two years), which, on its own, might have had a significant effect on the prices of Taiwan's exports. However, simultaneously a severe labour scarcity emerged and, as a result, wages increased on average by 12.2 per cent per year for the four years up to 1991. Unit labour costs increased by 27 per cent in the years between 1986 and 1992. The labour-intensive manufacturing industries that had been the foundation of Taiwan's export successes were hammered. This had two results.

First, Taiwanese companies began to relocate capacity abroad where labour costs were lower. Between 1987 and 1993, over 4000 firms set up operations in Southeast Asia where wages were, initially, one-tenth of the Taiwan level, and over 7000 invested in mainland China. In some cases, virtually whole industries moved – for example, 80 per cent of Taiwan's shoemaking firms are said to have shifted their manufacturing capacity to China. By 1990 Taiwan had become the second largest foreign investor in the Philippines, Malaysia, Thailand and Indonesia.

Second, there was a great shortage of labour for those activities which could not move (services to the Taiwanese population – for example, construction, domestic service, hotels and restaurants, personal, business and social services) or which were insufficiently capitalized to risk a

movement (leather goods, electronic assembly, plastics and metalworking). Particularly hard hit were some of the government's major infrastructural projects: the Taipei underground railway, a new freeway, the
Central Railway Station, the rapid transit system. The number of
vacancies in 1989 was put at between 100,000 and 200,000, increasing
by some 50,000 per year (Stahl, 1991).

The results of this conjuncture are familiar: a rapid increase in illegal
immigration, usually through people overstaying their visitor's visa.
Insignificant before 1986, the average annual inflow of visitors between
1985 and 1988 was 89,000 for Malaysians, 34,000 for Filipinos, 27,000
for Indonesians, and 24,000 for Thais (Tsay, 1992).

Once again, it was businesses – particularly small-scale firms – that
were active in pressing the government to allow legal worker immigration. A government corporation, BES Engineering, applied for permission to bring in 300 men to work on the Taipei underground railway,
but the government's Council of Labour Affairs rejected the request on
the grounds that the company proposed paying the workers only 53 per
cent of the current going rate for such work. In fact, the pay for illegal
workers in construction was said to be 43 per cent of the Taiwanese
rate, a level still ten times the average income of a Filipino peasant
family. There was also pressure from women's organizations to legalize
the existing flow of foreign workers on the grounds that this would
allow Taiwanese women to work (immigrant domestics cost between
one-third and one-half of local rates for hired home help).

In general, the government stressed that increased immigration would
overburden social services, housing and medical care, and (another
audacious leap of faith) increase the crime rate. The trade unions strongly
opposed any relaxation of the rules, a position with which the government broadly agreed, adding that immigration would disturb a society
with a supposedly high degree of ethnic and social homogeneity. Nevertheless, adjustments were made. To complete the government's own
infrastructural projects, a certain number of one-year visas carrying the
right to work became available. The Council of Labour Affairs laid
down strict rules for this: workers were to be recruited only for projects
explicitly sanctioned by the government, after local advertising had failed
to secure applicants, after a deposit had been left with the government
for each worker, and on condition that the worker was paid at least half
the local pay rate, housed, and given seven days leave annually in his
or her country of origin. In 1991, the Council announced its willingness
to approve work permits for up to 30,000 workers in a dozen occupations. In 1992 a law lifted the ban on many contacts with mainland
China (Fong, 1993) and allowed the import of workers.

Furthermore, the government set about rationalizing the existing situation. In February 1991 it offered to repatriate illegal immigrants without penalty and without removing their right to return legally in the future. At the same time, new detention centres were constructed to house future illegal workers, and new penalties introduced for employers hiring such workers (up to NT$300,000 and three years' imprisonment; for labour recruitment agents, the fine was up to NT$1.5 million and five years' imprisonment). The amnesty was bedevilled by the lack of serious estimates of the numbers involved. The government estimated there were 12,000 Filipinos on the island, 11,000 of them illegally. However, a Philippines Immigration Commission which visited Taiwan to persuade the government to extend its deadline for the amnesty claimed there were up to 50,000. A total of 22,579 people reported under the amnesty.

At the same time, the government urged firms to automate their production processes to escape the need to employ illegal workers; to increase the training of Taiwanese workers; and to introduce flexible work schedules to suit part-time local workers. Furthermore, it offered a reduction in military service from three to two years to increase the supply of young workers. Even so, the numbers involved were quite insufficient to meet the vacancies. In the spring of 1994 the government's Council for Labour Affairs reportedly received requests from local companies or brokers for nearly 350,000 workers, and approved applications for one year for 170,000. Two-thirds of these were from Thailand, 23 per cent from the Philippines, and 5 per cent each from Malaysia and Indonesia. The official concerned admitted, however, that severe labour shortages would persist – particularly in construction, home care and the merchant marine.

As in Hong Kong, the apparent choice was between increased immigration and a slower rate of growth with significant export of capital. As the government equivocated, it was the export of capital which balanced this account. But even then, the demands of manning the service economy went well beyond the domestic supply of workers, and continued to activate the arrival of foreign workers, increasingly from more distant sources in South Asia and beyond (on one occasion a Ghanaian construction worker was apprehended).

Singapore

Singapore combines one of the most spectacular rates of economic growth in the postwar world with one of the most stringent regimes of control of both population and wages. The control of labour costs has

always been of great importance to the government (Harris, 1987: 60–
67), and this has been paralleled by one of the strictest population
policies in the world, founded upon a dogmatic interpretation of fash-
ionable population-control ideology, laced with a revival of eugenics
theory.

In the first phase of growth, the government made major efforts to
reduce the rate of population growth by legislating a maximum of two
children per family. In so far as this policy was successful, economic
growth in later years made the island increasingly dependent upon
imported workers. While the government was happy to accept educated,
professional and upper-income immigrant workers (on 'employment
passes'), it continually battled to curb the entry of manual workers (on
'work permits').

Singapore could not escape dependence upon foreign unskilled
workers. Yet, from the 1970s, the regulatory regime was draconian (see
Selangor Graduates Society, 1978). Such workers were not permitted to
change jobs within the first three years or to hold trade-union office,
and protests were liable to be answered with deportation. Women
workers were subject to six-monthly pregnancy tests, and could not
marry Singapore nationals without government permission – granted
on the couple's agreement to accept sterilization after the second child
(those on employment passes faced no such restrictions). In July 1983 it
was repeated that those foreign nationals marrying without permission
were liable to deportation; and if a Singapore national was involved, he
or she would forfeit their entitlement to cheap public housing, free
education for their children and subsidized medical treatment. In an
earlier test case in 1977, where a Singapore man refused to accept
sterilization, his Malaysian partner was expelled (and not permitted a
visitor's permit to re-enter the city) (*Straits Times*, 16 March 1977).

In the late 1970s, a different problem began to be identified. Despite
Singapore's high rates of growth, the productivity performance was
poorer than the city's nearest rivals – in the 1970s productivity advanced
by 3 per cent per year, compared with 7 per cent annually in Korea,
Taiwan and Hong Kong. This poor record was attributed to the ready
availability of unskilled foreign labour to meet shortages, and this in
turn was, paradoxically, attributed to the government's policy of holding down the rate of growth of wages. In 1979 the government's National
Wages Council abruptly reversed its former policy. It proposed to
increase wage costs by some 20 per cent per year for three or four years
in order to price out low-paid workers and force companies either to
increase their efficiency in the use of labour or move out of Singapore.
Thus, it was calculated that the demand for foreign workers would be

eliminated as the economy was upgraded in terms of skills and productivity. In practice, a large proportion of the increase in labour costs was to form enhanced payments to the Central Provident Fund (CPF), the government's social security fund; some estimates suggested that since the wage bill was between 8 and 15 per cent of total production costs, the maximum likely increase would raise total production costs by between 1.6 and 3 per cent (but in so far as the effects were small, the point of the policy was lost).

The government also sought to nudge the policy effects along independently. There was a sharp cut in the issue of work permits for immigrant workers, and the government campaigned to force construction employers in particular to divest themselves of immigrants (possibly four-fifths of construction workers were Malaysians). The many building employers who had not included their foreign workers in the Central Provident Fund scheme were now obliged to do so, a change which is said to have increased wage bills by a half, and building costs by 10 per cent. Singapore was not economically isolated, so planning by edict had severe limits. Other governments were eager to capture what Singapore might spurn. Sri Lanka, Malaysia, the Philippines, Fiji and Papua-New Guinea all made bids to attract Singapore firms threatened by the changes in the wage structure. The Singapore government, however, went some way to accommodate labour-intensive companies by reviving a scheme to industrialize a nearby Indonesian island, Batan.

While this extraordinary endeavour to force up the costs of manual labour was underway, a different preoccupation attacked the ruling order. The Singapore Census suggested that one-third of Singapore's graduate women failed to marry by the time they were in their 30s, while uneducated Singapore women continued to have large families. Prime Minister Lee Kuan Yew drew the inference that, while '[t]he better educated and more rational are not replacing themselves', a 'multiple replacement rate right at the bottom [of society, leads to] a gradual lowering of the general quality of the population'; and again, 'levels of competence will decline, our economy will falter, the administration will suffer and society will decline' (*Financial Times*, 4 June 1984). The fear inaugurated what became known as the 'Great Marriage Debate' on how to reverse the 'lopsided pattern of procreation' (Lee Kuan Yew, National Day rally, August 1983). The government experimented with dating agencies and sponsored weekend trips to encourage the 'more rational' to breed (it seems not to have occurred to the government that rationality might lead women to refuse to marry and breed; rationality, it seems, must be subordinate to patriotism). Procreation incentives were introduced to persuade upper-income women along the government's path, while lower-income women were offered nearly two years' salary to be sterilized. Lee and his colleagues, all social democrats by persuasion, did not, it seems, refer to the most famous precedent in this field, the eugenics policy of Nazi Germany –although the Nazis were dedicated only to the sterilization of the mentally and physically handicapped as well as, for a time, ethnic minorities, not of the whole working class.

In 1987, the Singapore Family Planning Board was wound up, and with it the old slogan 'No More than Two Children'; this was to be replaced now by the slightly comical 'At least Two. Better Three. Four if You Can Afford It'. By the 1990 budget, the procreation incentive, it was said, could be manipulated so that an upper-income woman could escape taxes for fourteen years. However, beneath these some-what risible issues was a more serious intent: the Singapore government wanted its graduate women to breed and to work. But the opportunity for a mother to work was closely related to the availability of domestic help – and hence to immigrant maids. Preventing immigration of the unskilled thus struck directly at the capacity of educated women to follow the government's policy. When, in 1989, the Singapore govern-ment increased the special levy or tax on foreign maids (and sought to expel the illegal immigrants), a newspaper interviewed an educated mother, Wong Siew Hoon, who was willing and able to have the govern-ment's third child while continuing to work, but now found it impossible since a legal domestic would take half her salary (*Los Angeles Times*, 14 May 1989: 26). The government quickly promised it would set up 200 child-care centres, but said nothing about who would staff them, who would care for children too young to go to such centres, let alone clean and cook for the employed mothers.

Singapore's elite had other fears concerning the available workforce. Among these was the fact that the population was ageing. Projections suggested that, because Singaporeans, and especially Singapore Chinese, were not reproducing fast enough, the population could be halved between the years 2010 and 2100. Furthermore, the burden of the aged could become extreme: by the year 2025, for every 100 people of working age, there could be 45 aged sixty or more. The process was accelerated in so far as Singapore was tending to lose through emigra-tion a significant number of its professional class (often also in the ages with the highest reproductive rate). For a long period, the government published no figures on the numbers involved, although the records of Singaporean entries to Canada and Australia suggested that 4000 families left annually for these countries (the city stock of graduates was some 55,000). Thus, along with the drive to get Singapore's educated women to breed, an effort was also made to recruit abroad professionals who might become immigrants (a special effort was directed at Hong Kong, where many professionals were eager to emigrate to escape any problems arising from Hong Kong's 1997 reintegration with China).

Alongside this care lavished upon the professional classes, Singapore's manual workers were regularly seen as letting down the nation. They were accused of refusing to do unpleasant jobs, so making immigration necessary. A government report of 1980 argued that the city's workers were going soft since they refused to work overtime or on night shifts; at least 10 per cent, it reported, were 'choosy, irresponsible and money-minded'. One presumes, by contrast, the 'more rational' were guided purely by altruism.

Singapore's rate of growth continued to be spectacular and this encouraged the government in its confidence that the effort to increase wage costs was the right approach. In 1981 it was announced that, with the exception of domestic, construction and shipyard workers, there would no longer be a need for foreign workers after 1991. In 1983 it was reiterated that no foreign workers would be required by 1992. However, the government was becoming more cautious, and no more 'wage corrections' (under the policy of increasing labour costs) were made after 1981.

In 1985, Singapore experienced its first severe economic contraction since the political independence of the city. An 11-person commission of inquiry under Lee's son, Lee Hsien Loong, was set up to diagnose the origins of the crisis and prescribe remedies. The commission concluded that the crisis was due to a number of factors which in sum had led to a sharp decline in Singapore's competitive strength. A key issue here was the increase in labour costs – by an average of 10.1 per cent per year between 1979 and 1984, while productivity had increased by only 4.6 per cent (whereas, the report suggested, Taiwan's wages had increased in total by 10 per cent, and those of Korea and Hong Kong by very little). The recommendation was to reverse the old policy and return to the former one of keeping wages down: there should be a wage freeze and a sharp reduction in payments to the Central Provident Fund. Simultaneously, 60,000 foreign workers were expelled to lower the unemployment figures.

The volte-face was as extraordinary as the original policy. The Singapore government's social-democratic and planning credentials were suddenly seen to be quite at variance with the running of an open fragment of a world economy. Singapore's output did not permit the government to choose freely the size and composition of its labour force; Singapore's markets decided that question. The government's ambitions were utopian. The problem was particularly severe since, one study suggested, the economy was peculiarly dependent upon immigrant labour; Stahl (1991) calculates that for every new indigenous worker employed, Singapore creates additional jobs for 2.54 foreign workers, compared to Hong Kong's 2.35, Taiwan's 1.62 and Korea's 1.28.

In the second half of 1986 the economy revived, and so did the demand for labour. The government set about searching for foreign electronics workers to damp down wage pressures resulting from a tight labour market. Officially, increased worker immigration was permitted, although the government ruled that companies must limit recruitment of foreign workers to half their labour force, and imposed on employers a per-capita levy for immigrant labour (a levy which, it was said, was frequently deducted by the employer from the pay of the hapless worker, thus neutralizing any supposed disincentive effect). Permission was granted for an increase in the number of daily commuters from Malaysia (to 20,000 per day), and in 1988 for an increase in the number of three-year work permits for Malaysians.

The government also urged housewives and the elderly to return to employment. Workers over the age of 55 were offered a reduction in their contributions to the Central Provident Fund as an inducement. However, in the sectors where labour demand was strongest (construction, electronic assembly), employers insisted upon young workers; here, it seemed, older workers could not be substituted – at least, certainly not at a wage for which they were prepared to work.

Despite the elaborate machinery of control (and Singapore's stringency of regulation was famous), it was inevitable that labour demand should continually spill out of the official market into the illegal. The penalties facing employers for hiring illegal immigrants were not inconsiderable – a S$5000 fine and/or one year's imprisonment (168 employers were found guilty of employing illegal immigrants in 1987); those who aided illegal immigrants were liable to six months' gaol and eviction from public housing. Yet the numbers, it was reported, seemed to increase continually. In 1989 the government legislated to make apprehended illegal immigrants subject to three strokes of the cane and three months' imprisonment. The Thai government was one of those which protested strongly at the treatment of its citizens, arguing that Singapore had introduced the measure only after the completion of a series of major infrastructural projects (Changi Airport, a stadium, the underground railway) had rendered part of the loyal workforce redundant. The Thai embassy in Singapore was swamped with panic-stricken workers, many of whom complained that the employment agents who had recruited them had assured them their Singapore status was legal. The Singapore government relented on condition that the illegal workers removed themselves by a deadline date; the Thai government despatched two naval ships, two aircraft, trains and a fleet of buses to collect its nationals.

The case of Singapore represents one of the more extreme attempts to plan a labour force and exclude, as far as possible, foreign manual workers. The demand for labour in Singapore was created by the demand for the city's output, yet the government continually refused to accept this, and battled to neutralize the implications of economic growth. It was continually defeated. In defeat it became vicious, displaying gratuitous cruelty to the workers who had contributed significantly toward building the power of the government and the prosperity of Singaporeans.

The Domestic Helots

The illegal international migrant by no means plumbed the depths of the world's labour markets, however. The legal international economy depended at numerous points on a black market, much of it within countries where workers and children were enslaved or bonded to work. We saw something of this earlier in developed countries, but in developing countries far larger numbers are involved. The Anti Slavery Society estimates that the number of 'slaves' – those obliged to work to pay off debts, either their own or those inherited from parents, grandparents or other close relatives; those bound by custom to perform obligatory duties; or child labour – is of the order of 200 million worldwide.

It is impossible to quantify the phenomenon; evidence is no more than anecdotal. For example, chattel slavery is said to persist in the Arabian peninsula; Amazonian Indians have been pressed into work on farms and mines in Brazil; refugees are frequently seized and forced to work. In 1990, in the Chinese province of Sichuan, the police reported liberating 7000 women and children who had been sold into slavery; in one county of Shaanxi, 2000 cases of trafficking were identified, many in girls sold by their parents for domestic service, forced marriage or prostitution (*China Daily*, cited in the *Guardian*, 2 February 1990). In the same year, the Johannesburg *Weekly Mail* recorded the exposure of a trade in children and teenagers stolen from districts of Mozambique for sale in South Africa as farm labourers or prostitutes. A year later, an international protest by the US Lawyers' Committee for Human Rights

against the sale of young Haitians (some as young as eight) for work on
the sugar plantations of the Dominican Republic led to the expulsion
of thousands of Haitians. Reports said the boys worked, cutting cane,
for up to 16 hours daily for seven days a week for no more than pocket
money; however, all Haitians stood accused on the grounds that,
according to the Dominican president, the Republic 'risked losing its
national identity'. In July 1992 the Bangladeshi police arrested 11 traf-
fickers in emigrants, identifying 74 adults and children 'tied up like
animals' awaiting dispatch – the women and girls destined for Pakistan's brothels, the boys for camel-driving in the Middle East. In 1985
the Sind police (in Pakistan) closed a 'prostitutes slave market' trading
in girls from India, Bangladesh and Sri Lanka for distribution in the
Gulf area; the following year, Karachi airport police arrested 147 Sri
Lankan women being brought into Pakistan for trading in the same
market (*Guardian* reports, 16 November 1990, 26 June 1991, 21 July 1992,
11 February 1985; *Far Eastern Economic Review*, 7 August 1986: 34;
Mendelrevitch, 1979; UN, 1980).

The evidence suggests a vast clandestine base to the world labour
market, which is illuminated only in fragments when the police choose
to intervene. There have been more attempts to quantify bonded labour
or debt peonage. There are said to be 8 million such workers in Latin
America, many more in sub-Saharan Africa, and possibly 5 million in
India (the government has admitted to 200,000). In Malaysia, Tamil
palm-oil and rubber-plantation workers were said to be bonded to local
gangsters, directed by landowners, police and politicians. In India, there
were particular concentrations in agriculture, quarrying and brick-
making, often the result of drought-stricken farmers and their families
trying to pay off crisis borrowings, but succeeding usually only in sinking
further into a debt inherited by their descendants (a study of stone
quarries outside Delhi found three generations of bonded labourers
working).

The International Labour Organization estimated in the late 1970s
that there were 44 million child workers worldwide who, while technically not necessarily bonded, were frequently in servitude. The Indian
Bonded Liberation Front puts the number in South Asia alone at 25
million. Children are vital in the manufacture of matches and fireworks
in Tamilnad (45 per cent of the workforce are under the legal age for
work), woodworking, embroidery, wool cleaning, basket-making, carpet-
and bangle-making, weaving, construction, fishing, manufacturing local
cigarettes (*bidis*), hawking and selling, and domestic work (Banerjee,
1979). There are said to be three times as many girls as boys employed;
in the Tamilnad match industry, the youngest child found was 4 years

of age, although more commonly workers began at 5 to 6 years. The phenomenon is not new; but what was once a home-based cottage industry has now become factory organized.

The carpet-making workers of the Varanasi area of India have received more intensive study (Anti Slavery Society, 1990). There are said to be 100,000 boy workers involved, aged 6 to 14, 15 per cent of them sold by their parents into bondage (the Bonded Labour Liberation Front reports 150,000, of whom 90 per cent are bonded). The conditions of work and pay are, by report, appalling, with numerous accusations of beating and rape, some of beating to death (Campaign against Child Labour in Maharashtra, reported in *Daily Express*, Bombay, 15 July 1993: 3; and *Far Eastern Economic Review*, 9 July 1992). An important part of the output of the industry is exported – that is, it is part of the global market for labour-intensive goods.

Perhaps more fortunate are those infants traded for adoption – or the notorious 'mail-order brides'. These are not necessarily part of the world labour market (although both children and brides can be put to work), but are certainly part of world trade and, more particularly, of the trade relationships between developing and developed countries. Scattered press reports record the movement of Mexican, Colombian and Portuguese babies to the United States; of Calcutta children to Milan; and markets between Brazil and Israel, Switzerland and Germany, China and Hong Kong, and between both Sri Lanka and Indonesia and Europe (*Guardian*, 18 September 1980, 25 July 1985, 30 August 1985, 19 June 1986, 1 July 1988; *Financial Times*, 1 December 1989; *Far Eastern Economic Review*, 10 September 1982). In Bangladesh, a director of social welfare was accused of stealing babies for sale to Dutch adoption agencies. In 1986, Sri Lankan women were reported to be carrying babies to Dubai for sale to West German agencies, and there were unsubstantiated rumours of special baby farms for this trade.

A World Labour Market

The labour market fades away from the formal, known area of registered workforces, supposedly working standard schedules, and the recorded flows of workers across national boundaries, into successive layers of grey that darken slowly into the black economy. The law, however, divides this single market only into legal and illegal spheres (with no one knowing how significant the illegal sphere is); it does not force an economic separation. The market linkages increasingly unify the whole, bringing into some collaborative relationship the highest and lowest levels. This may be direct, as in the dependence of the Singapore woman computer programmer on illegal child care, or the boy carpet-makers of Varanasi working for world markets. Or it may be very indirect, through unknown patterns of complex linkages. But linkage there is, so that the mastery of the working conditions in one part of the labour market sooner or later requires that control be extended to the most remote parts, or decontrol goes in the opposite direction.

International migration, with all its problems, is only for the better-off workers – those who have escaped the unremitting misery of labour experienced by the many millions of workers left at home.

4

Immigration and the State

Introduction

This entire work is, in one sense, about the relationship between governments and migrants. Furthermore, much of the public discussion of the issues is implicitly presented in terms of the interests of the state. Indeed, it appears that on the issue of the free movement of people, the problem is the state rather than those who are mobile.

Immigration has become an issue of central political concern in developed countries. It is obsessive, punitive, neurotic and, in its own terms, largely inexplicable. A fantasy world has been created in which the most remote fears – hordes of rootless savages tramping the world – become the immediate stuff of practical political discussion. In 1992, in the European Union, upwards of a dozen intergovernmental bodies were examining the issues involved, and there were over one hundred ministerial and official meetings on the question. All this suggests a society so insecure, so vulnerable, that a handful of foreigners – the size of a small city or a respectable football crowd – can overturn it.

The issue was presented as a threat to civilization itself. Whereas the Europeans strove to prevent any immigration, in the United States the focus was on controlling the flow – but the terrors were the same. Consider Senator Alan Simpson of Wyoming:

> Uncontrolled immigration is one of the greatest threats to the future of this nation, to American values, traditions, institutions, to our public culture and to our way of life ... we intend to clearly exercise the first and primary responsibility of a sovereign nation which is to control its borders. (On the Simpson–Mazzoli bill, Immigration Reform and Control Act, 1982, reported in *The Economist*, 21 August 1982: 32)

Fears such as these turn upon the fantasy that millions of people in poor countries either wish, or are driven, to move to rich countries.

The cause is held to be 'population pressure', an obscure concept but vital to the validity of the orthodox case against immigration. Thus the movement of labour is impelled by forces simultaneously overwhelming and outside the direct control of the government of the destination country. The migrants, being poor, come purely to be a burden on the state and its supposedly lavish welfare provisions, thus eating into the savings of the mass of the workforce. The appropriate response is there-fore to direct all efforts, regretfully but firmly, to prevent this move-ment. Yet the overwhelming majority of people in developing countries do not move and do not try to move. Despite the vanity of those who believe life in their country is so attractive that no one can resist moving there, most people do not wish to leave their homes (and usually have the same sort of vanity about their homelands). The tiny minority that do move include the best educated, the most energetic and enterprising people (they have to be to withstand the hardships and sacrifices of international movement), who, other things being equal, make a dis-proportionate contribution to the societies they join. However, the fears are usually so great that such arguments – and indeed evidence – carry little weight.

There is a more basic problem concerning the framework of thought here. For thousands of years, people have moved about the surface of the world. In the twentieth century, however, the world became fenced – much as the free ranges of the American West were cut up by home-steaders. States, like European landowners before them, seized the common lands (and inhabitants) of the world, converting them to their exclusive control. Initial acts of appropriation by the imperial powers of Europe and North America forced all others to react in an identical style by trying to establish exclusive enclaves of their own (and expel the imperialists). Thus, in a short time (not much over two hundred years), all the world's people were penned in, divided by boundaries of greater or lesser hazard. By the 1960s, most of the developing countries had been obliged to follow the same logic, basing their power on the same machinery of control over the inhabitants of their territories.

The norm of the world order has become the territorial state, an unlikely outcome given the historical record. States came to control all the territory, with associated waters and airspace, and a defined share of the world's population. The concepts – and thus the facts – are exclusively aligned with the interests of states, of national shares (and even commodities acquire a national identity, as in German steel or Japanese cars or Indian textiles). Each state seeks to constitute itself as an autonomous agent, governing a supposedly homogenous and distinct society. In such a context, the immigrant is not only anomalous; he or she undermines the conceptual assumptions involved in the territorial state and, by implication, its power.

By 'nationalizing' populations, states tried to enforce a kind of immobility on people. Indeed, some measure of immobility is the condition of stable conventional sovereignty, of loyalty and therefore power. The very word 'nation' has been suborned in the process so that it no longer primarily refers to a separate people but is tacked on to the word 'state' as a kind of sociological shadow of political authority. The state reserves the exclusive right to decide who belongs to the nation, and then claims that it is created and sustained by those whom it has so recognized. Thus, in sum, the 'problem of immigration' is wrongly specified. The problem is that of the state and the social foundations of its power.

It seems, in theory at least, that it is sovereignty which is at stake. Consider the version of the US Constitution presented by Senator W.L. Scott:

> The power of Congress to exclude aliens from the United States and prescribe the terms and conditions on which they come in is absolute, being an attribute of the United States as a sovereign nation ... If it could not exclude aliens, it would, to that extent, be subject to the control of another power. (US Senate, 1976: 19).

Could the humble Mexican fruitpicker, the Korean grocer, the Afghan taxi driver, the Indian doctor, be seen in such a heroic light? In realistic terms, there are hardly any modern examples of immigrants affecting the power of the state – although there is at least one example of emigration doing so. The flight of the citizens of the former East German regime in the early 1990s led to a kind of implosion of the regime and its dissolution.

However, the simplicities of the discussion of sovereignty are remote from the emerging practicalities. Even the most powerful governments can no longer determine their economic policy independently of the rest of the world. They depend increasingly on flows of capital, goods, services – and workers – from abroad to secure the prosperity of their domestic economies. That is, the state has become dependent upon foreigners, whether owners of capital, traders or immigrants – on people whose political loyalty cannot be assumed. Only the world's markets, it seems, exercise any control.

The tensions over the nature of sovereignty arise because of the changes in the supposed social basis of the state. In the past, the construction of the social foundations of the state was a long and complex process which involved the invention of a social uniformity. The changes

88 THE NEW UNTOUCHABLES

were frequently challenged along the way by those who were excluded by the choices made in constituting that uniformity. For the means to unite some are no less the means to exclude others: 'ethnic cleansing', or at least harassment of those who find themselves a minority, is an essential part of the creation of a mass loyalty to the state. The minorities are created precisely to allow the invention of the homogeneity of the majority, and, regardless of their real attitudes, have to be, at least implicitly, identified as disloyal. A commentator on US immigration notes something American which is in fact common to almost all modern states: 'Charges of disloyalty and subversion against the aliens repeat a familiar American pattern of blaming domestic problems on foreign contagion' (Archdeacon, 1992: 54).

The drive to social uniformity is not an irrational matter. It is impelled by the need for loyalty. The matter is made urgent by the collision of competitive states, of rivalry and warfare. Supposedly, in the past the power of government ultimately turned upon its ability to call upon the adult population to defend it and prosecute its interests against other states. Loyalty was seen as a product of social 'homogeneity', the recognition of a common interest. Thus racism, ethnic, cultural or religious discrimination are not generated by inherited prejudice (that may provide the immediate pretext) but by the rivalries intrinsic to a world order of competing states.

Defining what constitutes the principle of the nation's homogeneity cannot be done in isolation from the characteristics of the population; the characteristics selected are a matter of political choice, the outcome of political struggle to establish and enforce one view over all others. Inevitably, measured against independent evaluations of a people's cultural distinctiveness, the choice will be arbitrary. Inevitably, too, weaker versions of what constitutes 'common values' or 'culture' are chosen. Consider, for example, the Republican Senator Alan Simpson's meditation:

> Americans in the fullest sense ... adopting not only our obvious political values but our social public values, things like fair play, compassion, consideration for the rights of others.... If our values change as a result of immigration, can we reasonably expect that the true freedoms and the things that we have that are dependent on those values will survive the change. (cited in *The Economist*, 6 June 1981: 47)

The self-indulgence inherent in Simpson's definition of 'American' is paralleled in every country, and suggests that boasting is as powerful an element in the definition as establishing a criterion of identity. An extraordinarily high murder rate or neglect of the poor might just as reasonably be included in the definition of 'American values', if such were not discourteous.

Since defining either values or culture as a criterion for true membership of the nation is in practice so difficult, it usually becomes no more than background talk (although the Nazis did go further and legislated the ethnic definition of 'German'). But this does not prevent continuing attempts to lay down criteria in order to exclude (or, rather, to win or defend political dominance). Thus, a certain number of English-speaking Californians have decided that an ability to speak English adequately must define who is an American, a choice designed to exclude both as many Hispanics as possible and the possibility of Spanish being introduced as an official language, so excluding the non-Spanish speakers. The definition is advanced to say who has the right to belong and to participate, no matter how nominally, in the exercise of political power.

At various times, public authorities in the United States have excluded (or failed to include) as part of the nation American Indians, black people, Irish Catholics, southern and eastern Europeans, Japanese, Chinese, Filipinos, and possibly others. Large numbers of Mexicans have been expelled. Each occasion involved a complex of rival interests struggling to establish their definition of 'American', and by so doing exclude all others. Defining outsiders thus plays a dual role: it defines the majority and establishes domination of the majority by one group. As Hans Ulrich Wehler writes of the first, in the process of creating Germany in the late nineteenth century:

> By defining deviants [including ethnic minorities, women, criminals and migrants – NH] as the proverbial 'negative other', the dominant majority actually uses them to define itself ... to strengthen the majority's sense of togetherness and sameness. (1972)

The process is never complete since there is no constant that characterizes the majority. Threats to the state raise the need to reinvent social homogeneity as an aid to maintaining loyalty. For example, in the 1930s the Nazi Party was able to select one group of Germans, those of Jewish origin, and isolate them as 'native foreigners' as a means to fortify the control of the state and, through this, of the majority.

However, the issue is not simply conceptual. This can be seen most clearly and painfully where minorities are forcibly driven out of a country, and others take their land, houses or businesses. The regime concerned, in legitimating (or even initiating) this theft, thereby secures for itself a group of citizens of unquestioning loyalty. In sixteenth-century England when King Henry VIII nationalized the Church, the distribution of Church lands to his friends and followers created a new stratum of the aristocracy, loyal both to their royal benefactor and to the new religious order. Four hundred years later, the partition of British India and creation of two new states – India and Pakistan – might appear on the surface as a religious dispute between Hindus and Muslims, but it also involved large-scale theft of the properties on the other side. In conferring legitimacy on these acts of spoliation, new ranks of loyalists were created whose commitments went well beyond the sympathy they might feel for co-religionists. In many new states the attack on minorities and the seizure of their property is a key episode in the manufacture of a strong loyalty to the state which legalizes these acts of theft.

If the attack on domestic minorities is a fundamental part of creating the social foundations of new states, many poorer developing countries do not define sovereignty in terms of controlling immigration (although, as we saw in Chapter 3, the Newly Industrializing Countries are emulating the developed in this matter). Pakistan came to host over 3 million Afghan refugees, and Iran over 2 million, without this overturning national sovereignty (or indeed the question even arising). The flight of Somalis and Ethiopians to Kenya, of Mozambicans to Zimbabwe and Malawi, of Tutsis to Zaire, Guatemalans to Mexico, whatever the severe difficulties in short-term adjustment and pain to both newcomers and natives, did not present a fundamental challenge to these states. In this respect, the developed countries appear weak and vulnerable, the developing secure.

In practice, governments in the developed countries equivocate between preserving social homogeneity and taking in scarce labour. On the one hand, ministers insist on keeping the door open for selected scarce categories of labour, and, despite furious public assurances, also tolerate a measure of illegal immigration. On the other hand, they fiercely affirm the tightness of controls and institute periodic crack-downs. Tough talk on immigration woos one audience; soothing insistence on the need to integrate immigrants convinces another. The persistence of immigration is concealed to avoid offending one audience, while the often brutal and dishonest methods employed to exclude or expel people are hidden lest they offend another audience. The fudge feeds both sides.

It seems the obsession with immigrants and refugees increases with the material power to cope with such flows: the richer people are, the greater the exclusionary motive. Thus, perversely, the stronger the state concerned, the greater, it seems, are its fears of vulnerability. The paradox arises because the domestic audience needs to be provided with popular diagnoses of current problems which do not undermine the basic order. Before exploring this, however, we need to look more closely at the issue of governments and population.

Population Control

While control of immigration has become an important political issue, there is an older tradition of treating the domestic population as a target for public action – to increase or decrease its size, to change its composition, distribution and density. Population has been used histori- cally as a means to occupy territory or to clear it for other political purposes. Emigration was employed to occupy new territories in the belief that this would lead ultimately not to rebellion against the im- perial power (as occurred with Britain's American colonies and, finally, with all the European empires) but to an extension of the political and commercial power of empire.

However, governments in modern times have been less consistent about emigration. For periods of time it has been banned (for example, Algeria, Yemen), selectively controlled (Egypt, Syria), or positively encouraged (Jordan, Tunisia), or subject to periodic shifts between these different stances. In essence, however, the state assumes a sort of owner- ship of its nationals and control of the exits. On the other hand, if the Europeans and Japanese in the past encouraged emigration as an instrument to take over other territories (in this respect, they all failed), the United States government tended to see emigration as an act of disloyalty, a rejection of the 'American way of life' (the government of the old Soviet Union adopted a similar approach, using exile as the highest form of punishment under the penal code). At the other ex- treme, the opening up of the world labour market has offered some governments the opportunity to exploit their control of the exits to export their workers, and thereby, through the resulting remittances, increase the foreign-exchange earnings accruing to the government. Many governments went some way in this direction, as we saw in the last chapter, and possibly the most striking case is that of the Philippines.

Attitudes to immigration have also varied widely. The generalization that the developed countries can be divided into countries of emigration (Europe and Japan) and immigration (the countries of the Americas, Australia and New Zealand and so on) was, as we have seen, only a half-truth. When their economies expanded swiftly, the European countries have depended historically upon immigration. However, in the twentieth century, governments in both the developed and developing countries have shifted the emphasis to seeing an increasing population as a burden, rather than a source of economic and military strength. So powerful has this ideology become that some governments have gone to considerable – not to say, cruel – lengths to seek to cut the rate of increase in population. In the case of India, the notorious programme of forced sterilization during the emergency rule of Mrs Gandhi (1975–77) summarized some of the horrors involved – and rightly led to a devastating electoral defeat. In China, the attempt to enforce a one-child policy, with powerful sanctions on disobedience, has led to even worse savageries, best known in the cases of enforced infanticide (Aird, 1990). These cases are well known because the countries are large; but, as we have seen in the case of Singapore, smaller countries also have punitive regimes in this sphere. South Korea, for example, introduced measures to reward government officers with public housing if they agreed to have no more than two children, and even greater rewards if they volunteered for sterilization after the first child, and lesser benefits after the second child (*Korea Herald*, 29 July 1983).

The underlying approach here borrows from a supposedly scientific demography, a science of population management. Governments, it is assumed, can identify an ideal size or geographical distribution of population, and possess the effective power to achieve these aims. At the extreme, the Nazis adopted the prevailing medical ideology of the times in proposing eugenics, the sterilization of the 'substandard', moving on to the liquidation of the inferior species. In its milder forms, population management is part of the old ideology of scientific planning, most closely associated – as Dariusz Stola notes, in reflecting on population expulsions – with authoritarian regimes:

> The totalitarian regimes emphasized the belief in the malleability of human societies, a faith which, I feel, is at the heart of all organized population displacements. It was a belief in social engineering, in surgery on the body of peoples, a conviction that these amputations and transplantations of social tissue were necessary, justifiable and rational. (Stola, 1992: 338)

The results of population policies in our own times are unimpressive. Rates of growth are generally falling, but it would be a heroic inference to attribute this to the effects of policy (the declines occur with or without government promotion of family planning). The same is true of the lesser preoccupation with redistributing population – away from big cities to particular areas. Government aspirations are often spectacular, but the means to achieve the aims, let alone their desirability, are much more doubtful. The government of Brazil in the 1970s identified national schemes to redirect flows of the northeastern migrant population away from the traditional destinations in the south to the far west and the Amazon. The Indonesian government continued the Dutch policy of trying to shift people from Java to the outer islands and West Irian (a policy for some time supported by the World Bank, but now acknowledged as disastrous). Malaysia sought to open up under-developed farming land and move people there. China directed or induced people to move to the border areas, to the northeast, Mongolia and Tibet. Nyerere's vision of socialist Tanzania led to the rural popu-lation being obliged to regroup themselves in new towns far from their fields. South Africa, under apartheid, was forever forcing populations to be in one place rather than another; it made meeting the labour demand in white South Africa a constant war against the authorities.

There is frequently much cruelty involved in these forced movements. As so often, the extraordinary patience of people in the face of the fantasies of their governments prevailed, and there was little overt opposition (although many of the migrants voted with their feet and made their way back to their original homes). What is surprising is that governments should so often persist in claiming to know better than their citizens where they ought to be, and spend scarce resources in trying to achieve a given outcome. By the late 1980s, many governments came to recognize that it is not possible – or had become impossible – to predict the future output of goods and services in the economy, yet still persisted in the illusion that they could predict the size of the labour force (and population) required to produce it, and where, territorially, people ought to be. As with the Singapore government, growth is pursued while ignoring the implications for the workforce.

Immigration Control in the Developed Countries

The 'countries of immigration'

The United States was fashioned in a popular revolution which entailed the creation of a nation of equal citizens (albeit excluding the indigenous Indians and the black population) as the foundation of legitimacy. Apart from the Dutch Republic and, later, Revolutionary France, the concep-tion of a socialized people which emerged in America as the official order was shocking to contemporary opinion. It happened well before most Europeans moved from the idea that the inhabitants of a country were subjects of a monarch (and that the ethnic provenance of the subjects was irrelevant to their status) to the notion that they were equal citizens. In terms of immigration, this shift changes the terms of reference. A monarch may choose whom to regard as his subjects on any grounds whatsoever; personal loyalty would thus loom larger than the social, ethnic, religious or cultural origins of the person concerned. Citizens, on the other hand, in theory select new recruits to the national club on the basis of preserving a particular political order or society: in this case, to strengthen or perpetuate an 'American way of life'.

However, the struggle to establish a particular definition of a legitimate citizen becomes a preoccupation in most countries only in the late nineteenth century. The US federal government had no constitutional role in regulating immigration, so historically the issue could not have been seen as one fundamental to sovereignty. Responsibility for immigration became an exclusive prerogative of the federal government only through a Supreme Court decision of 1892. In mid-century, there had been an agitation – and the creation of the Native American Party – to prevent the arrival of both Irish and German Catholics, but it did not lead to legislation and died away in the 1860s.

By 1875 Congress was becoming more favourably disposed to the idea of exclusions. By 1882, convicts, prostitutes, lunatics and paupers had been banned (the poor implementation of this measure led in 1891 to the assumption of responsibility by the federal government). Excluding deviants was only a first step. In response to attacks on Chinese immigrants in San Francisco in 1877, the Chinese Exclusion Act of 1882 banned the landing of a whole racial group (the measure lasted until 1943). Subsequently, the Japanese were excluded under a 'gentleman's agreement' with the Japanese government to prevent emigration from Japan (a labour version of what later, in trade, became a 'Voluntary Export Restraint' – a government agreed to curtail exports to the US under threat of being banned altogether).

As in other developed countries, immigration law proper began in the United States with the First World War. In a furore of fears concerning the arrival of enemy spies, Congress in 1917 passed an act codifying past restrictions, introducing literacy requirements, banning 'Asiatic' immigrants, and requiring all arrivals to carry passports (this measure lapsed in 1919). This measure was superseded by further acts in 1921 and 1924. The 1921 Act introduced immigrant quotas proportionate to the national origins of the American population of 1910, with a total annual ceiling of 358,000 (200,000 from north and northwestern Europe; 155,000 from south and eastern Europe; the rest, 3000, from Asia and Africa). The 1924 Act intensified the conservatism of the regulatory regime – or, rather, the drive to recapture some imaginary earlier 'homogeneity' – by making the proportions of immigration correspond to the national origins of the American population of 1890 (that is, excluding the period of greatest immigration up to 1914). There was accordingly a drastic cut in the numbers permitted to land from southern and eastern Europe. All immigrants were now required to have a valid entry visa, issued in their country of origin; to pass a literacy test; not to belong to one of a number of inadmissible groups; and not to bring dependants. The Act also laid out the powers of deportation.

The legislation was somewhat irrelevant since the subsequent years of depression were marked by a low level of applications to immigrate, with, as we shall see, some disastrous exceptions. However, this did not discourage Congress from periodically seeking to block particular groups. Thus, a 1930 measure limited the admission of Filipinos to 50 per year (the Philippines were among US possessions abroad), and laid down measures to encourage repatriation of those already in the country (primarily in California). Up to 1946, Filipinos were forbidden to marry what were known as 'Caucasian' women (that is, white Americans), to own property or to vote. In 1942, as part of efforts to encourage wartime loyalty, Filipinos were allowed to take US nationality if they worked for the government; in 1945, they were permitted to own property in California, and in 1948, to marry Caucasian women. Perhaps no more was to be expected in a society which, like South Africa and the colonial empires of the European powers, was still thoroughly segregated by colour of skin.

There was, however, a politically more disastrous exclusion in the 1930s: of thoroughly white refugees from Germany and Austria (Britain was equally guilty in this respect). Despite the evidence of what was happening under Nazi rule, there was no increase in the immigration quotas to allow people to escape from persecution; on the contrary, existing restrictions were considerably tightened. Thus, in the fiscal year 1937, only 42 per cent of the German/Austrian quota for immigrants was utilized. In September 1930, the Hoover administration instructed consular officials to apply more stringently the clause of the 1917 Act that forbade visas to those 'likely to become a public charge', relating the refusal of visas to the level of unemployment in the United States. In practice, consular officials issued visas only to those with clear evidence of means to support themselves indefinitely without work, or with guarantees from relatives and friends. In fact, refugees were already forbidden – on pain of deportation – to apply for public relief within five years of arrival, so there was little possibility of them becoming a charge on public funds. In the first five months of the new policy, immigration fell by 90 per cent, and remained at a low level until President Roosevelt revised the instruction in March 1938, even though the demand for visas between 1936 and 1939 far exceeded the quota on offer (Mitchell, 1992).

The implicit or explicit racial criteria for admission were repeated in the first major piece of new legislation after 1924, the 1952 Act (the 'McCarren–Walter' Act). Here 150,000 visas were available annually for those originating in the eastern hemisphere, within national quotas based upon the proportions of the national origins of the American population of 1920. Within these quotas, criteria for admission included the possession of professional skills and family reunification (a criterion that repeated the 'social reproduction' qualifications contained in the quotas idea). Immigrants from the western hemisphere had no more than the customary exclusions (health, criminal record, means to support etc.), since the farmers of the south and southeast still depended heavily on migrant Mexican farm hands.

The postwar social and political context changed with great speed. Segregation of black Americans, in operation in the US armed forces during the Second World War as well as in the southern states, was becoming intolerable at home, and insupportably embarrassing abroad as newly independent black governments (and those from South Asia were so classified) emerged. The establishment of the formal equality of all Americans came with the assertion of the formal equality of all non-Americans in the rest of the world. In 1965, an amendment to the 1952 Act began the process of phasing out the implicitly racial quota system, and for the first time permitting significant immigration from Asia and Africa. A total of 170,000 visas were allotted to the eastern hemisphere (with a 20,000 ceiling for any particular country), 120,000 to the western hemisphere. Seven categories of entry were laid down, although family reunification became much more important than the possession of professional skills. Revisions were introduced in 1976 and 1978 when the two hemispheric ceilings were merged in one global ceiling of 290,000, exclusive of close relatives.

The 1965 amendment was required both for domestic purposes and in the interests of US foreign policy. But it was partly a face-saving formula that was not expected to change the composition of those arriving. Congress was not yet aware that the world labour market was changing and US immigration rules would follow suit. Robert Kennedy, attorney general at that time, reported to the congressional committee considering the bill that it was expected that immigration from Asia would rise to 5000 in the first year of the Act's operation and then decline. In fact, immigration from Asia in the 1980s was some 2.6 million (44 per cent of all legal immigrants). Immigrants from Europe and Canada, 60 per cent of the US total in the 1950s, fell to some 14 per cent in the 1980s.

Congress was continually divided between the requirements of nationalist populism ('protecting the American way of life') and meeting the demand for labour. It was an ancient dilemma. As Divine (1957: 61) notes of earlier debates:

Most evident were the petty and narrow motives which inspired the antagonists. The supporters of restriction, posing as the defenders of the American labourer and protectors of American society, seemed to be moved primarily by racial prejudice. Their opponents, ostensibly acting to prevent a serious dislocation in the nation's economy, appeared motivated by economic self-interest.

Immigration (including the issues of illegal immigration and refugee arrivals) became in the 1970s an increasing preoccupation of Congress, as shown in the frequency of both legislation and enquiries. Furthermore, disagreements within Congress seemed to make it increasingly difficult to achieve action. After 1977 three attempts were made to agree on new legislation, but they all failed. The bill which seemed most likely to pass both houses, the Simpson–Mazzoli bill, died in December 1984.

However, a subsequent set of proposals (the 'Wilson–Panette' bill) became the basis for the most comprehensive Act since 1952 – the 1986 Immigration Control and Reform Act. The Act was ostensibly a response to the steady growth in legal immigration – from 1 million in the 1940s, 2.5 million in the 1950s, 3.3 million in the 1960s and 4.5 million in the 1970s. Relative to the US population, these were still small shares. The 1980 census recorded that, for the first time since 1920, the foreign-born population had increased (it was just under 14 million in both years). There was also much wild talk of an extraordinary increase in illegal immigration, despite the increases in long-term unemployment that followed the end of the long postwar boom in 1973–75; the evidence however was – as we have seen – far from clear.

The bill's most important clauses permitted a major increase in the number of visas to be allowed annually – to 590,000 (90 per cent of admissions, however, related to family reunification); employers were to be fined or imprisoned for hiring illegal immigrants; and illegal entrants of six years or more residence in the United States were to be given the legal right to stay. In practice, the sanctions against employers were weakened on the grounds that it would be unfair to penalize them for hiring workers on the basis of easily available forged documents. In the event, 3 million illegal immigrants benefited from the Act.

However, it would be a mistake to see this as a clear subordination of employment to nationality issues. For the bill could only proceed with concessions to farm interests. Northwestern farmers (with early harvests of strawberries and cherries) argued that rumours of the bill's provisions had radically reduced their supply of workers. Between 50 and 80 per cent of the crop was normally picked by migrant workers, and few, it was said, reported for work in the relevant months of 1986. In Oregon, farmers persuaded the state to release prisoners and deploy the National Guard to help in harvesting, but alleged that one-third of the crop would still be lost. In California, farmer associations alleged that between a quarter and 90 per cent of agricultural workers were illegal immigrants, and further numbers were crucial in important industries – meat-packing, furniture, rubber, chemicals. The bill was revised to accommodate these objections: any illegal immigrant, working in agriculture (the US Department of Agriculture put the number at half a million), provided they had worked for 90 days in the year preceding May 1986, was eligible to become a legal temporary resident (and after holding this status for four years could become a permanent resident). However, the Department of Labour pointed out that the H-2 scheme, in operation since 1953, permitted the issue of temporary visas for farm work if it could be shown that the farmer concerned had tried and failed to recruit an American-born worker. There were 16,000 such workers in 1977, engaged mainly in seasonal work harvesting East Coast apples, cutting sugar cane in Florida, laying irrigation pipelines in Montana, sheep-herding in Idaho. The government estimated the number in this category at some 220,000 by 1990.

Along with the amnesty for illegal immigrants, steps were taken to strengthen the work of the Immigration and Naturalization Service (INS) to prevent the entry of those without documents. The press reported that the INS had been issued with M-14 rifles (with night-vision scopes and infra-red sensors) and two armoured personnel carriers. The announcement led to the formation in Texas of Civilian Militia Assistance, a squad of vigilantes armed with M-16 rifles, to help patrol the border and search out illegal arrivals (at the same time, a number of churches formed special centres to protect the clandestine movement and help place illegal entrants).

The reality of what the press persisted in calling a 'crackdown' was somewhat different. The number of INS patrolmen – let alone the two personnel carriers – was laughably inadequate for the 2000 miles of border with Mexico, let alone the legion of people who entered in other ways (particularly those who entered legally but overstayed their permitted time of residence). Even with the power of sanction, it was impossible for 900 INS agents to police over 9 million employers. With the wage bill for illegal workers reputedly at least one-third lower than normal (primarily because no other charges – social security, overtime pay, withholding taxes – were paid), the much lauded market in effect forced employers in certain sectors to break the law.

The 1986 Act was criticized on two main grounds. First, sanctions against employers would lead them to discriminate against any applicant for work who looked Hispanic. Second, the regulations ignored the long-term economic interests of the country. Business associations attacked those who framed the bill on the grounds that they had not tried to attract scarce skills from abroad to strengthen US competitiveness, particularly when the projected size of the labour force showed a declining rate of increase to the end of the century.

The attempt to cope with the issues involved in illegal immigration, however, suggested to the wider US audience that undocumented entry was a serious problem. Already in the 1970s, 13 state governments had introduced penalties for employers who hired illegal entrants. Some school districts redefined the category 'resident' or took other measures to exclude the children of illegal immigrants from free public schooling, even though children born in the country are automatically citizens. In 1994, in the 'Save Our State' initiative supported by 600,000 voters, the state of California was instructed to deny illegal immigrants access to public education, health care and other services; police, teachers and health care workers were obliged to report suspected illegal immigrants.

The combination of the 1965 measure ending racial discrimination in the issuing of visas, the continued strength of the 'family reunification' clauses, along with illegal and refugee flows, accelerated the cosmopolitanization of the big cities of the United States. Some argued, however, that it was precisely the family reunification clauses and the failure to make allowance for recruiting people with scarce skills that were leading to a decline in the average quality of immigrants (measured in terms of skills and education). This, it was said, had numerous ramifications in terms of the labour market for unskilled workers, particularly where unemployment remained high. However, while economic criteria did not loom large in the formal legislation, there had always been a surprising amount of room to manoeuvre for particular categories of workers (as seen earlier for H-2 agricultural workers) – for doctors, nurses, scientists, and so on.

In the 1980s, there was a different mood in Washington. Immigration, as a political issue, was increasingly becoming one of the points of focus for a generalized insecurity about the position of the United States in the world. International competition for markets and influence, particularly with Japan and other East Asian countries, had become a preoccupation of Congress. The quality of the labour force was one issue in international competition, and was measured by a number of indices – the proportion of young people achieving high-school graduation, the numbers reading science and engineering in tertiary education, and so on. Immigration provided a cheap, albeit (in terms of numbers) limited means to increase both the skills and youth of the labour force, particularly given that the closest rivals to the United States – Europe and Japan – remained trapped in the old traditions of hostility to immigration.

The government's General Accounting Office reported that the sanctions against employers hiring illegal immigrants had, as feared, led to discrimination against all minorities, legal or not. Employers reported that they checked the papers of – or refused to hire – only those whom by appearance or accent they had reason to suspect (Perotti, 1992: 99). Those representing minorities, lawyers and civil-rights organizations, pressed for the repeal of these clauses, arguing that employers should not be used to implement Congress's immigration legislation.

Thus, the 1986 Act was not fully effective before Congress returned to the issue with the 'Simpson–Kennedy' bill (ultimately the 1990 Immigration Act). This involved a major expansion in the numbers to be admitted (from 530,000 to 700,000), and the legalization of the status of several hundred thousand Salvadorean and other refugees (the numbers of which had doubled since 1987). Furthermore, the number of visas issued to applicants because they possessed desirable labour-market skills (as opposed to rejoining their families in the United States) was nearly tripled (from 54,000 to 140,000). There was also a limited reversion to the old criteria: Senator Edward Kennedy secured a special provision to permit the entry of 40,000 Irish without relatives in the United States; and a further 40,000 Italians and Poles were to be admitted because, supposedly, they were relatively disadvantaged in terms of having kin already in the country.

A 1991 change in the law also promised priority visa consideration to 10,000 individuals willing to invest $1 million in the United States and create ten jobs within six months. Great hopes were expressed for this change and Hong Kong – scheduled to rejoin China in 1997 – was targeted as a key source of wealthy immigrants. US firms are said to have dispatched headhunters to Southeast Asia and Taiwan to find potential investors. The INS somewhat rashly predicted that the scheme would lead to an inflow of capital of $8 billion annually and the creation of 100,000 new jobs. However, the results were disappointing: by the spring of 1993, only 283 visas had been approved (and this included spouses and children of investors) out of 698 applications. The INS lowered the minimum capital threshold to half a million dollars but without striking results. It seemed that in a global competition to attract the rich, the United States' terms were inferior to its nearest rivals – Australia required only the transfer, not the investment, of US$390,000 (30,000 business migrants were accepted between 1981 and 1991); Canada, in its 1986 scheme, required a transfer of US$220,000 for three years (with a lower sum required in poorer provinces), and the creation of a business that employed at least one resident within two years of settling. Others had even better terms: countries in the south Pacific and Latin America did not require residence, so the beneficiary could continue to live in Hong Kong; Tonga promised to issue a passport in six weeks if the intending citizen purchased a 20-year lease on land (with a minimum value of $23,000 per family).

The 1990 Act marked the beginning of a recognition that immigration was becoming a matter of international competition rather than a residual to family unification, or governed by the interests of defending a way of life. It was a victory for the pro-immigration lobbies – from free-enterprise thinkers and institutes (the American Enterprise and Cato Institutes), some business interests, minority and religious associations, and some of the liberal left. The opposition was led by environmental and trade-union interests. But the alliances cut across traditional politics, separating old-style nationalists, whether liberal or conservative, from a heterogeneous group who advocated less stringent or no immigration controls.

The beginnings of the transition in the United States from conservation of a historic nation to replenishing the national labour supply were paralleled in other countries of immigration, although doubts and countertendencies continued to recur. For example, as late as 1975, in a green paper prepared for the 1977 Immigration Act, the Canadian government publicly aired an ancient fantasy about 'assimilability' and the need to preserve the 'somatic identity' of Canadians:

> A person's identity includes a sense of one's body. These in turn are determined not only by one's physical traits but also by the socially provided standards and ideas with regard to what is physically normal, fit, beautiful, clean and pure.... Of particular interest in the present context is colour and other physical characteristics used in a group or society to define racial identity. (Bakan, 1978)

With even more daring, the writer alleged that 'mixed marriages' 'frequently' lead to a 'confused somatic self-image', and observed that '[n]ot knowing where you really stand with respect to accepted norms is anxiety-creating'. Thus did ancient bigotry don new garments of pseudo-psychological science, with as little evidence – or common sense – as in the past.

Nonetheless, the inexorable expansion in the numbers of immigrants, legal or not, continues, and with it an increasing effort by governments to use economic criteria to choose those they will admit. As the problem of ageing becomes better recognized in North America, the highly skilled labour required to care for the aged also tends to be drawn from immigrants. Canadian policy has been particularly successful also in attracting a capital inflow from East Asia, which has transformed Vancouver and British Columbia (an area which supposedly prided itself on its British character). By the early 1990s, some 40 per cent of the 53,000 children in school in Vancouver spoke English as a second language; in some schools, the proportion is said to be as high as 90 per cent. Two-thirds of the city's hotels are owned by East Asian groups, and in 1990 a Hong Kong Chinese was nominated as lieutenant governor of the province (*Far Eastern Economic Review*, 20 February 1991).

In Australia, immigration policy evolved in a comparable direction, perhaps accelerated as the country's ruling order reduced its historical ties with Europe and came increasingly to see itself as part of the dynamically growing economy of Asia. Policy shifted from an exclusive emphasis on immigration from Britain to one restricted to Europeans (embodied in an explicit White Australia policy – even Asian wives of returning Australian soldiers were at this stage excluded from citizenship [Castles, 1992: 551]), to one where, in the 1970s, the racial categories were ended. Immigration was supposedly linked to domestic unemployment levels, but in practice it is impossible to manage flows relative to such short-term issues.

Historically, many Australians associated increased immigration with rapid growth in the economy, and some attributed boom to expanded labour supply. The cosmopolitanization of Australian cities proceeded as swiftly as in the United States and Canada and, despite those perpetually gloomy at the prospects, with remarkably little strain. With settlement, immigrants came to play a larger political role, and were thus able to adjust the process of change, to institutionalize it.

Europe and immigration

The transition from being a self-sufficient sovereign people to representing a national share of a world labour market was painful and difficult in the 'countries of immigration', but stands as a model of flexibility in comparison to the entrenched conservatism of Europe (and Japan). America wanted settlers and resented temporary migrant workers; it therefore required 'family reunification'. Europe – like the South

African mines – wanted only workers on temporary contracts, and therefore resented 'family reunification'. Indeed, in Europe it appears implicitly to be the case that economic growth – and therefore the competitive standing of countries – can be sacrificed, at least in theory, to defend an imaginary ethnic homogeneity.

Among European countries there was a great diversity of response, differentiating particularly the empire models (France, Britain, Holland, Portugal) and the single 'nation-states'. At one extreme, Britain initially accepted in theory all legal members of the Empire, and later the Commonwealth, as equal British subjects, with a right to settle and work within all British territories (a right that was, however, heavily qualified in practice). France fashioned a republic of citizens, many of whom were natives of colonies but shared the right to settle in France. In both cases citizenship was a political status conferred by the state, rather than exclusively inherited by birth.

At the opposite end of the spectrum, Germany, Sweden, Switzerland and others defined nationality as, in theory, entirely coterminous with a supposed ethnic descent. In practice, Sweden was much more liberal in accepting people for naturalization without consideration of ethnic descent. In the German case, on the one hand, the government was constitutionally obliged to accept for citizenship all those who could validly claim to be of 'German' descent, regardless of their legal nationality (as the State of Israel was constitutionally obliged to accept as citizens all who could validly claim to be Jews). However, the German government was under no obligation to extend citizenship to those who lived and worked in Germany but could not claim 'German' descent; and, in theory, any number of generations of such people could live in the country without acquiring any right to citizenship. Hence the German figures for 'immigrants' cover all those of non-German descent resident in Germany, but exclude the much larger number of foreign immigrants who have German descent; the two groups together constituted about a quarter of the population of West Germany by 1960. On the other hand, the German constitution – like the Swedish – had more favourable conditions than most other European countries for the entry of those seeking refugee status.

However, all countries retained a widening range of exceptions to capture special categories of skilled labour or follow particular foreign-policy objectives. In time, this led to a 'fracturing' of entry requirements; in the case of West Germany, as Blaschke (1993: 380) notes, by 1990 there were 11 or 12 different entry categories, and the procedures had become so complicated that few understood them in their entirety:

The gates of entry are virtually beyond counting and hard to describe. They have developed in different ways in the course of the last two hundred years or have been created ad hoc in the past few months. (ibid.: 383)

Over time the various traditions have converged. On the one hand, the ethnic concept has become increasingly important in the definition of British and French citizenship in order to exclude Asians and Africans with an inherited right to settle in the imperial centre. On the other, there has been great pressure on the 'ethnic' powers to accept all those settled within their borders as citizens in order to reconcile the nature of the existing population with the political order.

Furthermore, almost all governments have employed arguments about the control of immigration as a way of escaping the inevitable problems of adjustment, and at times as a form of play-acting, when in reality government power to end immigration was limited. All maintained, from time to time, that immigration was a problem, or even *the* problem, and in so doing focused public attention on the issue. In this way government rhetoric 'helped to create the anxieties it was intended to calm, with the curious result that public concern was eventually prayed in aid of policies that had helped to create it' (Rose, 1969: 228).

Restrictions on immigration did not, as Saggar (1992: 17) notes, follow an increase in public concern, but preceded it – indeed, created it. In Britain, only two years after a very small inflow of immigrant workers (some 3000 in all in 1950), the government established an inter-departmental committee to study the question, leading to a recommendation to colonial governments to cut the issue of emigration permits and to disperse immigrants in Britain (Layton-Henry, 1990). When Mrs Thatcher made a notorious speech in 1978 in which she claimed to understand the fear of people that they might be swamped by immigrants, those affirming that immigration was an urgent issue facing the country rose from 9 per cent before to 21 per cent after the speech (Saggar, 1992: 125). White (1986) similarly notes that restrictions on immigration tended to precede economic crisis and increases in unemployment, rather than follow them (as with the 1971 UK Immigration Act): the worries were social, and unemployment was used as a rationalization after the event.

In the case of Britain, workers had been recruited from the West Indies, Asia and Africa during the Second World War (the restrictions on their entry to Britain were removed in 1942). In the immediate postwar years, while emigration continued to be encouraged, the government made significant efforts to recruit displaced – but white – persons in Europe (for example, 170,000 Poles and Italians were brought in). However, from 1948, the spontaneous arrival of West Indian workers began a process that expanded to include those from the Indian sub-continent, parts of Africa, Cyprus, and so on, and continued up to the ending of the automatic right of entry for Empire subjects in 1962. Up to that time, immigrants from the Empire were automatically citizens with the same rights as those born in Britain (including the right to vote and stand for public office).

The 1962 measure by no means settled the issue, since many groups in the former Empire retained the status of British nationality, and it was thus necessary to remove from this status any right to enter Britain. Through successive crises, leading to the flight of British passport holders – particularly those of Indian origin living in Kenya, Uganda, Malawi and, later, Chinese from Hong Kong – two types of British passport were created: one carrying the right to enter and live in Britain, one without it. The unfortunates who gained the second type were thus unilaterally deprived of their former rights. For the first time, a specific British nationality was invented, based upon a quasi-ethnic origin or 'patriality', turning upon the nationality of a parent or grandparent.

With the 1973 entry of Britain to the European Union, citizens of the European member countries gained rights of entry which were better than Commonwealth citizens had. However, the exceptions remain significant. First, as we have noted, citizens of the Republic of Ireland are excluded, and this covers a large number of unskilled and semi-skilled workers – there were some 640,000 Irish nationals in Britain in 1990, compared with 136,000 Indian nationals and, the second largest group, 87,000 American nationals. Second, retaining the British role in the world economy, particularly as a financial centre and as the domicile of the European headquarters of many international companies, requires ease of entry and departure; thus intra-company transfers are excluded from immigration controls (Salt and Kitching, 1990: 267–94). Third, the large tourist trade is similarly protected from excessive border restrictions. Fourth, education is an important export sector of the economy – in 1992, there were 85,000 students in the public sector, and nearly half a million in the private sector (the estimated contribution to the 1990 gross domestic product was £1167 billion, or 4 per cent of British export earnings [Wilson, 1992]). The volume of movement involved in these large categories – 46 million entries in 1991 (Spencer, 1994) – makes elaborate controls impossible to operate without severe economic losses. Finally, particular categories of labour are specifically excluded: doctors and dentists arriving for professional appointments are not required to hold a work permit and can stay for up to 12 months on a current entry certificate; those searching for work can stay for 6 months. At the other end of the spectrum, there is virtually free entry for seasonal migrant workers in agriculture (usually travelling as students).

If the British, at least in theory, accepted Empire or Commonwealth citizens resident in Britain as British, and then sought to identify new-comers as foreigners (other than those entering for family reunification), France identified those with French identity cards (including, for example, the inhabitants of the four main cities of Senegal) as having the right to settle in the country. Furthermore, the efforts to incorporate Algeria into France led in 1947 to the recognition of Muslim Algerians as French citizens. Yet severe conflicts of interest remained: the French Algerian authorities at various stages discouraged migration to protect the local labour supply; however, as the movement for an independent Algeria developed, they began to encourage movement to France as a safety valve, while Paris shifted from seeking labour to trying to discourage the spread of sedition to metropolitan France. Later, under the Evian Agreements (1962) which ended the war in Algeria, Paris agreed to the free movement of labour to France in return for Algerian protection of French interests and population in Algeria, and in particular, French oil and gas installations; in the event, the Algerian government nationalized these assets in 1971. Only two years after the Evian Agreements, Paris tried to restrict the movement in a new bilateral agreement with Algiers – an annual quota of 35,000 was laid down as from 1968 (under separate agreements with the relevant governments, France agreed to accept 150,000 workers from Morocco and 100,000 from Tunisia). In practice, the Algerian government saw the outflow of workers, particularly the skilled, as deleterious to Algeria's economic development, and eventually suspended the arrangement just ahead of a decision by Paris to do so.

For Germany, as we have noted, under the federal constitution, workers drawn in by the extraordinary growth of the economy remained temporary or 'guest workers' (Gastarbeiter). Political and economic status, citizen and worker, remained distinct. While by 1960 possibly a quarter of West Germany's population had been born abroad, by 1990 there were some 5 million 'immigrants' (including those born in Germany of non-German parents). The initial movement had been started and regulated by bilateral government agreements. The rush of agreements came after the main supply of labour, from East Germany, ended with the building of the Berlin Wall in 1961. However, once established, direct relationships between employers and source areas tended to take over – up to 35 per cent of the migration of Turkish workers to Germany took place outside the bilateral agreements, and two-fifths of these were requested by companies rather than being recruited by

German government agents (Wilpert, 1992: 184). The agreements, however, restricted the freedom of the government to act unilaterally on the flows.

What had been created by government action tended to be sustained by employers, even after the government had reversed its position. As we have seen, as controls tightened, so the exceptions increased, particularly for seasonal workers in construction and agriculture from Poland and the Czech and Slovak Republics. Companies also recruited workers from Albania, Bulgaria, Poland and Hungary. It was still insufficient and reputedly the numbers of illegal entrants continued to rise.

In Europe generally, from the early 1970s and shortly before the onset of the largest recession since the Second World War, increasing attempts were made to end immigration, deter the arrival of newcomers with a right of entry, and encourage immigrants to leave. Britain was among the first to seek to suspend the process with the 1962 Commonwealth Immigration Act; Denmark temporarily suspended new arrivals in 1970; Norway increased the restrictions on the issue of work permits in 1971; West Germany ended the right of foreign tourists to apply for work permits in 1972, with other disincentives to those with the right to enter Germany under family reunification privileges; the Netherlands restricted entries from 1973, France from 1974. Thus, within a very short space of time, the desperate search for workers was replaced by a no less desperate struggle to exclude them. In December 1978, the French government suspended the granting of extensions to ten-year residents' permits which were due to expire in 1979, affecting some half a million North Africans; in the spring of the following year, Paris eased the provisions to expel immigrants without judicial appeal (the same innovation took place in Britain), and tried to introduce summary detention (a measure subsequently defeated in the Assembly). Governments tried also – unsuccessfully – to pressurize governments in source countries to restrict emigration (without an increase in foreign aid to compensate for the loss in emigrant remittances). Some also penalized the carriers, forcing airline officials to implement immigration legislation, and thus avoided the legal complexities of expelling landed immigrants (the US Coastguards, for similar reasons, arrested suspected immigrants on the high seas and expelled them – acts that might be construed as acts of piracy). As we have seen, employers were also used to help implement immigration law by making them liable to charges for hiring illegal immigrants.

Governments also, as we have seen, tried to encourage existing immigrants to give up voluntarily their residential rights and leave.

Britain made provision for this under the 1971 Act, but, as has been frequently noted, those who utilized the provisions usually intended to leave the country in any case. Similarly under the West German regulations of 1984–85, most of the 180,000 immigrants who left seemed to have decided to do so independently of any incentives offered. In 1977–78, the French government offered financial help to encourage unemployed immigrants and their families to leave; out of the targeted 100,000, some 45,000 – mainly Portuguese and Spaniards – responded, but again, it was thought the beneficiaries had already decided to leave.

The context of increased control, in conditions of world recession from 1973, ensured that the question of immigration was interwoven with increased economic insecurity among the population at large. If this were not enough, in almost all European countries there were political leaders to urge on the process, to seek to stimulate sudden waves of panic at the 'foreign invasion' (the words used by former President of France, Giscard d'Estaing). Former British cabinet minister Enoch Powell spoke in 1968 of British decline in terms of the fall of the Roman Empire, overwhelmed by barbarians. Edith Cresson, prime minister of France, promised the mass expulsion of illegal immigrants. Some British borough councils refused to implement their legal obligation to rehouse the homeless if they were foreign-born; French local authorities also refused the citizens of French overseas territories the right to public housing.

Having established the context of the public debate, governments feel obliged to proclaim, at one- or two-year intervals, a complete end to immigration, knowing full well that the promise cannot be fulfilled. In the jostling for a political edge, the lies are traded without a flicker of shame. French minister Charles Pasqua in mid-1993, preparing for the presidential elections of 1995, announced the government's target as 'zero immigration' and promised legislation to legalize random identity checks and introduce an accelerated expulsion procedure; such measures were necessary because illegal immigrants were responsible for crime and drug dealing.

This verbal froth may have been effective in directing public attention to some of the more defenceless members of society, but it had little impact on the number of arrivals. According to one of the better estimates, the entries for residence of non-Europeans into the European Union increased from 1 million per year in 1985 to 3 million in 1992 – with legal immigration increasing from 700,000 to 1 million; the number applying for asylum from 170,000 to 690,000; citizens of former Yugoslavia with temporary protected status from 100,000 to 300,000; the entry of 'ethnic' Germans (nationals of countries other than

Germany but claiming German descent) from 100,000 to 300,000; and illegals from 50,000 to 400,000 (Widgren, 1993). Of course, figures for arrivals say nothing about the stock of foreign residents, since the numbers leaving were also rising; by 1990, there were only about 8 million resident aliens, or just over 2 for every 100 of the population of the European Union.

The numbers of illegal entrants seemed to be rising and, as in the case of Canada and the United States, governments in Europe were periodically obliged to regularize their status in order that they could be brought into the area of public supervision. Regularization was a recognition of the failure of immigration regulation to control the labour market.

Public attitudes

Yet while there seemed an inexorable drift to the political right on the question of immigration, there were always significant forces that were either indifferent to it or sympathetic to a more liberal regime. Indeed, despite appearances, particularly as reflected in the press and television, the indifferent may have constituted a majority for much of the time. Those who regarded immigration as a threat to sovereignty or national identity were always more assertive than those who did not, since fears take precedence over indifference. Those whose national identity was too secure to be threatened by the presence of foreigners were similarly silent. Employers with an interest in easing the supply of labour were normally unassertive, or afraid of being characterized as unpatriotic. The champions of the free market in Europe, unlike their co-thinkers in the United States, rarely urged an easing of immigration controls, and the exceptions to regulation – maids for the richer families, hotel and restaurant workers or seasonal labour – were established quietly as exceptions and not made into issues of principle.

However, a few small voices did seek occasionally to present counter-arguments. For example, a French government report in the early 1990s argued that immigration had been an important component in sustaining the size and youthfulness of the French population since the mid-1970s, and that there was no evidence that high immigration (as in the 1960s) had created unemployment, or that its supposed suspension in the 1970s had reduced unemployment. The report argued that ageing in the French population would make the resumption of immigration necessary; to offset the expected decrease in the size of the labour force up to the end of the century, the retirement age would need to be raised, the participation of women increased, and 100,000 immigrants admitted annually (Blanchet and Marchand, 1991). The argument hardly registered in the torrent of the reverse flow. Few were prepared to allow immigrants to be converted from instruments of national destruction to saviours of the nation. Europe's rulers had for too long exploited anti-foreigner feelings to relinquish lightly the old populist card.

Nationality

If immigration is in the foreground of public debate, the underlying issue appears to be different. Nationality or citizenship is defined relative to those excluded from it – that is, from full and rightful participation in the supposed life of a country, usually involving rights of self-government. Indeed, the defining of non-citizens, resident aliens or foreigners is one of the rare instances in which the definition of citizenship is made explicit. The status of native is most commonly inherited by birth rather than choice (in contrast to the position of the immigrant); and the rights and privileges of that status, in the absence of foreigners, do not need to be specified. The debate about citizenship is thus concerned with the nature of the state and its social basis in the citizens – that is, with sovereignty.

Large-scale immigration challenges the conception of citizenship in a modern 'socialized' country. Attempts to reconcile the coexistence of those with and those without the rights of citizenship have led to a breaking down of the boundary between the two – between, on the one hand, nationals (born to parents and grandparents of nationals, permanently resident in the country of nationality) and, on the other, nationals resident abroad, those with dual or more nationality, foreigners with permanent residence, temporary residents, seasonal migrants, those attaining and those claiming refugee status, illegal immigrants (of several kinds), and non-natives resident abroad. Colonies and dependencies, special arrangements between countries, and so on, make the situation even more complex. Each category has, supposedly, different attached legal and political rights and obligations. But the growth of immigration and of categories forces a redefinition of citizenship; forces the Europeans and North Americans – as Brubaker (1989: 3) puts it – 'to reinvent themselves ... as nation-states'. Thus, out of the wide variety of subject nationalities within the British Empire and Commonwealth – with four inhabiting the United Kingdom (Welsh, English, Scottish, Northern Irish) – Commonwealth immigration forced the invention of a British nationality that had not previously existed. Indeed, the 'British' are in legal terms one of the newest nations in the world – so much so

that some international sports have not caught up with the new definition (witness the separate teams for England, Scotland, Wales etc.),
and many people, to the understandable irritation of the non-English
British, still refer to the British as the English.

Nevertheless, the norm remains the born-and-bred citizen, a supposed
model of genealogical immobility over centuries. The world's population is assumed to be divided up into clear-cut groups of nationally
defined inhabitants, countries. Again in Brubaker's words, membership
of each national state is presumed to be 'egalitarian, sacred, national,
democratic, unique and socially consequential' (ibid.: 3). Members are
assumed to enjoy a set of clearly specified rights (including political
rights) that distinguish them from everyone else; a common loyalty or
allegiance (which carries with it the obligation, if required, to bear arms
for the state and, if necessary, to die in defence of the state). Membership has to be exclusive; that is, it excludes membership of (and therefore loyalty to) another state, thereby in theory rendering dual nationality
an impermissible status (except for minors, who are excluded from the
rights and obligations of adult citizens).

However, in so far as a significant proportion of the population of a
country leads exactly the same life as everyone else (including working,
paying taxes, receiving social welfare benefits etc.), but is denied the
rights of participation in self-government, there is a disjuncture between
the reality of daily practice and legal status, the foundation of sovereignty.

Thus, in most countries practice is continually changing, seeking to
accommodate a changing reality, and thereby making a mockery of
legal definitions of citizenship. Inevitably, foreigners who live and work
in a country tend through custom and practice to acquire rights which
are virtually indistinguishable from those of the natives, whatever the
law says, and in doing so, blur the distinctiveness of being a full member
of the national society, or at least, devalue its significance. Indeed, the
position can sometimes be reversed so that the foreigners become privileged. For example, in those Muslim countries which ban the consumption of alcohol, foreigners are quite often allowed to drink; or again,
not to have to bear arms for the state under which one resides might
also be considered to be a substantial privilege, the value of which is
far greater than the right which is in return denied, the right to vote.

For different political reasons, as we have seen, privileged access is
also retained for selected entrants; this overrides the simplicities of
immigration regulation and the distinction between native and foreigner.
Algerians long retained the status of being French; citizens of the Irish
Republic, under British law true foreigners (that is, not members of

either the Commonwealth or a British dependency), retained the right to live and work in Britain, regardless of immigration law. Other governments have enshrined the right of entry to foreign nationals who claim a common descent – as we have seen with 'ethnic Germans', who may be, in legal terms, Russians, Romanians, Poles etc. On the same basis, nationals of Latin American countries retain the right to enter Spain, Brazilians to enter Portugal, Russian Greeks to enter Greece; those of claimed Italian origin, retain the right to enter Italy, and those of Japanese origin (as with some Brazilians and Peruvians) the right to live and work in Japan.

However, clear distinctions exist between the way different governments define the rights of entry. Take, for example, two extremes: the United States and Germany. In the case of the United States, while the overwhelming majority of the citizens do not choose their nationality (they are born Americans, just as the majority of Germans are born German), there is a powerful liberal tradition that people do choose their nationality. Immigrants are therefore people who choose to become Americans – and are perverse if they do not become naturalized. In Germany, it is assumed that foreigners are temporary visitors who have no wish or expectation to become citizens, even if they work in Germany.

Despite the expectation that immigrants will want to become citizens, US law does not impose great restrictions on foreign residents. They are not permitted to vote; but only a bare majority of those with American nationality vote in presidential elections, and even fewer in other elections, so the privilege is not, in practice, highly valued. Nor may they serve on juries, run for high elective office, or occupy certain administrative positions. They are, unlike the natives, in theory subject to deportation for certain offences against the law, but the miracle of US litigation imposes powerful constraints on the exercise of this sanction. Furthermore, before military conscription (the draft) was abolished in the early 1970s, resident aliens were obliged to undertake military service as were citizens. In this case the idea of an exclusive loyalty to the state that issues a person's passport was clearly infringed – residents were assumed to be loyal to the state in which they lived, not the state of their legal status. It might seem that the privileges of being an American national are so slight that there is little to gain from naturalization. As Peter Schuck puts it:

> Citizenship represents an increasingly hollow ideal. It neither confers a distinctively advantageous status nor demands much of the individual who possesses it. (Schuck, 1989: 65)

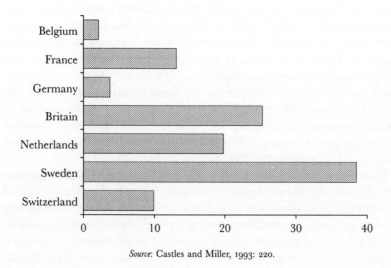

Source: Castles and Miller, 1993: 220.

Figure 4.1 Naturalization rates, selected countries, 1988/90 (naturalizations per thousand foreign residents)

Paradoxically, the advantages of being an 'American' derive not from enjoying the status of a citizen within the United States so much as from the status a US passport accords while travelling outside the country (more freedom, for example, from the need to obtain visas for entry to other countries), and in the ease of entry to the US. Thus, an alternative basis for nationality becomes not sacred loyalty but legal convenience. However, such considerations concern only what is still a minority who wish or are obliged to travel abroad frequently. For those who want to remain in the United States, the privileges of being an American hardly seem significant. On the other hand, the disadvantages of being an American may be considerable. It may restrict an immigrant's ease of entry into his or her country of origin; and if that country restricts the right of foreigners to own or inherit property or land, becoming an American may exclude an immigrant from property ownership in his or her country of origin.

It is hardly surprising therefore that a significant number of legal immigrants to the United States do not opt to naturalize. One might expect the numbers to increase. Even under the 1980 census, over a quarter of those identified as foreign-born and resident in the United

States for ten years or more did not apply for naturalization (that included 56 per cent of those of Hispanic origin, and 44 per cent of those aged 20 or more). Nor is the situation confined to the United States. In Australia in 1988, 43 per cent of permanent residents born overseas had not taken naturalization even though they were eligible (some 1 million people – 60 per cent of them of British or Irish nationality). A parliamentary committee reported that there was doubt about the commitment of this group to the country, and proposed that they should be denied certain privileges (for example, the right to sponsor relatives for admission, welfare and other benefits).

For other countries, the naturalization rate varies widely (see Figure 4.1). The constitutional basis of a state – supposedly founded upon government by consent and representation – is, in theory, undermined in so far as there are significant numbers of people living in the country who are excluded from the vote – and may wish to remain so. Governments have reacted in different ways to this situation. The Nordic countries, the Netherlands and two Swiss cantons allow resident foreigners to vote in local elections, which presumably do not touch on issues of national sovereignty. New Zealand permits them to participate in all elections. In Britain, traditionally, Commonwealth citizens have been permitted to vote in all elections, and this has not been superseded by the European Union arrangements. Different French governments have decided several times that it is unconstitutional to give a local vote to resident aliens, a ruling reiterated in a German Federal Constitutional Court decision of 1990 when the Schleswig-Holstein State endeavoured to introduce this right.

In representative voting systems, the changing composition of the population offers political opportunities for opposition parties to build support by bringing in new groups of voters. For example, the French Socialist Party committed itself in 1981 to securing the right of resident foreigners to vote in municipal elections. However, fear of the rising anti-immigrant National Front tempered the promise. While President Mitterrand continued to urge the reform, Prime Minister Michel Rocard in 1990 renounced the promise as an inducement to opposition parties to participate in a national debate on immigration.

Today, the balance of opinion is changing. In so far as mobility increases and the role of states in sustaining the material condition of their citizens declines, it could be that people will become increasingly indifferent to the preoccupations – if not the fantasies – of their governments. Instead of the vote being a singular privilege, extended to newcomers only with great reluctance and care, governments may well become eager to find any audience to legitimize their preoccupations and will thus be driven to include all residents – at which stage, the idea of nationality will need revision.

At the opposite extreme, as we have seen, the Federal Republic of Germany defines itself as the state of all Germans, whatever their original nationality. Like the elect of God in the Calvinist persuasion, one cannot earn this status through good works, but only through the divine benediction of the state, and the criterion for the bestowal of this privilege is ethnic descent. The small number of foreigners permitted to naturalize are obliged to prove their 'Germanness', their assimilation, in advance of attaining German nationality (whereas, in the United States, naturalization is the route to assimilation). After a minimum of eight years' residence, applicants must demonstrate a capacity to support themselves and their families, be of an 'irreproachable' way of life, 'integrated into Germany and German culture', show a 'lasting orientation to Germany and German culture', competence in the language, knowledge of the German state, and an active commitment to the constitutional order of the Federal Republic. However, even if conformity with these vague and subjective criteria of 'Germanness' is demonstrated, nationality is granted only if this is seen to be in the interests of the German government.

Thus, the immigrant has to be, by one subjective measure of Germanness, more 'German' than the majority of those born in Germany and claiming German descent. Indeed, the naturalization law seems designed to perpetuate an extraordinarily narrow definition of Germanness, quite removed from the heterogeneity of the inhabitants of the Federal Republic. The naturalized suffer a severe disability compared to the natives. Faced with these obstacles, it is not surprising that, of those immigrants living in Germany for ten years or more, so few secure naturalization – 1 in 200 Yugoslavs, 1 in 500 Greeks, and 1 in 600 Turks (Halbronner, 1989: 71). Indeed, even gaining the right of permanent residence without naturalization is difficult – in the early 1990s, some 71 per cent of Turks who had lived in Germany for ten years or more had still not attained permanent residence.

However, life is not simple for the 'ethnic Germans'. To obtain German nationality, they are required to complete satisfactorily a 59-page questionnaire. Even then their application may not succeed. Whenever numbers wishing to enter Germany become significant, the government seeks to qualify its constitutional obligation. In 1989 Bonn cut social and housing benefits to discourage arrivals from Eastern Europe (100,000 in 1987; 250,000 in 1988; and 360,000 officially predicted for 1989). Furthermore, the criteria of German descent are vague enough to allow both ambiguity and official discretion. Thus, after the Soviet liberalization of October 1956, there was a considerable increase in the migration of those claiming to be ethnic Germans from the Soviet Union to West Germany until Bonn suspended the programme for two years on the grounds that a high proportion of the applicants were in fact 'ethnic Poles' (the concept of German ethnicity obliged everyone else to acquire some distinct ethnicity). The ambiguities are part of reality, even without the problems of subterfuge. It was estimated in 1988 that 68 per cent of men with German nationality in the Soviet Union (all Soviet citizens were legally members of a Soviet nationality – Russian, Ukrainian, German etc.) married non-Germans, and 58 per cent of men with Jewish nationality married those with German nationality (cited in Brubaker, 1992: 269). Soviet citizens born to such unions but abroad can on defensible grounds choose whether to be Jews (with, if their mother was Jewish, a right to enter Israel) or Germans (with a right to enter Germany) or some other Soviet nationality. These options are doubtless among the simpler alternatives facing a population with inevitably diverse ethnic origins that only with falsification can be forced into the rigidity of the available legal categories.

The German case is an extreme one, although it represents something in the subjective perception of most peoples – nationality is primarily a function of ethnic descent rather than social existence, and legal status follows upon this. It is assumed this descent is self-evident so that it is simple to identify who is rightfully a member of the nation. Frequently it is not.

However, it is not inevitable that the principle should be as restrictive as German practice has made it. The concept of Swedish nationality is similarly based upon the idea of a common Swedish descent; but admission to this group by those of a different descent does not depend upon the requirements of language competence, knowledge of history and culture, a commitment to the constitutional order, and tests of assimilation and loyalty, that feature in German law. Five years' residence and a record of good conduct are the main criteria.

In practice, the system adjusts through complexity and discretionary power. The theory might suggest that foreigners can not be trusted since they retain an overriding and exclusive loyalty to a foreign state, and therefore, as immigrants, always constitute a fifth column in the host society. Yet where the numbers are great (and the national origins so hopelessly diverse that foreigners have no allegiance to one foreign state), governments are obliged to seek means to bring them into forms of participation. Where naturalization involves significant losses (for example, the right to inherit land in the country of origin), governments compromise on the idea of nationality as an exclusive status by conceding dual nationality. There are possibly a million people in France with both French and Algerian nationality, for example.

It is unclear how far the multiplication of nationalities can go with the creation of new categories (for example, 'non-resident Indians', which includes foreign nationals) or secret affiliations. Consider a person born in the United States to a couple, respectively from Tanzania and Kenya but originally born in parts of former British India which became independent India and Pakistan, who migrates to Canada. Six claims on national status are possible, provided five of the claims are kept secret from the sixth. Over a few generations, a mobile family might build up a significant portfolio of passports to ease the tiresome rigours of international travel, broaden the potential for work, and avoid irksome legal obligations (such as the commitment to military service) – and assist tax evasion. The growth of the black economy in nationality must parallel the increasing lack of coincidence between a hetero-geneous reality and the simplicity of national theory.

Elsewhere in the world, the collision between ethnic claims and the realities of settlement provides an almost endless source for political struggle – and savageries. In particular, this has been true for the de-colonized territories of the European empires through to the break-up of the Soviet Union. Often the new ruling orders in the national fragments of the old cosmopolitan imperial territories were willing to sacrifice significant proportions of the inhabitants of their territory in order to secure the unity of the rest and their own position in power. The Chinese of Southeast Asia, the Indian minorities of East and Central Africa, the Tamils of Sri Lanka, like the Jews of Russia, Poland and Germany before them, became the anvil on which the unity of the rest could be forged (Harris, 1990). In most cases, a thread of class struggle was interwoven with the minorities accused of being alien capitalists exploiting the true natives (although only a minority of the minority owned any capital).

In defining citizens, once governments leave the firm terrain of all those who inhabit a given territory, the door is opened to the impos-sible pursuit of an ethnic essence; to what in Israel became a question which could never be answered with justice and without the arbitrary 'What is a Jew?' (Orr, 1983). The problem becomes acute in the lands of the old Soviet Union where the real differences are slight, but where Soviet passports made claims of legal nationality which obstructed assimilation. In the Ukraine, despite the generations of intermarriage that long preceded the invention of modern nationalities, more than one-fifth of the population are 'Russian'. In Belorussia, although 30 per cent of urban dwellers claim Russian as their first language (and 60 per cent speak Russian), only 13 per cent are Russian.

The issue can never be settled by fiat. In so far as Moscow continues to harbour ambitions to restore its power over the territories of the former Soviet Union or parts of it (as with the Ukrainian Crimea) and to employ ambitious 'Russians' to achieve this, the newly independent governments are inevitably driven to regard those of its citizens who claim to be Russian as actual or potential traitors. The potential for collective insanity is most appallingly shown in old Yugoslavia's Bosnia.

The Baltic Republics showed different reactions to the new situation. All three new states were fashioned in opposition to Russia. Yet in all three, 'Russians' were a significant minority (in the case of Latvia, perhaps as much as half the population) and, as in the Ukraine and elsewhere, many Russians strongly supported the break away from Russia. In Estonia 28 per cent of the population is said to be Russian (staffing many of the managerial jobs), and the new state therefore defined citizenship in June 1993 as those living (or descended from citizens living) in the country before 1940, when some 8 per cent were said to be Russian. Within a month, the absurdity of this position, which excluded from citizenship such a significant proportion of the inhabitants, led to an amendment allowing all those 'lawfully employed' in the country to be admitted under a quota system (provided they passed a language test). In Latvia and Lithuania, even this nominal flirtation with mass exclusion was not attempted. In November 1991, Lithuania admitted to citizenship all who requested it; thereafter, applicants were required to have been resident for at least ten years, and to pass a language test.

The mixing of peoples continually changes the definition and significance of nationality. For most countries the privileges of membership, if such they are, cannot be denied to those who live, work and pay their taxes simply because they were born abroad. But this then devalues the rights of the natives – every movement of opposition to immigration is implicitly one in defence of supposed privilege; as the French ultra-right leader, Le Pen, proclaimed: 'Être français, cela se mérite'. Yet the privileges have always been doubtful, and economically – in so far as they exist – they now depend in part on immigrant labour.

In an open political system with rivalries between neighbouring states, the definition of citizenship is a weapon in the struggle for power, and is never settled. Increased international mobility exacerbates this instability, undermining an increasingly archaic conception of sovereignty. But the instability of states in turn forces increasing mobility – the flight of those unfortunates who become, for whatever reason, the lightning rod of social conflict.

Refugees

The phenomenon of people in flight internationally brings into sharp and painful focus the contradictions implicit in the subject of immigration. The issues no longer concern the supposedly temporary worker, a unit of the economy, in search of work rather than the rights of a citizen, but are matters of compassion. If the case of the temporary worker can supposedly be judged on reasonably clear-cut grounds of economic utility, the possession of desired skills, that of the refugee is, in principle, a matter of ethics. In practice, however, governments have been so concerned to prevent the entry of aliens that the distinction between the two categories has become increasingly unclear – worker migrants are viewed as people in flight from poverty, and those seeking asylum are all too often regarded as 'economic migrants' who are really also fleeing poverty. If it is impossible for governments to avoid accepting people as refugees, then they are appraised as immigrants in terms of their economic utility, with special favour reserved for young professional men without dependants (Salomon, 1991).

International refugees are the result of the breakdown of the state system and the capacity – or willingness – of governments to protect their citizens. New – and sometimes old – states, as we have seen, in struggling to establish a social basis for authority (often in conditions of economic decline) define the criteria for membership of the nation in order to force social unity through discrimination against those who do not conform. In extreme cases, such governments make it impossible for the nonconformists to remain in their homelands. Wars are also prodigious manufacturers of the stateless, like the medieval ronin of Japan, those without a lord. Given that the world is now officially parcelled up between states, there are no free territories where the expropriated can find refuge.

Although the persecution of peoples is an ancient practice, no international legislation was required to respond to it until boundaries were laid down. Even so it was not until after the Second World War that it was found necessary to formulate some principles. Article 13(2) of the United Nations Declaration of Principles affirms that 'everyone has the right to leave any country, including his own, and to return to his country' (by implication, everyone has a country). The affirmation was meaningless however, for the right is empty if simultaneously there is no right to enter another country. Nevertheless, when the war ended the Great Powers sought to lay down a settlement for the problem of 'displaced persons'. They accepted the obligation to consider for settlement anyone who, 'owing to a well-founded fear of being persecuted for reasons of race, religion, nationality, membership of a particular social group or political opinion, is outside the country of his nationality' (United Nations Convention Relating to the Status of Refugees, 1951). This was applicable to movements in Europe before 1 January 1951, but it was stretched to include Hungarians, responding to Soviet invasion, up to 1956, and then scrapped; it was replaced by the 1967 Protocol to the Convention (Rogers, 1992).

The postwar European settlement embodied an attempt at a once-and-for-all reorganization of the European state system – as did the Versailles Treaty of 1919. It failed to achieve this since the underlying problem is not so much the distribution of peoples as the powers and prerogatives of states. As we have seen, the break-up of the Soviet Union and the political transformation of Eastern Europe has reopened many of the issues supposedly settled after 1945. In addition, the ending of the European empires in Asia and Africa spread identical questions round the globe.

The decay of the state system over the past 20 years is reflected in the dimensions of the refugee problem. The United Nations estimates that there were 2.5 million in 1970, 11 million in 1983, and 18 million in 1994 (compared with 25 million displaced within their own borders) (Ogata et al., 1993). But these figures are thought to underestimate considerably the real situation. Other sources suggest that today there are some 70 million refugees (that is, outside their own borders), with possibly the same number in flight within countries. The majority are in developing countries, fleeing civil war, repression, military conscription, forced resettlement, drought and famine (Desbarats, in Kritz et al., 1992: 279). In some cases, the numbers involved have been extraordinary – possibly 9 million fleeing from what was then East Pakistan to India in 1971, and 6 million fleeing the civil war in Afghanistan, half to Pakistan and half to Iran. Turkey accepted 1 million Iranians, 36,000 Iraqi Kurds and 10,000 Afghans. The numbers dwarf those which have caused such panics in Europe and North America in the 1990s. Looking at the refugee problem from the perspective of the host country, in the late 1980s in Malawi there was 1 refugee for every 9.8 of the population – compared with 26.7 in Sweden, 48.2 in Canada, 97.0 in Germany, 252.3 in Switzerland (UNCHR, 1993: 154). Yet quite small numbers – 2000 Cubans arriving in Miami per day – could be declared a national emergency for the mighty United States.

The geographical distribution of refugees maps the areas where states are weakened by warfare, the intervention of the Great Powers, or other political or economic crisis: the Horn of Africa (Somalia, Ethiopia, Sudan, Uganda), Mozambique and Angola, the Middle East (Palestine,

Lebanon, Iraq, Iran), Central America, Indo-China, the Caucasus and the Balkans.

Historically regimes claimed, as part of their sovereignty, the right to move populations at will, to occupy or evacuate territories, to extend or withdraw protection from groups of their inhabitants. The withdrawal of protection from one group allowed them to be assaulted, robbed and raped with impunity by those with protection. Theft, as we noted earlier, created new interests in defending the new status quo.

However, despite appearances, the *relative* scale of flight is not new; similar movements have occurred wherever and whenever there has been an attempt to fashion a modern state. For example, Eastern and Central Europe has for much of this century been racked with the problems of decaying empires and attempts to fashion new states. It is little wonder that, as Dariusz Stola (1992: 324) puts it, '[d]eportations and evacuations, exile and forcible repatriations, compulsory transfers and panic-stricken flights are an essential part of Central European history.' From the Germanization of eastern Prussia and the attempt to expel the Poles in the 1880s, to the Russification of the Tsar's domains leading to the expulsion of the mass of Polish Jews, to the continuing reorganization of the Balkans before 1914, the creation of 'national identity' was a brutal, bloody and never finally accomplished process. In the First World War, half the Serbian population was driven to march to the Adriatic (possibly 200,000 perished *en route*); 3 million people were displaced in Russia; 800,000 were driven from Austrian Galicia; the Russian military advance on eastern Prussia drove out half a million people.

The Treaty of Versailles after the First World War settled little. With the dissolution of the Ottoman and Austro-Hungarian Empires and the struggle of the successor states to establish some measure of authority, the peoples of the Balkans continued to be shunted about on the map. Some 200,000 refugees fled to Bulgaria, while 95,000 Turks and 30,000 Greeks were expelled (Stola, 1992: 329). Anti-Semitism provided an excellent tool for forcing the social solidarity of the new states of Romania, Hungary and Poland, driving out many thousands of inhabitants long before Hitler made the persecution of Jews an important means to secure his power. In 1933, after considerable emigration, 700,000 Germans were enumerated as Jewish; by 1939, when Germany had come to include Austria and Czechoslovakia, there were 300,000 left. In war, the Final Solution constituted the most extraordinary act of destruction upon any group of people, not just in the scale of its cruelty but in the exemplary character of its injustice: the wound the Europeans inflicted upon themselves by this peculiar act of self-destruction became a psychic trauma bequeathed to subsequent generations.

At the time, governments showed remarkable equanimity in refusing to recognize the terror inflicted upon part of the German population – and continued to refuse entry to the refugees. The main preoccupation of the British Foreign Office (Wasserstein, 1979) was to prevent European Jews reaching Palestine lest this anger Arab opinion and so threaten British interests there. Much effort was devoted to blocking the escape routes of Jews through eastern Europe, epitomized in the story of the SS *Struma*. This vessel, carrying 769 refugees from Romania in December 1941, broke down in Istanbul, where it was marooned for ten weeks while British diplomatic representatives pressed the Turkish government to return it to the Black Sea into the arms of the original persecutors. In the end, the Turks compromised and consented to tow the ship out to sea, where it foundered with the loss of all on board except one.

The British government also encouraged a national hysteria about 'infiltrators' from the Third Reich – hence the arrest and internment of 30,000 'enemy aliens', including Jewish refugees, on suspicion of spying for Germany (just as the United States interned its citizens of Japanese descent). So far as entry procedures were concerned, Britain came to distinguish between 'war refugees', accepting some 30,000 from Holland and Belgium, and 'racial refugees'. Only 2000 Jews were accepted under this provision, although some 40,000 had gained entry to Britain between 1933 and 1939 before this distinction was introduced to stem the flow.

Other governments were no less firm in setting their faces against serious help to refugees from the Holocaust. Thus, Argentina attempted to block the entry of Poles and Jews, as earlier it had obstructed the landing of refugees from the Spanish Civil War. In the United States, as we have seen, the issuing of visas was sharply reduced to prevent the arrival of European refugees. In 1939 a bill was presented to Congress to allow the admission of 20,000 children from Germany, but it was defeated – 'the cruellest single action in US immigration history' as the Select Committee on Immigration and Refugee Policy put it half a century later (US Congress, 1989b: 199).

The fate of Europe's Jews, however, was only the most extreme expression of a social collapse of extraordinary dimensions. Possibly 60 million people were displaced during the war (Proudfoot, 1957: 340), and 20 million more in the immediate aftermath of the war. They included people in flight from the hostilities, those forced to migrate, and those who were persecuted. The Ukrainian nationalists, for example, tried to drive out possibly 300,000 Poles. Hungarians and Bulgars (possibly 60,000) were driven from Romania; Romanians (possibly 100,000) from Hungary and Bulgaria; and an unknown number of Greeks from Macedonia. Poor Yugoslavia, dismembered by Germany, Italy, Hungary and Bulgaria, was subject to violent population persecution and redistribution. Perhaps as many as 8 million people from the Soviet Union and Eastern Europe were conscripted as forced labour to work in Germany. Stalin, on an apparent whim, punished whole peoples for alleged collaboration with the German invaders, so that at the end of the war 'ethnic Germans' fled westwards – 350,000 from the Soviet Union, 300,000 from Hungary. By 1950/51, some 11.7 million had been expelled or had fled. Finally, in the postwar settlement, there were again major transfers of population within Eastern Europe and the Soviet Union.

Yet the truce was not a permanent settlement. Significant minorities remain outside what is supposed to be their state – as with Hungarians in Romania, Yugoslavia, the Czech Republic and Slovakia, Germans in the Soviet Union – or had no state. Ambitions to power could remanufacture ethnic issues without minorities, as when some Bosnian Serbs endeavoured to destroy their Muslim neighbours. And it would be wrong to underestimate the ingenuity of governments in inventing new minorities if the need arose. The illusory pursuit of 'national identity' (or, more precisely, loyalty to the state), sanctioned untold atrocities upon masses of the innocent.

Europe was not alone in these 'final' solutions. The end of the colonial empires spread the virus implicit in the creation of the modern state. As we have noted, theft sealed the redistribution of land and property in the flight of refugees in the partitioning of India and of Palestine. In Korea in the early 1950s, the savageries of the Great Powers led to the flight of 4 million (and the slaughter of possibly 3 million). Ghana expelled its Nigerians in 1969, and Nigeria its 1.5 million Ghanaians and others between 1983 and 1985. Burma expelled possibly 1 million of its citizens of Indian origin between 1963 and 1964, and about 200,000 Burmese Muslims (Rohingyas) in the early 1980s. Uganda ejected its citizens of Indian origin in 1969; Saudi Arabia expelled 800,000 Yemenis during the Gulf War (1990–91) as a punishment for their government supporting Iraq, and Kuwait similarly punished its Palestinians. Libya punished Egypt, Tunisia, Mali, Mauritania, Niger and Senegal by expelling its citizens who were immigrant workers in 1976, 1978 and 1980. Ethiopians and Somalians were driven out of their respective countries to each other, and also to Sudan and Kenya. Bhutan drove out its Nepalese, Mauritania some 50,000 Senegalese and 25–30,000 Malians (1989). The 6 million Afghans who fled to Pakistan and Iran have already been mentioned, as have the 9 million Bengalis

who sought refuge in India during the military repression of East
Pakistan. Some 100,000 Tibetans fled to India with the Chinese con-
quest of Tibet and the subsequent invasion of Red Guards during the
Cultural Revolution; 90,000 Sri Lankan Tamils fled the civil war to
India; 1 million Salvadoreans and Guatemalans escaped military
repression and civil war to Mexico and the United States. Repression
in Brazil, Argentina, Uruguay and Chile led to large-scale flight;
Albanians surged into Italy, Cubans and Haitians to the United States.
Some 600,000 fled abroad from the former Yugoslavia (and nearly 4
million were displaced domestically). Over 2 million Rwandans were
forced to flee their country in 1994. This list has no pretension to being
comprehensive.

Groups of people became trapped in a legal limbo while governments squabbled over them – as with the Indian Tamils of Sri Lanka,
accepted by neither India nor Sri Lanka (Tinker, 1977), and the Biharis
of Bangladesh. Immigrant populations were used as scapegoats to
establish or perpetuate the power of a ruling order, as Bengalis were
used in Indian Assam. Targeting them was a favourite way to punish
an errant government – as when Iran threatened reprisals against
Filipino workers in Iran in 1982 following the ill-treatment of Iranian
students in Manila; or when Saudi Arabia banned Thais seeking work
in retaliation for the murder of a Saudi diplomat in Bangkok; or when
Argentina instituted a ban on residence rights for Chilean immigrants
following the 1978 clash between Chile and Argentina.

It is an appalling history. Governments ritualistically condemn Nazi
Germany, yet it seems everywhere have followed comparable principles,
and sometimes a not dissimilar practice. Consider as prototypical the
treatment by the Bulgarian government of those of its citizens who
claimed Turkish descent. With the general crisis of Communist regimes
in the late 1980s, part of the old leadership tried to stabilize its power
and ward off the demands for reform by directing attention to what
was alleged to be the continued refusal of those citizens of Turkish
origin (850,000 in a total population of 9 million) to conform to Slav
Bulgar norms (Vasileva, 1992). The government demanded the elimina-
tion of 'cultural differences', or 'integration' – the use of Turkish names
in public places was prohibited. Turks were instructed to adopt Slavic
names, and there were general complaints of police harassment. Foreign
protests prompted the government to change tack: the leader of the
ruling party, Todor Zhivkov, demanded that Turkey open its borders to
receive 'its citizens'. Some 370,000 were forced to flee, abandoning
houses, land, shops and work. The government assured the rest of the
population that, as a result, the housing shortage would be relieved.

Scarcely six months later, the government fell and reforms began. Turks were allowed to return, to resume their original names and to speak Turkish. Within one year 42 per cent of the refugees had returned. However, the non-Turkish beneficiaries of the flight refused to return the houses and land they had acquired through forced sales at government instituted prices, and in 1990 it was estimated that some 72,000 Turkish Bulgarians were homeless.

The Turkish government, whatever its misgivings, tried to give a sympathetic reception to the Bulgarian immigrants. Other governments have been much less sympathetic. Most regarded the acceptance of refugees as an adjunct of their foreign policy. Thus, up to the end of the Cold War, the United States accepted as 'refugees' only those in flight from the Eastern bloc countries (so there were, by definition, no refugees from non-Communist countries). Everywhere the springs of compassion are rapidly exhausted by sheer numbers. The spirit of international agreements on refugees is constantly qualified, ignored or defeated.

The story of the Vietnamese 'boat people' exemplifies the world's embarrassment or cruelty. From 1978 onwards, three years after the end of the Vietnam War, a million or so people were forced out of their country, most of them drawn from the educated or better-off classes of the old regime of the former South Vietnam. The countries immediately receiving these seaborne victims – Thailand, Malaysia, Indonesia, the Philippines – in general came to refuse landings by anyone who did not already possess the legal right to enter a third country. Notoriously, the Thai government tolerated the depredations of Thai pirates who searched out and seized refugee vessels, slaughtering the men, robbing, raping and seizing the women for sale into prostitution. The Malaysian government, trapped in policies to favour Malaysian Malays as opposed to Malaysian Chinese, identified the refugees as Chinese, and the navy towed their boats back to sea. Between 30,000 and 40,000 boat people are estimated to have perished *en route* from Vietnam. Lee Kuan Yew, then prime minister of Singapore, refused to accept any of the refugees, while acknowledging that they were highly skilled, and did not allow ships that had picked them up at sea to anchor in the port unless a bond of US$4665 was first deposited with the government. Lee, ever an inventive politician, formulated a novel moral proposition to justify this approach. If refugees were accepted, he said, then 'we would not only be encouraging those responsible to force even more refugees to flee, but also unwittingly, demonstrating that a policy of inhumanity does pay dividends.' Lee's policy of inhumanity, however, was supposed to 'pay dividends'. The prescription could be extended almost indefinitely

– one should not help those injured in road accidents lest this encourage bad drivers. His foreign minister, Rajaratnam, gave a hint of the extraordinary paranoid fantasies of Singapore's leadership when he alleged that the flight of the boat people was a deliberate attempt to destroy the Southeast Asian countries by trying to force them into a race war.

The North American and European governments, being further away and disciplined by a less pliant citizenry, were less tempted to emulate this public display of heartlessness. However, with the initial notable exceptions of Canada, the countries of Scandinavia, and especially the United States – which took in half the Vietnamese in flight, including boat people, along with 130,000 Cambodians and 150,000 Laotians, accepting its responsibility to its former client states – the reaction of governments in most developed countries was to work mightily to sit on their hands. Many gave up any responsibility for saving those at sea, leaving this to the judgement of captains of passing vessels in the area; the captains, for their part, were pressurized by ship owners (and the refusal of ports in the area to accept refugee landings) not to pick up refugees, regardless of the state of their small boats. With a few remarkable exceptions, compassion was reduced to the exercise of individual conscience, snared in thickets of official discouragement.

The Vietnamese government, at the Geneva conference of 1979, offered to honour the United Nations Charter of Human Rights by allowing all who wished to leave Vietnam to do so freely. The Great Powers, in panic at this generosity, demanded much tighter Vietnamese controls on the flight, then running at about 50,000 per month. Later, Hanoi, in response to Washington's protests at its treatment of political prisoners, offered to release them all if the United States would take them; Washington accepted a selected 10,000.

The British government, then under Mrs Thatcher's prime ministership, accepted 10,000 Vietnamese (under 3 per cent of the total). With the Hong Kong government (which at this time had interned 54,000 Vietnamese for screening), the British now pressed for a radical redefinition of the flight. It appeared on this reading that the Vietnamese boat people were astonishingly light-minded, not fleeing terror or persecution at all; they were, rather, simply illegal immigrants who had deliberately chosen an eccentric method of travel. Being illegal, they could then be legally expelled by force, or rather repatriated. There were strong protests, particularly from the United States. The British were quick to point out that Washington had expelled 20,000 seaborne Haitians between 1981 and 1989 by the simple expedient of not allowing them to land, turning their vessels round. At the appropriate time of 3.0 a.m. when the world's press might be expected to sleep, on 1

December 1989, 17 women, 26 children and 8 men were manhandled onto aircraft for return to Hanoi – 'a shaming spectacle', as the *Financial Times* editorialist put it.

The straight rejection of the claim to refugee status was part of a general process in the developed countries of escaping any responsibility for people in flight by refusing to believe that they were in reasonable fear of persecution. The extraordinary privations and dangers suffered by these people did not count in weighing the plausibility of the claims, even though informed opinion suggested that no more than 10 to 15 per cent were bogus (Khan and Talal, 1986: 42). Furthermore, to back up the allegation that such refugees were really illegal immigrants, it was suggested that they were poor and unskilled, driven to flee poverty not the danger of persecution – when again all the evidence suggested that they were better educated than the average, had often paid to fly to Europe, and, if permitted to work, were unlikely to be a charge on public funds. Governments could not allow such reality. In trying to increase the disincentives to migrate, arrivals were – if they could not be expelled immediately – increasingly interned in prison conditions indefinitely. Many countries came to prohibit asylum applicants from working and supporting themselves – for example, West Germany in the early 1980s, France in 1991 – and then complained that the burden on the public exchequer of maintaining them as internees forced the government to expel them. Few areas of public policy exhibited such aggressive hypocrisy.

In the late 1980s there was a rapid increase in the numbers of people seeking asylum, both from some of the more notorious trouble spots (Somalia, Ethiopia, Sudan, Sri Lanka) but also and increasingly from within Europe. In the eight years to 1991, the number of people applying for refugee status in Europe increased from 65,000 to half a million (the bulk of them entering Germany), and to nearly 700,000 in 1992. In the United States over the same period, applications increased from 25,000 to 100,000. The press and other commentators had a field day in highlighting this as a matter for panic, promising that the sheer demography of the world must ultimately produce 'devastating mass immigration'. Yet even if we count all those applying to enter one or other of the 16 leading countries of Europe and North America (and this is far in excess of the numbers actually accepted), the total (Widgren, 1993: 91) still reaches only about one-fifth of the refugees received in Pakistan during the Afghan war, and three-fifths of the number of Iranians taken in by Turkey (and well under 5 per cent of the world's total refugees).

Yet, whatever the numbers, the erosion of the system in the developed countries continues, apparently inexorably, through a series of means:

1. The bulk of those seeking asylum are defined as 'economic migrants' and therefore governed by immigration, not refugee, law. This allows arrivals to be expelled to their country of origin. When Britain repatriated five Tamils to Sri Lanka and two were arrested and tortured (as they had said they would be), an independent tribunal found the government in error. Nothing daunted, the administration revised the rules to allow expulsions while applications were being considered. The new procedure has the merit of testing claims to persecution by placing the applicant directly under the authority of the alleged persecutor; if his or her claims are borne out, they are thus physically removed from any claim on British hospitality.

2. All governments use administrative means to reduce the numbers being granted refugee status, apparently without regard to the circumstances of the case. As a proportion of applicants, the numbers accepted in France fell from 60 per cent (1983) to 30 per cent (1987); in Switzerland, from 16 per cent (1984) to 8 per cent (1987); and in Britain, from 40 per cent (1982) to 8 per cent (1987) – from 45,000 to 9,600. On this evidence, the world is clearly becoming a much safer place.

3. However, domestic opinion is sometimes outraged by summary procedures that endanger lives. Enquiries take much time, producing a backlog of applications. Governments are therefore obliged to create legal limbos where applicants are neither accepted nor rejected – in Germany, this is known as 'tolerance'; in Britain, 'exceptional leave to remain'.

4. However, to hold out for a long period is usually difficult, especially if the applicant is forbidden to work. If applicants can work, they relieve the public exchequer of the cost and reduce what are said to be the resentments of the local population at meeting this cost. They also build up their assets, and there is evidence (Harrell-Bond, 1993) that increased assets make refugees much more inclined to return home when it is feasible.

5. Governments also increase the legal requirements to enter their country. Applicants for asylum are thus required to obtain a visa before departure (the absurdity of this provision for someone seriously afraid of persecution seems not to occur to immigration officials). Several governments (Britain, the USA, Canada, France) force airlines and shipping companies to implement controls by fining them if they deliver anyone with defective documents. Britain fined arriving airlines £30.7 million between 1987 and 1991 on this count.

6. Some governments try to divert potential applicants for asylum to other destinations. The United States coastguards seek, as we have seen, to turn round ships at sea suspected of carrying refugees so that they

cannot land and thereby acquire rights to defend themselves against deportation. The USA also asked Mexico to receive Chinese arrivals, and Panama and others to take in Haitians. Germany offered Croatia help with refugee housing if the refugees stayed there.

7. Increasingly, discretionary powers devolve upon the immigration official, who is rarely competent to judge the claim that, in a particular country, someone is threatened with persecution, particularly if the applicant's command of the local language is imperfect. Administrative pressure to speed up procedures invariably led to an increased rate of rejections, regardless of the validity of the case.

8. There are other transparent dodges. The European powers agreed that if the potential applicant had the misfortune to land in any other country *en route* to their final destination, they could be deported to that country while their application was considered. Thus, for example, a Bosnian fleeing by land is obliged to cross another country, often Croatia, but can then be returned there – in which case, the Croatian government has a strong incentive to refuse to accept the Bosnian in the first place. It was, as Edward Mortimer argued in the *Financial Times* (9 December 1992) 'an obscene game of pass-the-human-parcel'.

9. As noted earlier, governments also increasingly appraise refugees as if they are immigrants. Thus Britain endeavoured to exclude elderly parents and unaccompanied minors from the Vietnamese refugees offered the right to enter. The French similarly tried to exclude families until the Constitutional Court struck this practice down. Others evaluate the applicant's economic potential before considering asylum, and so exclude most of those in most need.

10. The law is revised with the sole aim of reducing the numbers admitted. The British Asylum bill of 1991 withdrew financial aid for applicants to argue their case, and laid down a procedure whereby judgements were reached without a verbal hearing or the right to challenge the judgement – the 'National Humbug Bill', as a *Guardian* editorial put it (3 November 1991).

Increasing numbers of refugees, governments agreed, threatened the survival of countries. Much of their populations did not agree. Some actively disagreed, but the majority were, despite the media, indifferent. Particular issues, however, ignited campaigns of opposition – around, for example, Kurdish or Sri Lankan refugees in Britain, or 70 Palestinians interned for two years in Denmark and then threatened with expulsion. Campaigns of fund-raising evoked much sympathy, particularly given the dense media coverage of particular crises (as for example in Bosnia, Rwanda or Angola). Popular generosity was often well ahead of government gestures; thus, when the Canadian government, among the more generous, was spurred in July 1979 to offer 50,000 entry permits for Vietnamese refugees provided localities in Canada volunteered to take them, Canadians considerably overfulfilled the target (to the embarrassment of the government). There were other cases – sea captains who defied owners and ports to fish Vietnamese refugees from the sea; the French volunteers who purchased a special ship to go to the South China Sea and the Gulf of Thailand to rescue boat people.

In the United States in the mid-1980s when, as we have seen, officially only Communist countries produced 'refugees', American churches organized a clandestine system to bring refugees from Central America and provide them with sanctuaries; some 281 churches, meeting houses and synagogues are said to have been involved, even though Washington roundly declared that those in flight were not refugees but only economic migrants (and the Immigration Service duly laid criminal charges against offenders in October 1985). In Germany in 1994, the head of the Catholic Church called on priests to find sanctuary for refugees facing deportation (more than 200 churches – Protestant and Catholic – sheltered refugees on the run).

These were scattered incidents, as scattered as the neo-Nazi clashes which attracted much greater attention. They indicated that at least some people did not accept that national sovereignty and survival depended upon increasing cruelty towards those in flight. Indeed, some pointed out that refugees could have valuable effects in stimulating economic growth – as the economy of Miami had been restored by Cubans. On this issue, governments were singularly impervious to costs and benefits. The Europeans supposedly spent on refugee control and assessment some $5–7 billion dollars (Widgren, 1993: 91) or, according to another estimate, $7–8 billion (Intergovernmental Interior Ministers, 1992), a sum roughly equivalent to one-seventh of the combined development-aid budgets in 1990.

The world labour market increasingly collides with the traditional prerogatives of national states. In so far as the state system itself weakens, there are increasing numbers in flight. In principle, the world can cope with the movements of both worker migrants and refugees – at maximum, they are tiny proportions of the population of the world and of the countries directly concerned. The alternative to accepting worker movement is to impede the world rate of economic growth – and thus the creation of employment and incomes for the mass of the world's population. The permanent policing of migration requires the restoration of some kind of imperial order. Neither option is realistic. A competitive state system means the pursuit of economic growth is intrinsic to the system; no one can contract out except at the risk of their survival. As for policing the world, the cost is beyond the power of even the most powerful state, and rivalries mean that no one power or group of powers can be entrusted with the task.

5

Social Networks and Migration

Recruitment

For those who migrate, the experience is primarily social, not a response to some unseen labour market. When people move, they change both the world they leave behind and the society they enter. Cultures are made, unmade and remade, and new syntheses are created which bind source and destination in new relationships. Social networks emerge linking a few streets in a city in a developed country to the quarter of a small town in a developing country. The networks are unseen by all except the participants; they mediate elaborate exchanges and inter-actions of people, goods, information and finance, thereby linking, as Douglas Massey (1990) puts it, migrants, former migrants (and their descendants) and non-migrants through friendship, common experience and material transactions. What is extraordinary is that this common phenomenon is seen as unusual, a deviation from the norm of genera-tions living a settled life in one place.

Passports, the pre-eminence of national interest, conceal the specificity of migration links between localities. It is 'Indians' who travel the world, even though departures are limited to a handful of localities in that vast country of different languages, scripts, cultures, cuisine and dress – Malaysian Indians are drawn from a few districts and castes of Tamilnadu and Kerala; British Indians are Gujaratis from East Africa and Indian Gujarat, and from Jullundur in the Punjab; people from five rural districts in Kerala, and others in Andhra Pradesh and the Punjab, work in the Gulf; there are Sindhis and Sikhs in Hong Kong, Taiwan and Indonesia; Gorakhpuris from Uttar Pradesh sell peanuts on the streets of Bangkok. The Mexicans who work the farms of the southern United States are drawn from the rural middle class (Stark, 1991: 289) of districts in the central states (Michoacán, Jalisco, Guerrero); they are not interchangeable with the young women who staff the factories in the boom areas of the north, nor the poor fruit and vegetable pickers who move seasonally to Sonora and Sinaloa on the west coast (Cornelius and Martin, 1993), nor the better educated who move to the capital or other big cities in Mexico. Half the 8000 Italian brickmakers of Bedford in Britain come from four villages in southern Italy. The German Greeks hail from Thrace and the German Turks from western Anatolia. Of Bangladesh's 21 regions or districts, only four supply emigrants, 43 per cent from the better-off rural families of Chittagong, and many of the rest from rural Sylhet. Four-fifths of the Filipina maids of Hong Kong are of rural origin, most of them from the north (villages in Ilocos and mountain provinces).

Almost invariably migrants are deliberately recruited in response to a specific demand for workers, whether the recruiter is the employer or his agent, or some kind of broker linking demand and supply. Agents for jobs in Venezuela scout villages in Colombia, Ecuador and Peru and provide transport to the destination. In some cases, friends and relatives do the recruiting – in the 1960s, as we have noted, larger German employers allowed their foreign workers to fill vacancies, and they brought people from their places of origin. The Macdonalds (1964) have shown historically how *padroni* organized and supplied labour from particular Italian towns to employers in the United States, acting as recruitment agents, bankers, landlords, foremen, interpreters, legal advisers and political ward bosses, simultaneously protecting and exploiting newcomers.

Something not dissimilar seems to occur in Java (Spain, 1994). Village headmen or sheikhs, usually large farmers and now important in the local network of political power, have for a long time acted as recruiters of labour for foreign destinations. They partly developed from the pioneering routes through Singapore to escape Dutch restrictions on Muslim pilgrimages to Mecca, but then moved on to supply labour to Singapore (from 1825), and bonded labour to Johore in Malaysia. Today the trade is partly funded by moneylenders and merchants – and the costs for the villagers concerned are high (the rupiah equivalent of US$110–220, with a rate of interest of between 300 and 500 per cent [Spain, 1994: ref. 106]). Destinations are commonly in Sabah, Johore, Selangor, Perak and Kuala Lumpur in Malaysia (for plantation and construction work), in the Middle East (as domestics and drivers), and some in Europe.

The costs and risks involved in moving between countries are far too high to think the traffic would be other than highly organized. No one would move to a foreign country on the off chance of finding work; and even if they set out, they would likely be defeated by the physical, financial and legal obstructions encountered *en route*. The agent is vital to the whole process of migration, and often arranges not only a job at the destination but also the loan required to sustain the migrant. Michael Piore (1979) notes how old this system is: steamship companies recruited workers in Europe for employers in the United States before 1914, as other agents hired rural southerners for work in the north in the 1920s. The deliberate role of the agent (and his or her contacts or origin) explains the apparently arbitrary character of the links – why, for example, factories in Southall in England drew workers from parts of Jullunder district in the Indian Punjab, rather than from the many much poorer parts of India.

Once the idea of working abroad becomes widespread in a particular district the numbers involved can become very large, and the competition to get work fierce. The possibility of fraud is great even where a government seeks to police the system and outlaw unlicensed agents. Take, for example, the Philippines where, in the early 1990s, some 2.5 million people were seeking work abroad. The government estimates that there were 679 registered and 700 unregistered agencies (others claimed over 1000). The officially recognized brokers are, in theory, limited to maximum charges of P5000 (then US$194), but the illegal agents charge between P10,000 and 150,000. Many of the unregistered agents collect fees to process applications and then disappear. Some recruits are provided only with one-way tickets, and on arrival have no work or entry visas; they are therefore arrested and deported (in 1978, 200 Filipinos were stranded in Singapore by a bogus employment agent).

The agents shift destinations according to demand – by the early 1990s, Hong Kong and Japan had overtaken the Middle East as the most important destinations for migrant workers, each taking between 50,000 and 57,000 workers from the Philippines. The shift in destinations is an underresearched area. Do the brokers search out new markets, or do agents in the destination areas seek new sources of recruits? The success of the agents in the sending areas depends upon stabilizing flows, and this depends on the timely identification of new destinations as old ones decline. For example, as the demand for Middle Eastern construction labour has declined, have agents identified new types of labour to supply to the Middle East, or new destinations?

In an excellent study, Singhanetra-Renard (1992) shows the stages of the development of international migration from selected villages in the northeast of Thailand. Traditional seasonal migration (to herding for trading caravans in the 1930s) gave way to movement to Bangkok when one of the villagers was sent there as a monk and summoned his relatives and friends. Modern migration, however, developed from the

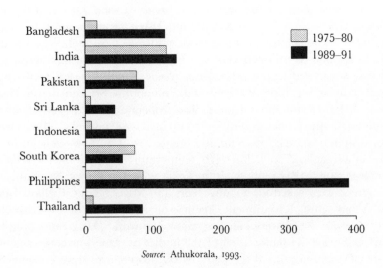

Source: Athukorala, 1993.

Figure 5.1 Labour emigration: eight countries in Asia, 1975/80 compared to 1989/91 (thousands)

construction and maintenance work on a US air base at Udon Thani (during the Vietnam War, between 1964 and 1975). Some of the US companies building the air base subsequently took local workers on to Middle Eastern construction projects, and this set off large-scale emigration from the mid-1970s; by 1986, Thai workers worked in at least 28 countries.

However, the recruitment syndicates encountered increasing competition between labour suppliers to the Middle East and this threatened profit margins. The brokers tried to raise the charges levied on the workers, but this led to their impoverishment and so to a declining incentive to migrate. In the 1980s, the agents spread out to link new sources of supply and demand – bringing workers from Indo-China to construction sites and plants in Thailand, illegal Indonesian, Filipino and Thai workers to Malaysia and Singapore; maids, barmaids and prostitutes to Japan and Europe, and so on. The Thai case – working with crime syndicates in Japan and elsewhere – suggests a vast unseen international network underpinning a global labour market; a horde of termites – as we put it earlier – boring through the national fortifications against migration, and changing whole societies. Certainly, the numbers are tending to increase (see Figure 5.1).

The temptation for the agencies to break national laws in a fiercely competitive market was overwhelming. Take, for example, a test case mounted by a Danish newspaper. In mid-1983, an agency called the Multinational Recruitment Group (MRG) based in Jeddah in Saudi Arabia advertised in the *International Herald Tribune* 'quality manpower from Bangladesh, India, Pakistan, the Philippines, Sri Lanka and Thailand' (MRG claimed to act for 47 government-approved agencies in 14 countries). In Copenhagen, a company was invented, Dangreen Construction, to ask MRG for 100 manual workers to work a 16-hour day in Greenland in below-zero temperatures – making for a high accident rate. MRG replied within hours with an offer of Sri Lankans. Dangreen then asked for 2000 workers and MRG offered Pathans from the Vinex Gulf Recruitment Agency of Lahore, Pakistan, with the proviso that, if any were killed or injured at work, Dangreen would be responsible for the repatriation of the bodies or those who were injured. When Dangreen refused the offer, MRG proposed to transfer the payment of its agency fees from Dangreen to the workers and to cut their monthly pay rate from £160 to £140 as an inducement to Dangreen to hire. The deal was entirely contrary to Pakistan's laws on the issue (Rosemary Righter, *Sunday Times*, 19 June 1983).

Destinations

The agent's choice of locality for recruitment makes the source of migrants highly specific. The same is true, at least initially, of the destination. The thousands of Fujianese travelling illicitly to the United States go to New York, not to California, where the famous China towns are, since New York has the largest group of people from Fujian. Sometimes the linkages between immigrants persist for lifetimes – a study of a Canadian home for the elderly containing 33 Filipinos, found that 28 originated in the same village.

The links are not simply social. Migrants move to work, and indeed their movement itself shows where the demand for their labour is strongest. In developed countries, this is usually in the cities. For the past two decades, 71 per cent of official immigrants to the United States have headed for only six destinations (with 27 per cent going to California and 19 per cent to New York); 40 per cent went to five metropolitan areas (New York, Los Angeles–Long Beach, Miami, Chicago and Washington DC).

The same tendency affects those refugees who are not recruited for work but are driven by fear of persecution, and who are often dispersed by governments under the illusion that this will increase 'assimilation'. Refugees then redistribute themselves towards the standard destinations. In the USA, for example, of refugees from the countries of Indo-China (Laos, Cambodia, Vietnam), 45 per cent changed their state of residence in the five years after arrival (compared to 9 per cent for the US-born population) to re-create specific concentrations. The case of the Miami Cubans is also an example of this phenomenon.

The demand for a worker simultaneously defines the level of education, skill and experience (or lack of them). This is true even though the majority of migrants are downgraded in terms of their original qualifications. Martin's study of Turkish migration to Germany (1991: 30) cites an estimate that one-third of the 800,000 Turkish emigrants between 1964 and 1976 had some skill (the number included between 5 and 10 per cent of the Turkish stock of plumbers and electricians in 1965, and between 30 and 40 per cent of carpenters, masons and miners), but almost all went into unskilled or semi-skilled jobs. As we have seen, Filipina maids are another example – a study of Hong Kong domestics showed that 55 per cent were college graduates, 12 per cent had started college, and 21 per cent were high-school graduates; before emigration, 40 per cent had worked as professional workers, most of them as teachers (Lane, 1992). A study of Filipino workers in Korea showed that 55 per cent were college graduates or higher, and 39 per cent high-school graduates (and on average they had paid US$1798 to work in Korea) (Park, 1993).

In the United States, the census of 1980 showed that immigrants were disproportionately bunched at the extremes of the skill/education spectrum: of those aged 25 or more, 8.7 per cent of the US-born had four years or more college education, but the figure was 9.7 per cent for immigrants (and 17.6 per cent for immigrants from Asia); 2.9 per cent of the US-born had less than five years elementary education, but the figure was 12.8 per cent for immigrants (and 7.4 per cent for immigrants from Asia) (US Bureau of the Census, 1984)

Occupations

Labour demand in the destination countries continually sorts workers into different roles, and in some cases this involves using – and sometimes exploiting – national, ethnic, religious, gender and social differences to organize work. On the other hand, some migrants 'capture' specialized niches in the labour market, building up patterns of skill and experience which fortify their dominance. Such patterns sometimes create stereotypes – a striking historical example being the association of Italians with ice-cream making. In the late nineteenth century, people from two districts in the Italian Dolomite mountains came to specialize in ice-cream making and retailing, organ-grinding and chestnut-roasting in Western Europe. In the case of ice-cream making, this connection has persisted to the present (Bovenkerk and Ruland, 1992). To take a different example, the Sus valley in the Anti-Atlas mountains of southern Morocco has, since before the First World War, supplied a large number of the grocers in the north of the country. Grocers from Sus are now important in France as well. The valley is very poor; amid the im- poverished hovels of those who live there permanently, the palatial villas of the absent grocers stand as monuments to the value of migration.

The labour market continually leads to the identification of particu- lar jobs with specific minorities. In France, Malians tend to work in the car industry, Senegalese in cleaning (in Rome, Senegalese migrants are often street traders). People from South Asia (Pakistanis, Indians, Bangladeshis) are assuming a dominant position in the running of New York's taxis: whereas only 10 per cent of new applicants to drive cabs in 1984 were born in the subcontinent, the figure is now between 40 and 45 per cent (20 per cent Pakistani, and 10 per cent each Indian and Bangladeshi); one-third of the 12,000 yellow cabs and 30,000 'for hire' vehicles are owned by people from the subcontinent (in total, South Asians constitute under 0.5 per cent of New York's population).

For employers, utilizing people of one origin has advantages. Foremen can be appointed from the same community and can communicate with workers in their own language. Social events can be organized that fit the culture of the workforce (for example, Friday prayers for Muslims) without offending people with different customs. Furthermore, where different shops are manned by different ethnic groups, the chance of unified action during industrial disputes is reduced – although indi- vidual departments may be particularly stubborn in their resistance since long-established social loyalties come to underpin worker solidarity.

More visible than occupational specialization by ethnicity in the rapid cosmopolitanization of the cities of Europe and North America is the creation of ethnically identified localities. Particularly in the United States, with its old traditions of ethnically differentiated neighbourhoods, the residential changes are striking. The Jewish population of New York's Brooklyn is declining, being replaced by a multiplicity of other groups. The Bronx has acquired 3000 Cambodians, served by Korean grocers and Indian newsagents (replacing Jewish delicatessens).

Residential ethnic clustering in declining areas has created new markets for foreign foods, grocery stores, restaurants, opportunities for foreign banks and specialized travel agencies. Los Angeles has become a mosaic of Mexican towns, Korean towns, Salvadorean towns, a Japanese high-rise financial quarter, and even an Iranian village (Westfield). Clustering provides a physical frame for protection, a defence against intrusions and an area of confidence which allows the transition from immigrant to native without exposure to the harassment some-times suffered by foreigners. It also provides the opportunity to establish cultural facilities (churches, mosques, Hindu temples, libraries, reading rooms), and for self-employment. About a quarter of Korean immigrants in the United States are self-employed – in Los Angeles the figure for Korean men is as high as 40 per cent – as are 16 per cent of Chinese, 11 per cent of Indians and 10 per cent of Japanese.

In sum, far from producing a dull homogenization of cultures, the international circulation of people re-creates a cultural kaleidoscope, involving occupational roles and residential areas. It speeds up the processes of social fission and fusion, of innovation, which are the essence of dynamic cultures. After the long period in which governments have tried to impose cultural uniformity on their populations, international migration now stimulates both cultural diversity and enrichment.

Politics

Immigrants are often fashioned by the wider society into socially close-knit groups with a high degree of internal self-dependence. Associations are set up to create a community, particularly for those who are restricted by a lack of competence in the local language; they may provide play groups for children, places for mothers or old people to meet and talk. Others form sports, social and cultural clubs (including cinemas or video shops supplying films from the home country). There may be savings and credit associations, sometimes linked to local branches of banks from the home country. Almost everywhere the more devoted form religious associations to establish places of worship, bring in priests hired to officiate, hold commemorative ceremonies for the great festivals of the year.

Often, the associations are unseen in the wider society, until a challenge occurs which appears to threaten the position of the immigrant group. Then the association may produce a lobby to press local councillors, MPs or government officers. In the football World Cup, held in the United States, many Americans were astonished at the sudden appearance of a vast array of immigrant organizations, mobilized to support their home teams in the contest.

Some immigrants with a command of the local language come to act as brokers to the rest of society. Immigrant associations provide a training ground for political participation in the wider community, for those wishing to become local councillors or MPs, or to participate in community-relations organizations. Immigrant voters in a few constituencies can also exercise leverage in tipping the balance of the vote. In some political systems, national origin may provide a crucial basis for an established politician to create a coalition of voting blocs. New York provides examples of this. In turn, established politicians are obliged to relate to the interests of the group and to elements of what passes for its culture – the mayor of New York, Irish or not, must join the St Patrick's Day parade, and in some British cities, politicians with a significant number of Hindu constituents will expect to celebrate Diwali. Immigrants reshape not only the dominant politics but also the culture.

However, immigration also creates transnational politics – with Turkish political parties operating in Germany and Pakistani parties in Britain, much as Spanish and Italian political movements were active in Latin America at the turn of the century. Mexican presidents now campaign in the United States among Mexicans settled there. Groups become active in raising money or participating in 'home' struggles – as Sikhs in Britain and Canada played a role in the campaign to create an independent Sikh homeland, Khalistan, in India; or as American Irish raised money for arms to help the Irish Republican struggle in Northern Ireland. The Armenian diaspora kept Armenian nationalism alive for many long years in the exile communities of Syria and California.

Indeed, successive waves of exiles from oppressive regimes build 'reserve armies' abroad for the day when liberation comes. The disintegration of the old order in eastern Europe allowed many émigrés to return to an active role in home politics. Thus a Canadian businessman campaigned to be prime minister of Poland, and a former Peruvian businessman briefly became president of what was left of Yugoslavia. A foreign minister of Armenia hails from Fresno in California, and an energy minister from elsewhere in the United States.

Cosmopolitanization makes politics more complicated, with elaborate new bonds and loyalties cutting across the old exclusivities. Dual or multiple nationalities accurately reflect these differing allegiances.

The Homelands

The impact of emigration on the places from which the migrants originate is complex; it differs relative to the area, the type of worker, and the continuing relationships between source and destination. One of the more obvious and well-documented effects is the flow of payments from worker to his or her relatives left at home – 'remittances'. Indeed, the economic importance of these flows to governments has prompted much more research on this topic than on most others concerning migration.

Nevertheless, this is still a poorly understood subject because of the difficulties in identifying the scale, frequency and form of the flows. There is a large degree of concealment to escape taxation and un-favourable exchange rates, and this sustains a large parallel black market. Often, in any case, banking facilities are poorly developed, and migrants are not familiar with the procedures and distrust bank officials. Sometimes bank charges are high. For example, Indonesian banks in the mid-1980s were said to charge US$15 per transaction, whatever the sum concerned. On an annual basis such deductions could reduce by up to 10 per cent the savings of an Indonesian domestic working in Saudi Arabia. Difficulties such as these led the Philippines National Census and Statistical Office at one stage to add 50 per cent to their calculation of the contribution of overseas workers to the gross national product to accommodate a guess at the scale of clandestine payments. A 1979 study of Sudanese abroad estimated that only a quarter of emigrants used the banking system to transfer funds home (Galaleldin, 1979); another suggested that the official share of funds transferred was no more than 11 per cent of the total remitted in 1980 (Choucri, cited in Russell, 1992: 268). In Pakistan, the 'hundi' system eliminated flows: workers paid an agent wherever they were abroad, and another agent within Pakistan advanced rupees to the final recipient. Some countries do not record the arrival of cash remittances below a certain level (for example, in India in 1980 sums of Rs 10,000 or less were not checked).

Workers often avoid the problems of transfer by saving in the coun-try where they work and then carrying back the total in a lump sum when they return. Others invest their savings in durable consumer goods and either send or carry these. Estimates of the proportion of remit-tances transferred in kind range from between 9 and 17 per cent for Pakistan, 8 and 10 per cent for Yemen, 24 per cent for Caribbean workers cutting cane in Florida, to 60 per cent for Egypt between 1979 and 1983 (Shahid, 1979; other citations by Arnold, in Kritz et al., 1992: 205).

Whatever the exact size of flows, the scale is not in doubt. A World Bank estimate suggests the global scale of flows increased from $24 billion in 1978 to 66 billion in 1989 (Russell and Teitelbaum, 1992). On a different basis, UNDP estimates that some $25 billion accrues to developing countries; and the IMF, extrapolating from a sample of

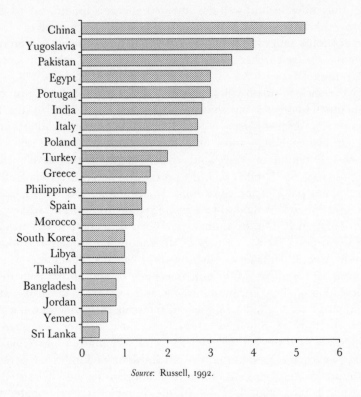

Source: Russell, 1992.

Figure 5.2 Top twenty remittance receivers, 1988 (US$ billion)

38 labour-exporting countries, put the total remittance flow at $33.8 billion in 1990 (a fivefold increase in real terms since 1969) (Elbadawi and de Rezende Rocha, 1992). In contrast to the figures for 1988 in Figure 5.2, UNDP estimates that Egypt received $4 billion, India and Pakistan $3 billion each. Thus the estimates leave a wide margin of possible error.

On average, according to one set of estimates, a worker remits some $700 per year, and possibly $1000 if unofficial flows are included. The range of estimates here is very wide – for Asia, unofficial flows are variously said to be between 10 and 60 per cent of total flows. In the narrower sense – the share of imports covered by remittances – the figures again vary widely between countries and years; in 1989, the figure was put at 43 per cent for Yugoslavia, 57 per cent for Egypt, between one-fifth and one-quarter for Pakistan (where it was 70 per

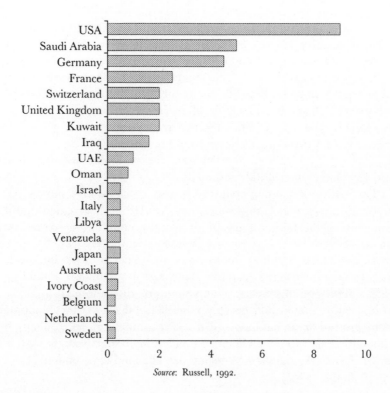

Source: Russell, 1992.

Figure 5.3 Top twenty remittance sources, 1988 (US$ billion)

cent in the early 1980s) and Jordan, and 27 per cent for Morocco, Bangladesh, Turkey and Portugal. In the extreme case of the Yemen Arab Republic in the late 1970s (when over one-fifth of the labour force worked abroad, much of it in neighbouring Saudi Arabia) remittances were 19,000 times larger than export earnings, and equal to 139 per cent of the value of imports.

There are few useful official figures for Mexico, but in the late 1970s it was estimated that illegal Mexican immigrants to the United States remitted or carried back over $2 billion annually (or four times the earnings of the Mexican tourist industry), and this affected directly about 21 per cent of the population of the country (Cornelius, 1979). A different study, based upon the flow of cheques and money orders in the mid-1980s, put the flow at between $1.5 and 2.5 billion; in the main, the funds went directly to the better-off families in poor areas in the central regions of the country (where over half the males in the age group 20–40 claimed to work regularly in the United States). Even a small country like El Salvador is said to have received in 1989 between half and one billion dollars (*Los Angeles Times*, 7 May 1989).

The size of flow does not indicate the scale of impact on the country receiving remittances. Expenditure of the sums employs many others in the making of goods and supply of services. An Egyptian study (cited in UNDP, 1992: 58–9) estimates this multiplier at 2.2 – that is, re-mittances of Egyptian £1 million would increase Egypt's gross national product by £2.2 million. For Pakistan, the multiplier was put at 2.4, and for Greece at 1.8 (Glytsos, 1990).

The loss to developing countries due to immigration controls in the destination countries is thus substantial. UNDP has calculated that if 2 per cent of the labour force of developing countries emigrated and earned poverty levels of pay in developed countries (say, $5000 per year), their total earnings would be of the order of $220 billion, and they could be expected to remit some $40 to 50 billion annually (or $200 billion over five years). The volume of direct foreign investment to equal this sum would be very large: $21 billion for the Philippines (compared to an actual inflow of direct investment of $0.9 billion); $19 billion for Pakistan ($0.2 billion); $3 billion for Bangladesh ($0.003) and for Sri Lanka ($0.02); and $8 billion for Thailand ($3.1 billion) (UNDP, 1992: 58–9).

Remittances fluctuated considerably over the years, particularly those derived from the Middle Eastern boom in oil production. Thus Tur-key's official remittances, $1.4 billion in 1974, fell by 60 per cent in real terms up to 1977, and the resulting balance of payments problem was a key element in the Turkish devaluation of 1979.

Many governments were taken by surprise at the growth in remit-tances – thus India's Middle East earnings rose from Rs1.3 billion in 1975–76 to Rs17.1 billion in 1984–85 without much serious considera-tion by the authorities. By the time governments began to establish schemes to capture an enlarged share of the new incomes, they were frequently caught by an equally unanticipated downturn. Thus, the Pakistan government, on the experience of the Fifth Plan period, prepared in its Sixth Plan (1983–88) a net increase of emigration to over half a million workers, and a growth in remittances of 10 per cent per year. In fact, remittances declined by 30 per cent. India experi-enced a halving of remittance flows between 1982 and 1986, and Thai-land a decline of 40 per cent. The Philippines, with significantly higher levels of education than its nearest rivals, was able to keep up the remittance flow.

In their fluctuations, remittance flows are no different from the earnings in other sectors. Unanticipated political crises periodically afflict all sectors. The 1991 Gulf War, for example, was an example of an unexpected intervention in the economic programming of ministries of finance. The Egyptian government claimed the country had lost $2 billion in remittances and $13 billion in the cumulative savings of its citizens. The Gulf War was one element that precipitated India into a balance-of-payments crisis which forced a programme of radical reform. Even recruitment in the Philippines reflected these events – hirings, running at 38,000 per month in June 1990, fell to 29,000 in February of the following year, before bouncing back up to 47,000 in June 1991.

If external events, economic or political, induce major oscillations in revenue, domestic policy for long operated to reduce national benefits from remittances. Policies of economic nationalism led to undervalued exchange rates (cheapening imports was more important than encouraging exports) and import controls, both of which militated against migrants returning funds or goods through official channels. Few governments could resist indefinitely the temptation to change policy to expand remittances, particularly when officials so often deplored the fact that migrant workers 'squandered' their earnings on private consumption rather than patriotic investment.

Fortunately, governments lack effective power to force emigrants to return their incomes if they choose not to do so. Not that they do not try – through bilateral agreements with other governments; but governments in receiving countries have little incentive to implement such measures, and the movement of earnings takes place so rapidly that remittances go underground wherever regulations become onerous. Governments are obliged to create incentives to persuade their citizens to conform without this jeopardizing the overall framework of economic regulation (for an overview of government measures in Asia, see Athukorala, 1993).

The incentives are usually designed to offset the negative effects of current arrangements for transfers or to enhance the returns. The 1974 Bangladesh Wage Earners Scheme offered a special rate of interest on remittance deposits; Pakistan's Bonus Voucher Scheme and Foreign Exchange Bearer Certificates (1985) offered for sale bonds with a high rate of return (which increased the longer the bonds were not cashed) which could be sold for foreign exchange. Governments set up a variety of funds (as in Turkey, to finance agriculture and allow the import of agricultural machinery), special banks, special housing schemes, apartments and even new towns to attract foreign earnings. The government of India created a separate regime for Indians living abroad, the Non

Resident Indian scheme, to attract foreign investment, allowing beneficiaries (of Indian descent, whether of Indian nationality or not) to
open high-interest tax-free foreign-currency accounts. The measures
perhaps help the substantial inflow of funds, especially from business
and professional migrants and their descendants in North America and
Europe (in 1985–86, the inflow was equal to 96 per cent of India's net
receipts of foreign aid).

Other governments exercise considerable ingenuity in trying to
appropriate or guide remittances to approved purposes. Thus, the
Turkish government opened a scheme in 1980 so that Turkish workers
abroad who were liable for military service could buy themselves out by
paying 440,000 lira (then £2840) in hard currency, which, the government said, would be used to purchase arms. Since the government
determined the issue of obligatory military service as well as the means
to annul the obligation, it was in the excellent monopoly position of
controlling this pure rent-seeking activity. We have noted in the last
chapter the schemes operating for migrant workers from Korea, China
and the Philippines to oblige the repatriation of a set share of earnings.

The adjustments required to sustain the flow of remittances drive a
wedge between the migrant worker, subject to a liberalized order, and
the networks of state controls. It has become increasingly difficult, both
economically and politically, to sustain this contradictory regime. It has
also become clear that the key factors determining what proportion of
remittance flows returned officially are not special incentives but stable
liberal economic regimes, free of the threat of devaluation. It would
have been absurd for Filipino workers to employ official channels for
remittances between 1976 and 1986 when there was a cumulative and
unanticipated devaluation of the currency by 176 per cent, an average
rate of inflation of 18 per cent per year, and a 3.9 per cent average real
rate of interest. Growing black markets, which in turn undermined the
official economy, were the result of failing to establish a stable regime.
Thus, the short-term need to sustain or expand remittances became yet
another force pushing virtually all governments to liberalize exchange
rates (and move to convertibility), trade policy and interest rates.

The New Rich

Remittances are large relative to local incomes in the home countries.
In the late 1970s, various studies estimated the annual remittance payment by workers of different nationalities (comparing these to local per-
capita incomes, a poor guide to incomes received by the majority in the

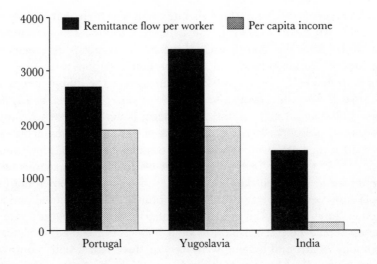

Figure 5.4 Annual remittance flows per worker, with local per-capita income, 1978/80 (US$)

country) (see Figure 5.4). A sample survey in the early 1970s of villages sending illegal migrants to the United States from the state of Jalisco in Mexico estimated that the average worker remitted some US$170 per month (or $2040 on an annual basis), sums that were the sole source of income for 70 per cent of migrant families (Cornelius, 1979: 78–9). Migrants in France in the 1960s remitted just over one-fifth of their incomes according to a government survey (Butaud, 1971).

However, averages are misleading. A Sri Lanka study demonstrates that the absolute size of remittances increases with the skill level of the migrants but declines as a proportion of his or her income. The average skilled Sri Lankan emigrant returns six times more than an unskilled emigrant does. The proportion of income remitted, according to occupational status, in Sri Lanka in 1983 was as follows. Those in the professional/managerial sector remitted 44 per cent of their average monthly earnings; technical/clerical grades, 38 per cent; skilled workers, 56 per cent; unskilled workers, 69 per cent; female domestics, 92 per cent (calculated from Korale, 1985). Higher skilled individuals may be accompanied by their families, so part of the change may be only a transfer of family costs from the home to the working country. On the other hand, domestics may live in and be entitled to full board, so their local living costs are peculiarly low.

The returns to labour through migration are high, but so are the costs. For Mexicans moving to the United States, the cost of reaching the border from the interior was some $200 in the 1970s, not including the loss of working days; and three or four attempts were often required to make the border crossing. In the case of the Philippines in the mid-1980s, when the rural minimum wage was equal to US$2.17 per day (1988), one estimate of the cost of legal emigration reached $1000: $100 for a passport, $150 for processing the required documents, $15 each for a medical examination and a training/briefing session, and a $600 'placement' fee (including the cost of air fares and agency fees). For someone living outside the capital, processing and expediting the application could involve several trips to Manila, costing in total perhaps another $200. To pay off a loan of that size, disregarding any rate of interest, could take seven months of a Singapore maid's full earnings (assuming board and lodging were free) or three and a half months in Hong Kong. If the rate of interest were high, then the debt might accumulate faster than it could be paid – a classic form of debt bondage.

In general, agents impose high charges on the migrant. In the late 1980s in Bangladesh, the cost of obtaining an overseas job as a proportion of expected earnings is said to have reached, in some cases, 40 per cent of the income of a skilled, and 50 per cent of an unskilled, worker (cited by Abella, in Kritz et al., 1992: 273). The ILO (1988) compiled a different set of estimates of the cost of getting a job: US$1–2000 in Bangladesh (1986); $800 in India (1985); $917 in Pakistan (1983); $400 for the Philippines (1987); $100–320 in Sri Lanka (1986); $900–1200 in Thailand (1986). However, we do not know how many migrants escaped from their brokers and did not return the credit and loans advanced, thereby making the risk premium very high.

The earlier migrants seem to do best. The first Thai workers who went to the Middle East made – by the standards of their home villages – their fortune. But as more workers became involved and agents competed to lower the price, the incentives declined over time – to the point where agents complained that they were unable to recruit enough workers. This led to a high rate of turnover: a quarter of Southeast Asian workers return after one year, and only one in five stays four years or more.

Workers' fears about migration are thus justified. The costs and the risks are high. As Martin (1991) notes of Turkish workers, 'even with wage differences of five or ten to one, most workers are reluctant to migrate abroad for employment if they have a secure job and a future at home.' On the other hand, the success rate is high, and many people have built periods of emigration into old ways of life and culture – as in the villages of Southern Ireland; of Al-Kuna, a subdistrict of north-western Jordan; of the Ilocos in the Philippines or northeastern Thailand. Indeed, Basson (1984) observes that in parts of Jordan 'emigration is a preferred state, hoped for, planned for and well integrated into family life'.

This pattern – away from home for work for a period of years abroad (often to save for marriage or a house) and then returning – is like customary patterns of seasonal migration, and rather different from the sudden competitive scramble associated with accelerated development in a foreign country (which is more akin to the old gold rush, varieties of Klondyke), especially where the migrants are drawn from only a few localities, age groups (usually 20–40), skills and sex.

The Caribbean countries, with a combined population of 30 million in 1980, lost 6 million to emigration between 1945 and 1980; between 1961 and 1970 nearly half a million left for the United States (or more than the total migration there in the 110 years before 1950), and others went to Britain, Canada, France and the Netherlands. New categories of workers were created with great speed – as with maids moving to Canada, a flow that increased rapidly after 1968, reaching between 10,000 and 25,000 annually up to 1987 (Simmons and Guengant, in Kritz et al., 1992: 94). In some cases, the movement represented absolute depopulation: official emigration as a proportion of the local population (and excluding those who subsequently returned) reached nearly 40 per cent for the Virgin Islands (1966–75), 14 per cent for Montserrat, and nearly a quarter for Surinam (1966–75). To some extent, the movement reflected the economic incorporation in the United States labour market of the independent territories on its periphery – Puerto Rico, politically within the USA, had by 1970 lost a quarter of its population to the States.

However, the impression is misleading simply because these very small countries are not comparable to larger ones. There we would have to compare localities. Thus, in Portugal, in the Trasos-Montes region (with a population in 1979 of 125,000), the six main municipalities near the provincial capital of Buganza lost 82,000 people between 1961 and 1970. The department of Drama in Macedonian Greece in the 1960s had between one-fifth and one-quarter of the population of Greece and produced nearly 40 per cent of Greek emigration; in eleven of the 69 communes at that time, over 80 per cent of males between the ages of 15 and 44 left; in another ten, 60 to 80 per cent; and in fifteen communes, half the women aged 15 to 44 (Kayser, 1971).

The migrants are concentrated in the most active age groups, so they have the greatest economic effect on the labour force. Indeed, immigration lowers the average age level of the developed countries. For the United States in 1980, 16 per cent of the native-born population were aged 25 to 35, but the figure was 26 per cent for immigrants (and 31 per cent for Asian immigrants). At the other end, emigration strips the labour force of its most active workers and women in the reproductive age groups. Where the demand is concentrated on domestics (as in Sri Lanka, the Philippines, Indonesia, Bangladesh and Colombia), the effects can be exaggerated. Some 40 per cent of Sri Lankan worker emigrants are women, two-thirds of them married, with over 60 per cent of those married having two or more children, and 22 per cent with children under the age of five.

The demographic effect is less significant than the economic. Emigration is concentrated in the more skilled and educated groups of the population. In the first wave of migration to the Middle Eastern countries, the effects on the construction industry were most clear. Thus Pakistan in 1978–79, out of eight key skilled cadres, lost to emigration 23 per cent of its masons, 26 per cent of its carpenters, 32 per cent of its electricians, 53 per cent of its plumbers and pipe fitters, 33 per cent of its painters, 50 per cent of its machine operators, 20 per cent of its mechanics, and 38 per cent of its engineers (calculated from the base figures in Gilani et al., 1981: 38).

For the professions, the 'brain drain' assumes even greater significance. In the 1970s, the United Nations estimated that 60 per cent of Pakistan's new doctors left; 25 per cent of India's new engineers; 35 per cent of Sri Lanka's accountants. By the end of the decade, Sudan had lost, mainly to the Middle East, 17 per cent of its doctors and dentists, 20 per cent of its university teachers, 30 per cent of its engineers, and 45 per cent of its surveyors. By the end of the 1980s, Ghana had lost 60 per cent of the doctors trained in that decade. Between 1985 and 1990, it is estimated that sub-Saharan Africa lost 60,000 middle- and higher-level managers (UNDP, 1992: 57). The losses were greatest for those who studied abroad – and therefore gained an internationally tradable qualification with the time, experience and opportunity to search out work abroad. It was a massive vote of no confidence in the prevailing regimes.

The losses are partly due to the overproduction of skills, brought about by governments concentrating on sectors of education that are the means of upward mobility for the middle classes rather than of mass significance. But another reason for the flight is that the highly skilled are, by world standards, so badly paid and supported (in terms of facilities). Overproduction is reflected in the continuing problem of educated unemployment. Somalia was estimated at one stage to be producing five times the number of graduates needed to fill existing jobs. In Côte d'Ivoire in the 1970s, up to half the graduates were said to be unemployed at any one time. However, some governments endeavoured to make up the losses from emigration by increasing output, particularly when it was realized that the export of the skilled could relieve bottlenecks in the supply of foreign exchange. In the 1970s, the Egyptian government planned to expand the output of teachers in order to supply 14,000 of them to the oil-producing countries.

With English as a national language, the Philippines had a considerable comparative advantage in supplying world markets. The Philippine Medical Association estimates that half the medical graduates of the 1950s were working overseas by the mid-1970s. The country also – following the US model – produces a very large number of college graduates – 100,000 annually in the 1970s. The result has been increasingly to convert the country into a world labour supplier. Occasionally, there were attempts to reverse this process by restricting emigration. In the early 1980s, the government complained that emigration was so reducing the quality of the local labour force that it was discouraging foreign investment. Efforts were thus made to reduce the outward movement. But by then emigration for work had become so entrenched that restrictions merely led to an increase in the black market in labour.

Following the theory of international trade, one would expect an open labour market to ensure that each country provided a specialized supply of labour; thus, while remaining competitive with each other, they would also be increasingly complementary. The world labour market is still far from open, but nonetheless, as we have seen, some specializations have emerged in developing countries at opposite ends of the skill spectrum – for example, doctors at one end, domestics at the other. There is some suggestion that, for example, the engineering profession is becoming more strongly associated with developing countries. Between 1960 and 1990, North America took in over 1 million professional and technical staff from developing countries; a United States Congressional Research Service estimate (UNDP, 1992: 57) suggests this represented a transfer from developing to developed countries of $20,000 per head, or a cumulative total of $64 million (at 1971/2 prices). However, these figures are misleading since simultaneously the output of US engineering schools (as well as their academic staffing) was being drawn from immigrants. In 1985, fully half the assistant professors under the age of 35 in US engineering institutions were foreign-born. It seems more likely that this is the result of the native-born deserting engineering than of cheaper foreign-born engineers displacing Americans.

The loss of skills is, at least in the short term, a problem for developing countries, although, given the oversupply of skills, the departures may provide opportunities for others. The employment of foreign or local consultants, expensive by the hour or day but cheaper than full-time permanent employment, provides some relief. It allows the consultant to escape from the low salaries for full-time permanent work by taking several short-term temporary jobs. Standards may be lowered also, or work redistributed between more and less skilled workers (for example, between doctors and nurses), particularly where on-the-job experience may lead to a competence equal to that learned through formal education.

For construction and other manual workers, the short-term effect of increased emigration has usually been a rapid increase in wage rates. In Sri Lanka between 1979 and 1981, the combined effect of a local building boom and losses of building workers through emigration pushed up daily wages by 65–70 per cent (the average price index rose at the same time by 49 per cent). Between 1969–70 and 1977–78, in Karachi, daily wage rates for carpenters increased 252 per cent (in current prices), 238 per cent for masons and 359 per cent for unskilled workers (Gilani et al., 1981: 43); there does not seem to have been much of a local building boom. In the market for drivers there was a comparable occurrence: in 1978, when 6000 Korean drivers were recruited for work in the Middle East, the wages of chauffeurs rose by over 45 per cent; Pusan bus drivers received a major pay increase above this level to dissuade them from migrating (it did not work, and the government was obliged to introduce a temporary ban on the recruitment of drivers for the Middle East). However, the effects were usually temporary, wage rates settling back after a time closer to the original level (although this depended also on whether emigration continued, on local market conditions, and on how the local supply of trained workers responded).

For construction workers, a powerful secondary effect of increased emigration is the building boom which follows increased remittances. Workers abroad or with foreign earnings spend on new homes, improving old homes, constructing farm buildings, small businesses or garages. In Bangladesh, in the main emigration districts (Chittagong and Sylhet), construction and service wages have both been pushed up by remittance spending. In Greece in 1965, 40 per cent of new buildings in Salonica were financed by remittances from Germany, and up to 80 per cent for the medium-sized towns of northern Greece (Kayser, 1971). Earnings from work abroad make it possible for families to continue to live in rural areas rather than migrating to the cities – that is, migration makes possible the survival of the villages and small towns.

Where a major part of the labour force has emigrated, rural areas become quasi-'dormitory suburbs', but with the city located in another country. The locality is a place where children grow up and adults spend periodic holidays, and to which the old people retire after an active lifetime working abroad. It is an ancient phenomenon connected with domestic migration, noted down the ages for those who went off to work in the city. In the mind of the migrant worker, the home village can hardly fail to become the place of humanity, far away from the inhumanity of work among foreigners – a place of home, of land and of the great transition points of life: birth, death and marriage. For the second generation, the loss of the romantic dream of a golden age may become a form of alienation from the present: a dream of the real that is only possible because it is far away and never tested by experience.

However, before we sentimentalize the contrasts, it may also be in some cases – as it was in colonial Africa – that, because pay to the emigrant is so low, the responsibility for the reproduction of the labour force falls exclusively on mothers left behind in the village and cultivating the soil while they raise families. In Africa under empire, the men were obliged to work far away solely for the purpose of paying colonial taxes (thus the costs of reproduction were donated freely by the family to distant future employers).

Today, more commonly, many emigrant families are relatively well off. In Bangladesh, emigrants earn abroad four to five times what they received before leaving (and they are in any case drawn from the better-off families). Indeed, families are promoted into the upper 10 per cent of income receivers (Mahmud, in Amjad, 1989: 78). Even for the un-skilled, family income is on average increased three times over relative to comparable national pay averages. For many Pakistani families – as for Mexicans, as we saw earlier – remittances play a key role in sustaining incomes; in the 1970s, for example, remittances increased the average household incomes of migrant workers by nearly 31 per cent (Burki, 1984; see also Oberai and Singh, 1980).

The resulting increases in visible prosperity are apparent in Kerala villages in the great boom in house rebuilding, in cars and motor cycles on the street, in new bank offices, shops, restaurants, theatres, medical practices and in the ownership of consumer durables (Mathew and Nair, 1978; Prakash, 1978; Nalapat and Radhakrishnan, 1978; Gulati 1987). Canadian earnings, it is said, have lifted Dayalpur in the Indian Punjab, now reputedly – allowing for journalistic licence – 'floating in foreign money' (Dasgupta, *Daily Telegraph*, Calcutta, 7 March 1993), with new trucks, jeeps and tractors, and a social life heavily sustained by inter-national telephone lines. At Ban Pak Tob, a cluster of villages in the

Thai northeast (just east of the provincial town of Udon Thani), the same wave of prosperity is visible: electricity arrived in 1983, and by 1985 most families possessed or were about to possess colour television sets, along with the same proliferation of pick-up trucks and motor cycles; the temples were being rebuilt; and the villages were increasingly preoccupied with a full education for their children. The typical Turkish returnee from Germany, who had left as a 25-year-old farmer to work on an assembly line or in construction, arrived back, according to Martin (1991), with savings of US$10,000 and retired at 50 to live off the returns on his investment.

It is not at all true – as so many critics maintain – that spending remittances does not stimulate the economy. Those with land improve it with irrigation and enhance productivity with new equipment and improved inputs. Emigrants build apartments as well as endowing temples and mosques. Almost universally they are persuaded of the value of education for their children and insist on upgrading local schools and improving local infrastructure. Kayser (1971) records that in Portugal 73 per cent of emigrants in the 1960s purchased or improved houses, 67 per cent increased their savings, 53 per cent purchased clothes, 52 per cent improved their food consumption, 39 per cent upgraded the quality of the education of their children, and 28 per cent purchased land. As Philippine labour minister Ople once observed, 'Overseas employment has built more houses, sent more children of the poor to college, and established more small business enterprises than all the other programmes of the government put together' (*Far Eastern Economic Review*, 17 October 1985: 51).

Many returnees experience higher than normal periods of unemployment in the short term, when they often refuse to do the same work they did abroad at much lower pay or return to the work they did before leaving. But, in the medium term, many employ their savings to start small businesses – as craftsmen, shopkeepers, taxi drivers, haulage contractors, managers of tourist hotels, small farmers, caterers. Many hire labour and increase the productivity of local operations through the experience of foreign work practices that they acquired abroad (Arnold, in Kritz et al., 1992). In some cases, they start factories; Piore (1979: 123) suggests that an entire garment industry in the towns of Mexico's Jalisco State has been fashioned out of remittances. Furthermore, the existence of communities of compatriots abroad provides well-developed markets for local produce, foodstuffs and clothing, connected by existing and former emigrants.

However, there can be reverse effects – most significantly, a relative decline in agriculture. A study of five countries in southern Africa

(Lucas, 1987) suggests this as an important short-term effect. But, in the medium term, remittances tend to increase investment in farming, improve crop productivity and, in southern Africa, expand the all-important accumulation of cattle. In former North Yemen, massive emigration led to the expansion of uncultivated acreage, a relative decline in infrastructure, and an increase in the employment of women and children. Cultivators abandoned their land in order to emigrate, and changed the cropping pattern from coffee (for export) to *qat* (a locally consumed narcotic). In the 1970s, ten-year-olds could earn the equivalent of US$200 per month as drivers and labourers. But again, these effects were short term; in the longer term there was increased investment in agriculture from remittances, particularly through the employment of workers brought into the country from elsewhere, and from mechanization.

The Yemeni phenomenon – the import of labour to make up for the losses of emigration – completes the circle, turning peasant farmers (in this case) into absentee owners. In many developing countries, as we have seen – for example, Jordan, Oman, Yemen, Greece – immigrants perform exactly the same role as in developed countries, supplying the bottom strata of the labour market so that the natives can be upgraded, but in this case through emigration.

The new wealth has an impact upon the social structure, disturbing (or reinforcing other factors which do so) ancient inherited privileges and status. The old village ruling class – of landlord, moneylender and merchant – finds new rivals, with an economic basis beyond local challenge.

Migrants are inevitably exposed to consumption patterns, styles of living and levels of efficiency which influence their behaviour when they return. In one sense, migration can be viewed as the training of a cadre which, on returning home, is capable of transforming economic back-wardness – or at least strengthening the processes moving in that direction. We have noted the way in which immigrants come to see the importance of the education of children, perhaps in the hope that through these means they will not have to emigrate to work. Women learn of new styles of behaviour, standards of health and family planning, all of which help the processes of change. Of course, there are many other factors here. Martin (1991) notes that in Turkey local life was changing rapidly in any case: television sets spread along the new highways, telephones, newspapers – all bringing new perspectives on social life. Furthermore, observers have noted the irony of educated women from the Philippines working as maids abroad in order to put their children through college – so that they in turn can work as maids abroad.

Social tensions go beyond the clash between old wealth and new. The new may excite envy and hostility. In Manila, there is a term that combines hostility and envy for goods purchased from Saudi earnings – 'Katas ng Saudi'. Others have suggested negative psychological strains arising from the long-term separation of families – Filipino marriages involving an emigrant are said to be more vulnerable to break-up; children grow up without mothers most of the time; and in other cases, absent fathers are replaced by interlopers. However, despite much imaginative – and plausible – reconstruction of these ills (and undoubtedly some must exist), the evidence does not go beyond the anecdotal, and may reflect resentment rather than reality. Long-term loneliness is surely a problem – although the same phenomenon occurs equally painfully with domestic migration, without drawing the same anguished attention. In Pakistan, doctors speak of a 'Dubai syndrome' afflicting wives left behind: the symptoms are said to include delayed menstruation, menstrual pains, periodic fits of crying (a diagnosis clearly fitting women only, and a particular medical version of women's health). In Thailand, the 'Saudi ladies' (Khun-nai-Saudi) are famous for wealth and idleness, and – as is typical in such situations – have earned a reputation for illicit sexual activity, even if the accusations are groundless.

However, for at least some of those who emigrate, psychic ruptures may be more severe than for those left behind. The loss of home, of a 'native place', may be damaging, and the scale of return migration may reflect this loss. Yet this is not a universal occurrence. Others – perhaps a majority – clearly rejoice to escape from the inherited prejudices, narrow-minded localism, bigotry and rigid moral constraints which so often characterize their 'native places'. Travel can then mean liberation – even if the emancipation is circumscribed by the toil of factory work and the grey tenements after work. There is an additional bonus if the traveller can return as a rich visitor, dispensing largesse and displaying the superiorities of a different way of life. On balance, migration is more liberating than damaging.

6

The Reproduction of the Labour Force

Introduction

International migration is in general excluded from generalizations about the economic value of liberalization and open markets – 'the most compelling exception to liberalism in the operation of the world economy', as Jagdish Bhagwati (1978) puts it. The freeing of trade and of capital movements is seen as leading to the most efficient utilization of the world's factors of production, an unequivocal good – in economists' jargon, approaching 'Pareto optimality' (that is, some are better off and none are worse off).

The same inconsistency is characteristic of those political leaders who have made their names as champions of general economic liberalization. Both Mrs Thatcher in Britain and President Reagan in the United States supposedly supported strongly the freeing of markets; yet the freeing of the labour market was to occur only within national boundaries. Indeed, in Mrs Thatcher's case, she presided over a regime which intensified controls on the movement of labour from abroad, and took special measures to curb the freest part of the labour market, the movement of illegal workers.

The world's powers have made major efforts to liberalize trade through the successive rounds of negotiation of GATT (the General Agreement on Tariffs and Trade), latterly in the most ambitious set of decontrols of all, in the Uruguay round. Yet there has been no proposal to negotiate multilaterally the easing of curbs on migration. On the contrary, the control of labour remains jealously guarded as an area of state egotism, with a growing proliferation of restrictions, visa requirements, police controls; the movement of workers remains as heavily regulated as trade and capital were in the supposed bad old days of high protection.

The theoretical justification for this inconsistency is rarely explained.

Henry C. Simons (1948), a founder of the Chicago School of economics (an important strand of opinion in the neoclassical tradition) attacks the need for consistency, but without providing an alternative argument:

> To insist that a free trade programme is logically or practically incomplete without free migration is either disingenuous or stupid. Free trade may or should raise living standards everywhere.... Free immigration would level standards perhaps without raising them anywhere ... not to mention the social and political problems of assimilation.... As regards ... our import of populations, our plans and promises must be disciplined by tough-minded realism and practical sense. (p. 10)

Three decades later, another member of the same school, accepting that migration controls did indeed reduce the world's efficient use of human resources, nonetheless repeated the same point:

> Free immigration would cause rapid equalization of per capita income across countries, accomplished by levelling downwards the income of the more affluent. (Reder, 1982: 31)

Yet advocates of managed trade can – and, indeed, do – argue exactly the same case: free trade will lead to the rapid destruction of domestic enterprise through imports from cheap labour sources; and the free movement of capital will lead to the country being stripped of its capital resources as investment goes abroad in search of the most profitable outlets.

Are the fears legitimate? It is an established theorem in economics that the free mobility of factors of production leads, other things being equal, to the equalization of factor prices (see Ohlin, 1967; Lerner, 1953; Samuelson, 1948;). But other things are not equal, and the proposition says nothing about whether factor prices are equalized upwards or downwards, nor what time period is involved, nor – as in the trade argument – whether the expansion in activity would be so great that it would more than compensate for any tendency to the equalization of wages.

Others have developed a theoretical case for restricting migration on the grounds that the provision of 'collective goods' (social and health security, educational services, subsidized housing etc.) in developed countries implies that open competition in the labour market cannot be allowed – those seeking to gain access to these goods would, in an open system, always be larger than the demand for labour. Thus, 'all relatively advantaged countries must adopt restrictive immigration policies to protect their advantages' (Zolberg, in Kritz, 1983: 36–7). But is the case valid? Is access to collective goods an important motive in migration?

For the poor of the United States, what are the collective goods which so seriously unbalance the labour market? Indeed, now that governments in the developed countries are almost universally seeking means to reduce the supply of subsidized collective goods, this argument, even if valid earlier, is becoming increasingly invalid.

The fears remain; fears embedded in an essentially political calculation rather than an assessment of economic gains. Indeed, the following statement from OECD epitomizes the doubtful – indeed hesitant – logic at stake:

> Restrictions on international labour flows are simply an obvious form of protection. The policy is intended to protect domestic jobs, wages and the 'integrity' of social transfer systems in the face of cut backs in the demand for labour, public budgets and medium-term growth prospects. The costs of these decisions – potential inflationary pressures due to a continued lack of responsiveness of domestic wages to international competitive pressures, growing job vacancies in certain sectors or occupations, illegal or 'black' markets, the failure of new labour and capital markets to develop within the OECD area, for example – may not have been given adequate consideration. (OECD, 1978: 2)

However, the argument against the free movement of labour is not universally shared. Professor Julian Simon (1989) pursues the neoclassical case to its logical conclusion: that the free movement of labour is beneficial both to the world at large and to each competing national unit (indeed, as with the trade argument, a unilateral freeing of labour migration should optimize the welfare of the country that undertook such a policy). Others argue, on the basis of a specific set of assumptions, that with a decreasing supply of labour the returns to capital and the aggregate income of society decline disproportionately (Bernard, 1953; Chiswick, 1982a), the reverse also being true. Hamilton and Whalley (1984) argue that, as long as the marginal productivities of labour in different places are not equalized, migration is 'welfare-improving'. They try to put some figures on the estimated gains from de-restriction. Depending on the elasticities of substitution of capital and labour and with 1977 data in a 179-country model, they estimate the efficiency gains from completely free movement at between US$4.7 and $16 trillion (the 1977 gross world output was some $7.8 trillion). With measures to redistribute income from the gainers to the losers, free migration becomes Pareto-efficient.

From a different tradition, J.K. Galbraith (1979: 7) draws attention to a different scale of costs borne by those denied access to the opportunity to work:

Migration ... is the oldest action against poverty. It selects those who most want help. It is good for the country to which they go; it helps break the equilibrium of poverty in the country from which they come. What is the perversity in the human soul that causes people to resist so obvious a good?

Substitutions

International trade theory in the nineteenth century assumed that labour and capital were immobile. Trade is the means by which differences in the endowment – and thus, the productivity – of these two factors is equilibrated, leading to the maximization of the welfare of trading partners (and a situation superior to one where there is no trade). Neither the movement of labour nor of capital is required in such a model.

However, even in the nineteenth century, in reality capital and labour had some degree of mobility; and in our own times, capital – as finance, rather than factories – has become almost completely mobile. The implicit principle embedded in the original formulation has thus become generalized to cover both traded goods and the two factors of production – all three should be exchanged until factor prices are equalized on a world scale.

As we noted earlier, theory implied – and many people assume – that these different elements can be substituted for each other. Let us suppose, by way of illustration, that goods from country A are relatively cheap because the local labour cost per unit of output is low, and part of this output is an important input to the exports of country B. If, for whatever reason, country B restricts these imports, then in order for an exporting firm to survive against third country competition – other things being equal – it needs either to import cheaper labour so that cheaper inputs can be made in country B or export capital to produce the finished goods in country A. If country B simultaneously prevents immigration, then the weight of competitive equilibration falls entirely on the export of capital. Thus, in this highly simplified example, the three elements can be completely substituted for each other, albeit not necessarily without increases in cost. In practice, people have identified increased immigration as the result of restrictions on imports (cf. Simon's discussion of the relationship between Mexico's agricultural exports and migration to the United States [1989: 265]), and increased capital exports as the result of immigration controls.

If in practice a measure of substitutability exists, then it is tempting to analysts to suggest that policy can be employed to shape what substitutions should occur – 'From a strictly economic standpoint,' Teitelbaum (in OECD, 1993: 181) argues, 'mobility of factors and the free exchange of products can be considered alternative strategies, leading to an identical result: the improvement in the well being of the trade partners.' Thus, governments can supposedly choose freely to eliminate immigration by substituting capital for labour without this producing either increased imports or major losses in competitiveness. The reverse proposition has also on occasions been popular: governments can substitute labour for capital without significant losses. In many developing countries, just such a strategy has frequently been attempted, most famously in China's Great Leap Forward.

However, the aggregation in the basic concepts – capital, labour, trade – is misleading, and the idea of complete substitution between them is accordingly also at fault. It is that aggregation which leads to people being puzzled as to why international exchanges in all three areas are required at all – Why does a country simultaneously import steel and export it? Why does it import labour and capital, and export them? In theory, capital is homogeneous and flows freely between sectors and locations. While there is a measure of truth in this so far as portfolio investment is concerned, it is not at all true of company investment, which is highly specific to the output of particular goods, technology and management. Textile firms, faced with declining profits, do not simply stay in the same place and move into making something else, the provision of computer software, for example. They are more likely to retain their role in textiles but change the goods produced or the location (to gain access to cheaper labour or inputs) – that is, the 'capital' is highly specific to one form of production, and it carries this 'comparative advantage' wherever it goes, endowing its location with that advantage.

The same is true of trade. The greater the degree of disaggregation, the more what appear as competitive goods become complementary, or at least, not necessarily competitive. Company A may make teddy bears and thus seem to compete with company B, yet A's bears cost $100 and B's $5, and each has a separate market without significant overlap because of the quite different quality of the two products. The more open the world economy, the more each national economy becomes specialized – and therefore the more dependent upon equally specialized imports of goods and capital.

Similar observations are applicable to labour. The illusion of homogeneity conceals the extraordinary complexities of specialization, including among the so-called 'unskilled' (a group sharply differentiated by education, age, aptitudes, physical endowment, energy, experience, etc.). No employer faces a homogeneous supply of labour, but rather a vastly variegated group of individuals; and selecting carefully between them can yield significant gains.

Thus, there are not only considerable limits on how far labour, capital and traded goods can be substituted for each other; even within these components, the possibilities of substitution are limited. Within the category of 'unskilled' there are enormous variations, from the completely illiterate to the highly literate (and developing countries' 'cheap labour' is of little economic value in most modern activities because of illiteracy). Take, for example, the crude difference between immigrant and native unskilled workers. Often the immigrants are younger, better educated, with fewer disabilities, and with a greater willingness to work hard in poor conditions. They do not share local assumptions on what is socially tolerable work and conditions, and may be more powerfully motivated to earn. Even if they cost the same or more, they might be preferred. But even this is highly misleading, since 'immigrant' implies again a spurious homogeneity – the aptitudes of different groups of workers make them unsubstitutable. Mexican wetbacks in search of agricultural labour have little in common with Turkish assembly workers in Germany or Indian grocers in Britain. We ought to have a classification system for labour which is as elaborated as the classification for goods.

The developed countries in general have failed to reproduce a labour force adequate for their expanded output. Their economies are, as it were, too large, so there is, despite long-run unemployment, persistent labour scarcity. On the other hand, the liberalization of economies opens up a world labour supply of enormous dimensions and greater diversity in terms of specialized aptitudes than ever before. The pressure on employers arising from competition in open markets is to import workers or relocate capacity abroad.

The Shortage of Labour

In a dynamic capitalist economy, as we have noted, there is a constant tendency to exhaust the available supply of labour. In the developed countries in the postwar period, this tendency has been exaggerated by the shrinkage in the available labour force and a decline in the available hours worked.

The first problem here is the low rate of increase in the population. By the early 1990s, the rate of growth in most of Europe was well below replacement levels, being below 0.5 per cent per year. By 2025, one estimate suggests, the rate of increase will be under 0.15 per cent annually (Zlotnik, in OECD, 1993: 47). First, the declining size of family, increasingly late marriage (in the 12 countries of the European Union, the average age of marriage is just over 25) and the increasing employment of women has tended to reduce the years of potential reproduction. It may also be the case that an increasing number of women are choosing not to have children at all. Second, an increasing proportion of the labour force is engaged in full-time education. Enrolments in education increased between 4 and 10 per cent per year for much of the OECD group of countries between 1950 and 1968. By the early 1990s, a typical German graduate took his or her first job at the age of 29.

At the other end of working life, early retirement has become increasingly common. For the European Union, the age of actual retirement in the early 1990s is four years below the statutory retirement age; for France, a third of men in the age group 55 to 59 are retired, and close to 86 per cent of those aged 60 to 64. The participation rate for Americans aged 60 or more fell from 65 per cent before the Second World War to 30 per cent in 1980; and for those aged 55 or above, from 61 to 40 per cent in 1985. A survey of leading pension schemes in Britain found that 80 per cent of participants took early retirement, two-thirds of them before the age of 60; in four of the schemes examined, 40 per cent retired before the age of 55 (Incomes Data Services, 1993). Withdrawal from work due to disability has also become more common, both because of the legal provisions of different types of pension and, so far as governments are concerned, as a means to keep down the politically damaging figures for unemployment. Thus, within 20 years, in Europe the normal length of the average man's working life (as we shall see, the situation is different for women) has been reduced by nearly one-third. This is reflected in the decline in participation rates for the population of working age – to under 60 per cent for much of Europe (but over 70 per cent in the United States, Japan and Scandinavia). Furthermore, the working time of those in work has declined – from an average of just over 48 hours per week in the early 1950s to, in Germany, 35 hours in the late 1980s. Holiday periods have increased remarkably, as have periods of leave from work for training, childbirth, and so on.

There are countertendencies, of which the most extraordinary is the prodigious growth in the productivity of labour. Military service in the United States and Britain was ended. Agriculture was stripped of much of its labour force; and with more 'casualization' of work, an increasing number of people took second and third jobs. However, much the most dramatic change has been, as we saw earlier, the acceleration in the long-drawn-out process of women entering paid employment. By the early 1990s, within the OECD group, nearly two-thirds of adult women were in paid work (and in Sweden, four out of five women). Indeed, the participation rate of women was fast approaching the lowered rate of male participation.

The entry of women into work has been made possible by an extraordinary increase in the productivity of household labour (sustained by a no less remarkable increase in the capital intensity of household work) and by a decline both in the numbers of children born to the average women and in the numbers of years devoted to each child. The growth in productivity has a long history; Long (1958) in the 1950s detailed the changes that had occurred over the previous 60 years, calculating that household equipment per woman home-worker had increased five times over with the transfer of many domestic services to outside suppliers, and the arrival of convenience foods.

Simultaneously, the standards of household maintenance and child care have continued to rise, with more maternal attention (although perhaps less time) devoted to a reduced number of dependants. However, married women with jobs are much more likely to divorce; indeed, marriage itself, compared to the past, is of declining financial significance, and more an issue of shared household maintenance and emotional support (if these are lacking, the incentive to divorce rises sharply). Half the current marriages in the United States are projected to end in dissolution, and two-fifths of those in Britain and in Scandinavia. One result is the rapid growth in women living alone with small children, the fastest growing group among the poor. In the USA, a quarter of all families with small children are headed by a single parent; in Britain, one-fifth. On average, divorced women experience a halving of their standard of living in the first year after divorce. Thus, even as women enter the labour force in unprecedented numbers, the countertendency following from the decline in marriage is affecting both their capacity to work full time and to prepare children for their role as adult workers.

The decline in the growth of the labour hours on offer is tolerable if productivity expands rapidly and/or governments are willing to accept lower rates of growth of output. But in an open and competitive system, slow growth entails relative decline, something few governments can accept. As the availability of equipment and infrastructural facilities spreads, the more labour costs, even if marginal elements in total costs, become key variables in competition. New entrants to the system of modern production, for example, the East and Southeast Asian 'dragons' – combining that equipment and infrastructure to attain levels of productivity as good as, or better than, American, Japanese or European levels, can do so at a fraction of the labour cost; they are immediately identified as rivals.

The changed economic structure in the developed countries allows the largest part of the labour force continually to upgrade its position, leaving sectors of unskilled labour unmanned. Such work is not just of low productivity, but very underpaid relative to its characteristics: what the Japanese call '3-D jobs' – dirty, difficult and dangerous (in Japanese, it is '3-Ks' – *kitanai, kitsui, kiken*). Such work is often characterized by low status, great tedium in unpleasant conditions, poor health-and-safety conditions, high pressure, inconvenient times (night shifts, work 'on call', etc.). Labour scarcity allows the mass of workers to escape these sectors. Yet often, these poor jobs are important for maintaining activity in the high-productivity sectors. Cleaners are vital if offices are to function, dishwashers are essential to expensive restaurants. It is here that new immigrants proved crucial.

However, there are some problems of theory here. If the poor jobs are needed, why does labour scarcity not impel wages to rise, conditions to improve, and times to be adjusted to a more convenient pattern so that native workers are willing to take these jobs? Alternatively, why is capital not substituted fully for labour in these sectors?

Reproduction Costs

Before the twentieth century – and in the British colonial territories in this century – the bench-mark wage for men was officially seen as one which should permit a worker to maintain himself, a wife and two children at a socially acceptable standard of living, with some modest provision for the maintenance of the worker and his wife for a short period after their working life had finished (although often here it was assumed that children would support their parents in retirement). Thus, in wage negotiations for the mass of workers, in the setting of minimum wages, and in establishing criteria for payments under systems of poor relief, much time was devoted to establishing what a minimum socially acceptable standard of living – maintenance and reproduction – was for a worker in a given position in society.

Setting this norm cannot be a simple objective measure of material needs. It needs allowances for adequate leisure for the worker to recuperate from work, special clothes to participate in religious ceremonies and festivals, funds for extraordinary events (births, deaths, marriages). The 'subjective' elements are socially important since they relate to what is seen as a 'fair' wage: that is, one acceptable to both employer and worker, and consistent with existing practice – 'customs and shared norms of fair treatment in employment' as Osterman (1984: 68–9) puts it in a modern context. 'Workers', he observes, 'expect a "good employer" to treat them equitably, make allocative decisions by rule, reward seniority and provide advancement opportunities and employment security.' The just expectations of the worker need to be met if he or she is to work well, hard and for long hours. It was assumed that one male wage should achieve this end, and that one male worker – with two children – required a full-time female worker to maintain the household.

This was only a bench-mark. In practice, achieving this level was a hopelessly utopian ambition for significant sections of society in the nineteenth century. Men, women and children worked casually at rates which barely maintained them round the year, let alone ensured any reproduction (the death rates showed the changing degree to which such pay did not even cover maintenance). The infant mortality rate and the abandonment of children to the mercies of nature and society at large illustrated that society had little interest in ensuring adequate standards of reproduction for this class of worker.

Let us suppose, as a theoretical exercise, that there are different bench-marks for different levels of work, forming a hierarchy of skill levels. Formally, the bench-mark is linked to the value of the work of the worker, to the average level of productivity in that occupation. Society needs to ensure that the labour force will be reproduced, which implies a higher level of wage than the employer would allow for. The employer seeks the lowest wage consistent with maintaining the work effort. The ideal from the employer's position is one where pay and output – at an individual level – are as closely linked as possible, so that increasing or decreasing effort is reflected directly in the worker's pay. Thus, there is likely to be a gap between the 'fair wage' (including socially accepted elements) and what the employer wants to pay – a gap crossed by bargaining, conflict, strikes, public regulation, and so on.

For a long period, piece rates ensured the linkage between output and wage. But often the nature of the output does not allow such rates: there is no 'piece', or work is collectively organized and it is impossible to measure individual contributions. Furthermore, wherever quality is important, piece rates become dangerous as a mode of payment since they are based upon a quantitative measure. The bench-mark wage also has a major disadvantage. It assumes a constant output, and is therefore a constraint upon the employer's capacity to lower wages when market demand for the company's production declines. To survive, the employer is obliged to seek both to contract the size of the labour force while keeping up output, and to reduce the pay of workers to below – and sometimes well below – the bench mark. The market transfers the worker abruptly from a position where it is expected he could maintain a family to one where no such expectation exists.

Theoretically in such a system the full cost of maintenance and reproduction is borne by the worker. While employment continues, it is a parental decision as to how much should be spent on raising and training children – that is, preparing the future worker to attain a given level of productivity in work. Booms and slumps are, in principle, reflected directly not only in the standard of living of the family but also in spending on health and education, on housing, recreation and leisure.

If we can imagine a closed economy, without technical innovation or competition, growth of population, natural disasters or changes in the occupational structure, incomes or employment, and where children inherit occupations from their parents, then the hierarchy of skills, representing a hierarchy of jobs and values of output, can – in theory – reproduce itself indefinitely. Each family receives income sufficient only to train a replacement for the male worker and the female household manager. As in the theory of a caste system, birth would completely determine occupation and income.

However, economies are not closed, and competition between firms, families and governments, with resulting changes in technology, incomes and employment, continually transforms the structure, making today's literacy tomorrow's illiteracy. The faster the pace of change, the less efficient the family becomes as a means to anticipate the skills required in the future, the more other agencies – firms, private and public educational and training institutions – must assume a major role.

From the late nineteenth century, the rivalries of the dominant states and the development of strong domestic class conflict led to the rise of what we have called 'the socialized state'. Governments tried to incorporate their populations in a consultative role (with the extension of the suffrage, mass political parties, a mass press) through measures of popular welfare. Furthermore, in conditions where it was expected that warfare would require the participation of a major part of the male labour force, the physical quality of the late-nineteenth-century working man became a matter of public concern. In Britain, following the Boer War, the Inspector General of Recruiting reported that 'the gradual deterioration of the working classes from whom the bulk of recruits must always be drawn' threatened the capacity of the country to defend itself (cited in Titmuss, 1958).

168 THE NEW UNTOUCHABLES

The type of economy emerging in the late nineteenth century required a much more stable workforce if the unprecedented levels of productivity now feasible within tightly organized but gigantic factory organizations were to be attained. In particular, some measure of protection from insecurity – whether at work, in old age or in terms of housing – came to be seen as a necessity for a significant part of the labour force. Increasing levels of education and skill are even more crucial for raising productivity, and governments compared each other in terms of the output of graduates, engineers, toolmakers etc. Indeed, in our own times, governments reproach Japan for unfair competition for failing to house its workforce according to modern norms.

Thus, the state increasingly intervened to secure a minimum standard of social provision for the population as a whole in what, in Britain, became known after the Second World War as the 'welfare state'. Questions of relative spending on the provision of health, education, social security, protection against unemployment or the rigours of old age were removed from the family and the market, and vested in government. The former supposed link between work and output, the income of the male parent and spending on his children, and the variation in spending with changes in the business cycle was broken: the state, it was expected, would continue to provide, regardless of changing circumstances.

State intervention introduced a voluntaristic element into the economics of the reproduction of labour, delinking provision from markets, and instead making it the subject of political discretion. In a competitive political party system, promises could be made independent of economic circumstances. The system of provision thus became rigid, with no means for downward flexibility in the event of economic contraction, and no apparent means to limit an indefinite expansion, as witnessed in the continuing disproportionate growth of health spending in all developed countries. The incentive to work and the fear of unemployment, it seemed, changed. Public housing provision tied down the workforce in places which were only by accident where employment was generated. State provision defied the economic and territorial variations which a market economy made inevitable. The rigidities, however, were tolerable in growing economies, which could to some degree be isolated from external markets.

Setting a minimum for society as a whole introduced both a measure of equality of provision and a degree of arbitrariness. Provision was related not to the productivity of different skills and their value to the economy, but dependent upon an aspired level of productivity for the economy as a whole. Thus, in comparison to the old market-based hierarchy of skills and provision, some of the population would be 'over-provided', others 'underprovided'.

The change did not take place in a neutral or technical context, but in a highly political one, so that provision which, on the surface, was supposedly supplied equally to all, in practice was skewed to some groups more than others. Free education and free health, for example, were heavily dominated by the middle classes. Governments, for similar reasons, sometimes neglected basic industrial skills – the extension of apprenticeships – for the expansion of tertiary education, a primary means of middle-class upward mobility. The state's discretionary power thus doubly defeated the market demand for particular types of skills: it disconnected supply of skills from demand, and biased the supply of skills in favour of the social groups which dominated its own operations.

There is much variation in social provision between different advanced economies. The United States has, compared to Europe, a much greater share of provision that is privately funded, so the market imperatives operating in the welfare system are stronger. However, the growth in health provision is much the largest of any of the developed countries (reaching over 12 per cent of gross domestic product in 1990, double that in Britain). In Europe, social provision continued to expand in the 1980s; in Germany, additional labour costs (including employer contributions to pensions, social security, health insurance) reached £14,377 per capita in 1993, adding an extra 84 per cent to the already high level of wages to make up total labour costs. In both the USA and Europe, the financial burden of provision – especially in health, pensions and education – reached crisis proportions in the early 1990s, precipitating major efforts at reform.

The extraordinary growth in state provision, however, does not reduce the burdens on family spending (nor does it mean all were covered). Indeed, the two – state and family provision – advance together. The growth in the productivity of labour imposes on families new standards and competitive pressures to upgrade expenditure on the raising of fewer children, in order to 'keep up with the Joneses'. In the early 1980s, the average family in Britain spent, in 1982 values, some £32,000 per child over 18 years (and £48,500 for two children). For a family then receiving some £6000 income annually, spending was some £850 for one child, and £1300 for two (or some 22 per cent of total income) (Consumers' Association, 1983). Ten years later, a family on a 'modest but adequate' income spent £3120 (at 1992 prices) annually per child up to the age of 11, and £3224 thereafter, or £56,888 over 18 years (Joseph Rowntree Foundation, 1992). For families living in or close to poverty, the cost of a socially adequate upbringing for their children is becoming an extraordinary burden.

The same is true for those on higher incomes. The competitive pressure was most notorious for Japanese middle-class families. To gain entry to university requires long preparation through expensive cramming schools, costing annually in the late 1980s an average of $650 part time and $3800 full time. Indeed, parents put their unfortunate offspring into cramming schools in order to cram to gain access to cramming schools. The costs of the competition can be seen in the annual toll of teenage suicides, nervous breakdowns and psychosomatic disorders at the time of examinations.

The costs of reproduction have grown well beyond the average male wage. The bench-mark pay rate is no longer expected to support a family of four. Thus the entry of women on a much larger scale into paid employment is fortunate. Whether women were 'pushed' by rising family costs or 'pulled' by expanding opportunities to earn, two earners are now required to meet the private reproduction costs of attaining society's aspired level of productivity (and, as we have seen, single mothers increasingly became one of the largest elements of the poor). However, this simple formula has to be qualified by the increased instability of marriage. A significant number of men slip out of the responsibility of reaching the old standard of maintaining a four-person household, and women, now required to work outside the home, refuse to accept the role of sole household manager. The old system of reproduction appears, as a result of the competitive context, rising standards and rising costs, to be breaking down for a significant part of the population.

In the heyday of the provision of a state minimum to all citizens, the distinction between citizen and noncitizen is considerably heightened. The minimum standard is determined by the supply of legitimate natives, not by the demand for labour or the productivity of the worker. The liberalization or opening up of economies renders impossible the maintenance of national systems on a minimum welfare standard, treating all citizens equally. The intervention of the state in, say, education, has led to an underproduction of workers willing to undertake unskilled labour at rates of pay which are below what is socially tolerable. In developing countries, the reverse phenomenon is an overproduction of the educated, offered rates of pay well below what is globally available.

The role of the state exaggerates the sharp differences between the reproduction costs of different countries. In a developing country, the average level of productivity is low, as also are the costs of reproduction and maintenance. The skills acquired there are thus substantially undervalued compared to the rest of the world. In a developed country, the average level of productivity is high, as also are the costs of reproduction and maintenance. In closed or semi-closed economies, incomes are geared to the average level of productivity – thus, in the obstinately persistent unskilled occupations, workers are, by world standards 'overpaid'. It makes sense, therefore, for a skilled worker from a developing country to migrate and thereby gain access to the higher level of productivity – and pay – in a developed country, without paying the local costs in terms of their own reproduction. Indeed, it makes sense to work at below the level of skill attained by the worker at home because the pay in a developed country is related to the average level of productivity in that society.

The political bargain – the social contract – between the state and the mass of the population becomes increasingly at variance with the average level of social productivity. In a fully closed economy, theoretically, this need not matter, but it would entail that shares of income must shift continually towards the most labour-intensive activities, to bring the least productive up to the average level. The public provision of social services must therefore expand disproportionately to establish the measure of social equality implied by the social contract at the heart of the 'socialized state'.

However, this is only a theory. There can never be, in a rigorous sense, a 'closed economy' to sustain such a model. The more productive workers, increasingly taxed to sustain those of low productivity, would move into the global labour market, taking their skills to wherever the reward is greater (as doctors from developing countries have done). Capital, if it could, would follow suit. There would be a low rate of technical innovation as the result of preventing imports, and a stagnating domestic market. As a result, profit rates would stagnate and investment fall.

Even more important, no state can preside over the continuing relative decline in its position in a world of competing states: it would be driven, as the old Soviet Union was, to make increasing efforts to reform the domestic economy in order to increase the rate of innovation and the rate of investment. What begins there would ultimately end in an attempt to transform the social contract so that society is no longer responsible for maintaining the least productive at the level of livelihood appropriate to the average level of productivity. The symptom of the welfare crisis is everywhere its escalating cost. The favoured remedies are to expose the system to market criteria (which, in practice, means making it subordinate to income inequality) either directly, through privatization, or indirectly, through self-financed trusts. The effect is to be a restoration of something like the nineteenth-century link between income (and productivity) and social provision.

Opening trade and capital markets can thus only be a prelude to the integration of national labour markets with the world. Domestic prices – including that of labour time – would then be related to world levels of scarcity and productivity. With that ruthlessness which has so frequently allowed the conversion of one age's 'common sense' into another's 'sentimentality', the ruling orders have written off their un-skilled – reducing welfare commitments as unemployment rises.

Too Many Workers or Too Few?

We have already argued that the heterogeneity of the labour force in a modern economy means that often, even in the category of 'unskilled labour', workers are not in competition with each other. Labour demand consists not of a set of sectors so much as a mass of specialized niches: workers are not necessarily substitutes for each other. If this is so, it is perfectly possible to find high labour demand as measured by vacancies (for unskilled labour) with high unemployment, labour scarcity and surplus. As US Congressman E. de la Garza from Texas noted with some exasperation in a 1978 discussion of illegal immigration with high levels of unemployment:

> [I]n Washington, you see 'Help Wanted' in every restaurant and every Macdonald's. Everywhere you go you see 'Help Wanted'. We know there are countless thousands of aliens illegally in the Washington area, apparently all with jobs. (US Congress, 1978: 25)

The same issue arises in every downturn. Thus in London, when un-employment was at historically high levels in the early 1980s, major shortages of labour were observed in key sectors (transport, textiles, metal manufacture, school catering services, hotels and restaurants, hospitals). In Germany, at the end of May 1979, total unemployment was put at 775,000 when unofficial business estimates of unfilled vacancies reached over 600,000 (*The Economist*, 9 June 1979: 94).

There are many possible explanations. At the extremes, some workers are clearly nonsubstitutable – in Britain, redundant northern miners in their 50s cannot work as dishwashers or short-hand typists in London. There are geographical discontinuities: job creation and unemployment occur in different places. In 1988, high levels of unfilled vacancies occurred in the southeast while the unemployment was in the north, and the difference in housing costs in the two areas (especially where the northern unemployed lived in secure public housing) more than eliminated any income advantage in moving. Without considering moving home, even within the same city, many women find that the costs of child care and travel to work take most of the income earned in part-time work – and certainly make it more sensible to draw public welfare benefits. Furthermore, the regulatory regime often makes for powerful disincentives to take low-paid work.

Yet, there is another factor, particularly relevant for young workers. They have been raised and educated to attain the average level of productivity in an advanced society – and to receive an income appropriate to maintaining and reproducing a family at that level. Just as doctors will not work as road-sweepers, nor higher civil servants as lavatory attendants, so workers in general have acquired from the society sets of expectations which cannot be reconciled with the pay rates and working conditions on offer in an open economy. It is easier, at least initially, to draw benefits accumulated by the payments of their parents into the system or to work in the black economy than to jeopardize any future possibilities of income by working now at well below the average rate. As discussed earlier, governments continually try to defeat this reasonable choice by increasing the barriers of access to social security, lowering the level of benefits, excluding classes of former beneficiaries, and generally harassing claimants in the name of 'preserving the incentives to work'. Yet those who work in unskilled occupations find themselves declining further below the average, slipping into poverty.

If native-born workers are unable or unwilling to fill the vacancies, the more mobile and active new immigrants could do so, particularly if they are illegal and not paying the normal additional taxes. Their income is increased, while the labour cost to the employer is lower. This affects new immigrants, those not raised in the society and therefore not acquiring the expectations of working for incomes appropriate to the average level of local productivity. The children of immigrants tend to have the same expectation as those born to natives, but as the children of unskilled workers they often fail to acquire the skills that many of the non-immigrants gain, with the result – no doubt exaggerated by prejudice – that the second generation has significantly higher levels of unemployment than the children of non-immigrants. In Germany, half of all German youth acquire skills, but only 20 per cent of immigrant children do so; in the late 1980s, when 21 per cent of immigrant fathers were unemployed, 38 per cent of their sons were also (Schulze, in Muus, 1993: 199). In the Netherlands between 1983 and

1990, the unemployment rate for the children of non-immigrants fell but remained high for immigrants, and two to three times higher for the children of immigrants. However, the comparison group for the children of immigrant workers should be other unskilled workers, not the children of non-immigrants in general.

There is, then, some divergence between the employment experience of immigrant parents and their children, allowing for the age differences. Unskilled immigrant adults often do better than highly skilled immigrants, suggesting that in many developed countries there is a greater shortage of unskilled immigrant workers than of the highly skilled. In Australia, for example, a study shows that at the highest educational level, immigrants receive lower pay and experience greater levels of unemployment than the native-born in that skill grade, whereas at the lowest educational level (eight years or less), immigrants do better than the native-born on these two measures. Furthermore, the rate of unemployment among immigrants increases with the level of education (Beggs and Chapman, in Abowd and Freeman, 1991: 379). Perhaps the unskilled immigrants are more willing to do jobs which the natives spurn, and are therefore not competing with native workers; whereas the highly skilled fill gaps only occasionally made vacant by the native-born and are thus competing with them.

The paradox – of high levels of unemployment among the unskilled existing with high levels of unsatisfied vacancies – is exaggerated by what educationalists see as a decline in the willingness of the young to acquire the education and skills needed. On the one hand, in the United States there is a clear correlation between levels of educational attainment and unemployment. Each downturn in the economy increases the unemployment level of the poorly educated, and each upturn rescues fewer of them. On the other hand, a quarter of the US student population fails to graduate from high school (45 per cent for Hispanic and 35 per cent for black school participants); 14 per cent drop out altogether. Employers complain that, even of those who graduate, the quality of the worker is so poor that office functions have to be located abroad or funds spent on remedial courses. Of course, this cannot be regarded as a disinterested point of view; nor is the evidence available that this is a different state of affairs from the past.

However, whatever the diagnosis, the outcome is not in dispute: an increasing inability on the part of the domestic unskilled labour force (particularly among the young and new entrants to the workforce) to meet the growing demand for unskilled workers. The gaps are jobs that cannot be relocated abroad, that are not moveable. As Böhning (in Bacci, 1972: 252) noted more than twenty years ago:

[Y]ou cannot transfer a coal shaft to somewhere in Turkey simply because labour happens to be abundant there; the solution is also irrelevant for the large number of building workers: you cannot build the houses needed in Frankfurt in Sicily; nor is the proposition applicable to migrant workers in private services, domestic work, public transport or other public service occupations: if dustbins needed emptying in Munich, the workers for the job must be found on the spot.

Nor are they jobs where capital can easily – or cheaply – be substituted for labour. Increasingly they are jobs which require an element of personal service – and personal service that is often of decisive significance for a skilled worker's capacity to work.

The Roles of Immigrants

Immigrant labour has played a number of distinct roles in the developed countries in the 40 years of postwar movement from the developing countries. The ending of some of these roles has not exhausted their function in the labour market – new needs have arisen almost as quickly as the old came to an end. It is worth summarizing some of them.

1. As the native-born labour force moved out of unskilled jobs, particularly the least desirable (the Japanese 3-Ds) – in brickworks, foundries, building sites, tanneries, coal mines, agriculture, hotels and restaurants, hospitals, railways and other public transport, assembly work in manufacturing, night shifts – immigrants have ensured that these sectors have been manned, thus making possible the rest of the economy's activity. This is particularly so where, with measures of protection (as is still true for much of agriculture) import controls make it difficult for imports to compete with domestic supplies.

2. Only some of these activities are in declining sectors. Immigrant labour has thus eased the process of structural change, reducing what might otherwise have been precipitate decline with a multiplicity of damaging effects in both nontradable and tradable sectors.

3. In performing these roles, immigrants provide a margin of 'flexible labour' where regulation has rendered the labour supply particularly rigid. They have functioned as what Böhning (Böhning and Maillat, 1974: 131) calls 'conjunctural shock absorbers' (*konjunkturpuffer*) – a margin of the labour force which can be induced to leave the country in the event of slump. Thus in the first major recession since the Second World War, in the early 1970s, the stock of foreign workers in Germany declined by 19 per cent, and in France by 16 per cent. The effects were

similar for the British merchant marine: non-British ratings were cut by one-fifth between 1976 and 1979 when the volume of freight carried also fell by one-fifth, but British-born ratings experienced no decline (although British officers declined by 5 per cent).

4. Underlying these roles is the enormous gap between more and less developed countries, in terms of the average productivity and cost of labour, and the mechanisms by which labour is maintained and reproduced. The income expectations of the skilled in developing countries are more than met, at least initially, by their working as unskilled workers in developed countries; the technically qualified gain even more. Neither has had to meet the local reproduction costs of the destination society; both are able to reach the same average level of productivity because of the social context of work. It does not make sense to describe this as either a net transfer of human capital from developing to developed countries, or the exploitation of the potential for high productivity in a developed country without having contributed to it.

5. The opening up of the world economy is vastly accelerating the processes of change, facilitated by the dramatic decline in the costs of transport. Increasingly, the role of immigrants is in the sector of personal services; this is discussed in the next section.

The Future

Each developed economy is already dependent upon a labour force vastly larger than that which lives in the country concerned – that is, on the increasing numbers of foreign suppliers of inputs to domestic production and consumption. It is possible that in time much of the world's manufacturing may be undertaken in what are now developing countries, with the developed countries basically functioning as service suppliers. What has already happened in the long slow decline (in employment terms) of agriculture in the developed world may be repeated in manufacturing. As this occurs, the governments of the developed countries may become increasingly indifferent politically to the import of manufactured goods, since domestic manufacturing interests will no longer be of such significance in the economy as a whole, and will be of a type so specialized that competition is limited.

However, the decline of manufacturing by no means ends the demand for immigrant workers. A service-based economy seems to generate a strong demand for the most highly educated and for a mass of unskilled workers. Of course, as in manufacturing, some services can be relocated abroad, and in some cases consumers can be induced to travel to the service – as in medical, tourist and retirement services. But a mass of services are tied to where the consumers are, and, as Bhagwati (1978: 208–9) puts it, 'service provision cannot be separated from the service provided'. In this case, trade in services and the viability of a service-based economy are closely tied to the capacity to supply a labour force at a competitive price. It is here that temporary or immigrant labour becomes important. Few pay much attention to the issue; as Geza Feketekuty (1988: 9) puts it:

> [M]ost countries [by which is meant 'governments'] assign a high priority to the objective of controlling entry by foreigners and lower priorities to trade and other policy objectives. At the same time, international trade in services could not flourish if people could not move freely from one country to another for temporary periods.

The issue of the emerging comparative advantage of developing countries in some services surfaced during the Uruguay round of GATT negotiations. The United States representatives tried to press the larger developing countries to liberalize their countries' use of US traded services (particularly banking, insurance and shipping). In addition, Washington argued that companies exporting services should be guaranteed the right to post managers, executives, specialists and their families for between three and five years to foreign countries (the freedom to be limited only to those with higher-level functions – a company's 'principal software manager', not a programmer or operator). At first, in the main, the developing countries rejected these proposals until they came to recognize that they had growing strength in labour-intensive services and construction. A group of eight developing countries (Argentina, Colombia, Cuba, Mexico, Peru, Egypt, India and Pakistan) thus pressed the developed countries to stop immigration controls obstructing their service exports by preventing the entry of temporary workers. India's minister of commerce, Dr Subramanian Swamy, made the point that,

> Our comparative advantage lies in labour-intensive services. Unless adequate provisions are made for labour mobility, providing for temporary relocation of labour for the provision of services, particularly in the industrialized countries, we would be against instituting a fundamental inequity [by liberalized unilateral trade in US-based services]. (Ministry of Commerce, Press Statement, 1991)

In the event, the issue was left without being resolved. But it is unlikely to go away, and governments from developing countries will, sooner or later, press the case for the right to supply, for example, construction teams to bid for infrastructure and highway projects in developed countries, for contracts to run hospitals, clean cities, dispose of garbage, even man a major shopping or restaurant complex (as, for example, Filipino companies supply the labour to run the Bahrain free-trade complex).

There are other reasons why the pressures for at least temporary immigration seem likely to grow. In the developed countries, decreases in fertility are continuing to reduce sharply the growth of population and hence the supply of native-born workers. The number of children per family has fallen well below a rate capable of reproducing the population (the 'replacement rate') – an average of 1.6 for the European Union (compared to 2.6 in the 1960s) and 1.57 for Japan. The change has been most marked in southern Europe: in Spain, from nearly 3 in 1970 to 1.3 in 1995; in Italy, from 2.4 to 1.29. Indeed, if the whole of Europe were to have the fertility rate of the former West Germany for the next 300 years, the native population would be extinct (Johnson et al., 1989: 3).

The contrast with the developing countries is extreme. By the year 2000 the world's labour force will have increased by 800 million (from 1980), with 93 per cent of this increase occurring in developing countries. In 1960 the ratio of births in the developing and developed countries was 4.4:1; in 1970 5.7:1; in 1980 5.9:1; in 1990 7.3:1. In the year 2000 the ratio is projected to reach 7.9:1 (UNDP, 1992). The share of the developed countries in the world's population will accordingly fall from about one-third in 1960 to one-fifth in 2000.

The effect of these contrasting patterns of fertility is most marked for those in the working age groups, especially for the young. Between 1985 and the year 2000 the total population of the developed countries is projected to increase by 14 per cent, and that of the developing countries by 103 per cent; the working population (aged 15 to 65) is expected to increase by 6 and 130 per cent respectively; and the young population (aged 20–40) will decrease by 10 per cent in the developed, and increase by 108 per cent in the developing countries. The same three figures for the United States – 26; 16; and –9 per cent – are strikingly contrasted with those for Mexico: 86; 129; 87 per cent (in the combined area of the US and Mexico, the Mexican share of all the young workers will increase from 21.9 to 37.2 per cent between 1985 and 2025). In Europe, by the year 2000, the labour force of the nine original members of the EC is projected to be declining annually by 300,000 (Mitchell, 1993: 2). If, even with a growing population, economic expansion invariably spilled out of national boundaries, how much more would this be true with a declining population? Contracting the economy to the size of the labour supply would be a process so painful that it is hardly to be considered as a political option.

Of the developed countries, two of the most extreme cases in terms of size of labour force are Germany and Japan (the two countries most dependent upon manufacturing). The population of the combined Germanies is projected to fall (from 76 to 65 million between 1986 and 2010). But even by the 1980s, the age composition had changed radically: between 1970 and 1987 the proportion of the population under the age of 15 had declined by 40 per cent (to 8.7 million), while those aged 65 or more had increased by 18 per cent (to 9.3 million). In the case of Japan, the younger groups declined particularly rapidly – for example, those aged between 14 and 19 were 14 per cent of the population in 1950; 10.5 per cent in 1960; 6 per cent in 1970; and 2.7 per cent in 1980. The number of over-65s rose from 5.7 per cent in 1960 to 11.7 per cent in 1990, and is expected to reach 15 per cent by the year 2000 and 25 per cent in 2025. Within the group of over-65s, those aged 75 or more increased from 38 per cent in 1985 to 53 per cent in 2025. While Germany and Japan have been among the most affected, all developed countries are aging. For example, in the Netherlands in 1985, 364 per 10,000 were over the age of 60; by 2020 the figure will be 756 per 10,000.

Those developing countries which have reduced population growth most rapidly are also affected. In South Korea, the number of children per family is expected to fall from 2.8 in 1981 to 1.7 by the year 2000. By then the government expects marked labour shortages in manufacturing, mining and construction to have developed. As we have seen, the country is already becoming dependent upon immigrant workers, especially in the export industries (by the late 1980s, half the workers in Seoul's garment industry were said to be foreign-born). Whereas in 1993 some 9 per cent of Singapore's population were over 60, by 2030 this share is projected to reach 30 per cent. In Taiwan, those aged 65 or more formed 6.7 per cent of the population in 1992, and are projected to reach 10.2 in 2011 and 21.6 in 2036 (in absolute numbers, the growth is from 1.4 million to 2.5 million to 5.6 million). Lacking Taiwan's remarkable level of wealth, China, with one of the most rigorous population policies in the world, is prematurely ageing: by the year 2030, 14 per cent of the population are expected to be aged 65 or more, or between 220 and 240 million people (double the total population of Japan).

A number of studies have attempted the impossible task of quantifying the shortages of labour, with or without taking into account ageing. For the United States, Clark Reynolds (1979) in the late 1970s, assuming an annual rate of increase in gross national product of 3 per cent, in productivity of 1.38 per cent (the average for 1960 to 1970), a constant participation rate and net annual immigration of 400,000, estimated that by the end of the century there would be a net labour deficit of 5 million (mostly for unskilled personnel). A similar study by Wood (1976) came to much the same conclusions. In Germany, the Institute of Labour Market and Occupational Research (IAB) of the Federal Employment Agency projected that by the end of the century there would be 2.5 million unfilled vacancies, and a further 1.7 million by the year 2010; the shortages would be most acute in personal and social services, and manufacturing would in the main have relocated abroad. A study of Japan – by the National Council for the Development of an Economic Structure for the Twenty-First Century – estimates that there would be 2.7 million unfilled vacancies by the end of the century; indeed, at the height of the boom in 1990, the labour shortage was put at 2 million (*Far Eastern Economic Review* report, 26 January 1989). A French study, mentioned earlier (Blanchet and Marchand, 1991), projected that the working age population of France would reach a peak in 2005 and thereafter decline, with the labour deficit increasing from 142,000 in the first decade of the next century to 180,000 in the third.

The estimates are no better than the trends and assumptions on which they are based, and cannot take into account the booms and slumps yet to be. They suggest, however, that crude demographic factors will make for a continuing scarcity of labour, particularly in the younger age groups, which will restrict the capacity for economic growth in the developed countries – and, in a competitive world system, favour a continuing shift of the world's income towards the developing countries.

The implications of this change – leaving aside people's perception of relative national standing – are likely to be considerable. At the level of the economy, it is expected that consumption will increase relative to income, savings will decline (in fact, the savings rate in the developed countries has been declining since the mid-1970s), and a declining labour force will reduce the expected output. Social spending will shift away from education and towards health, with a major increase in pension and other transfer payments (Masson and Tryon, 1990; IMF, 1989: 32). Börsch-Supan (1991) foresees a significant increase in the demand for housing as the numbers of households increase as the result of longer survival of the aged.

The relative shortage of workers – and hence the greater competition between employers for the available labour – is expected to increase wages, accelerate the reduction in the working week, increase the relative pay rates of young and women workers, and increase the emphasis upon performance rather than age-related payment systems. The increase in the average age of the workforce may lower labour productivity (or reduce the rate of growth). The speed of technical change outdates skills quickly, and so far it seems that the cost of retraining older workers rises steeply with age – and a declining number of expected years of work reduces the incentive to finance retraining.

However, the overall shortage masks even greater changes in the structure of economies. A possible slowdown in the growth of productivity in manufacturing with a rise in unit costs of labour is likely to lead to an acceleration in the relocation of manufacturing and mobile services to places where young workers are abundant – the developing countries. On the other hand, the developed countries are not only likely to become more service-oriented; an increasing proportion of the services will be labour-intensive and health-related as market demand becomes increasingly dominated by the needs of the aged. For example, one estimate foresees nurses expanding to become some 5 per cent of the labour force – and doing so at a time when the relevant native-born age group is contracting.

The political discussion of the issue, at least in the United States, has included seeking access to the labour force of a developing country as the key to sustaining national strength. A witness to a US congressional committee (Crowder, in US Congress, 1990: 309) on relations with Mexico made just this point:

> As our population becomes older, the problem will not be to find jobs for people, but people for jobs. For many years, Mexico, with its relatively young and expanding population will complement and balance our own as well as provide a formidable defence to the attack on our position in world markets.

In the crude sense of the weapon through which the Great Powers ultimately exercise power, their armed forces, these draw disproportionately on the younger working age groups. In the case of the United States, the shortfall in recruitment was already apparent in the 1970s and was offset by a shift to recruiting women (by 1979, women formed 14 per cent of the army), and an overwhelming dependence on ethnic minorities and immigrants. Without a general increase in – or in the case of the USA and Britain, a return to – compulsory military service, it would seem the Great Powers must inevitably come to depend on young mercenaries recruited in developing countries (perhaps, given current styles, on short-term subcontracts to the governments of developing countries). The Koreans went in the opposite direction: the government's Economic Planning Board offered those liable for their 18 months' military service the opportunity to escape from this by agreeing to work for five years in manufacturing; the army corps of engineers was also to be employed on civil construction projects to alleviate the labour shortage.

However, many argue that the problem is spurious – there is no labour shortage, only poor organization. In Japan, the Ministry of Labour argues that the deficits can be eliminated if more old people, home-based women and the unemployed can be induced to enter employment. The same case can be heard in the United States. It is argued in Europe that if the Union can increase its employment ratio by 10 per cent, it will make up the projected decline of 20 million in the existing workforce. Cutting the rate of unemployment from 9 to 6 per cent will make for 6 million extra workers. An increase in women's participation in paid employment (to the US level), with a supporting increase in crèches, would virtually eliminate the problem.

David Coleman (1992), in a well-documented overview of the data for Europe, draws the same conclusion: the unemployed, women and the aged can more than make up for any deficits. However, all the cases relied on the idea of labour as a homogeneous entity, infinitely substitutable, and willing to work in whatever conditions or at whatever price is on offer. They assumed older workers can replace younger ones at tolerable cost to employers and will be willing to fill the vacancies that actually occur. Surveys regularly show that unemployed workers are 'willing to work', yet when faced with the bad conditions and the low pay see themselves as driven by necessity into unemployment. Coleman is right to say that 'claimed recruitment difficulties cannot necessarily be taken at face value as impeding output or productivity', but quite wrong in condemning 'the demand for low wage labour to carry out underpaid jobs in unprofitable, obsolescent and under-capitalized industries' (440). As argued earlier, those jobs make possible better-paying jobs for the native-born. High-productivity work still requires a mass of low-paid workers in order to be effective, some of whom have to be physically close.

Governments have tested the thesis that the labour force is already large enough. Incentives have been offered to increase the employment of women, the sick, disabled and aged, without significant effect. Some have tried to extend the retirement age; for example, in 1983 the United States abolished any mandatory retirement year (without noticeable effect), raised the qualifying age for the full federal pension (the age is scheduled to rise again from 65 to 67 in the next century), increased the penalty for early retirement and enhanced the gains for each year worked over 65 (by 8 to 11 per cent for each year worked). However, this situation has done little to offset the apparent incentives of employ-

ers to be rid of the aged as soon as possible (and encouraging retirement is politically easier than sacking workers). Both Japan and Singapore offer cash incentives to firms to employ older workers but without
significant effect – small firms in Japan continue to prefer the young,
even if they are illegal immigrants. In any case, the financial incentives
offered are small: there is a brute logic in the unwillingness of the non-
employed to take up employment at the price employers and governments are willing to offer. As an official of the Japanese Foreign Ministry
delicately put it: 'Japanese business operations in an exceptionally competitive market ... are generally cool to the idea of hiring women, the
elderly or others with the additional costs these groups entail' (Government of Japan, 1993: 437–8).

Social Security

Most attention has so far been devoted, however, not to the broader
economic implications of ageing, but to the financial problems of governments in managing the increased costs of providing pensions and health
care – summed up in Nathan Keyfitz's misleading rule of thumb that,
if one aged person is to be supported by five workers, the tax rate must
take 20 per cent of the income of the five (in Lee, 1988: 101). Bourgeois-
Pichat (1988) has countered on the basis of French data that, with an
18 per cent state subsidy, in the late 1980s it took two workers to pay
for one pensioner. The French government has projected that if the
value of the pension is kept constant, contributions must increase from
19 per cent of the payroll to between 31 and 42 per cent by the year
2040. Some estimates suggest that by 2030 there could be more
pensioners than workers. The IMF (1989) has calculated for Germany
that if social-security benefits are to remain at the relative level they
reached in the late 1980s, the proportion of labour costs involved would
have to increase from just under 30 per cent in 1980 to 40 per cent in
2025. In the case of the United States, health-care costs have already
grown rapidly, increasing by 5.5 per cent annually for 20 years, and now,
in per-capita terms, are double the average for the developed countries.
In the case of Japan, if incomes increase by 2.4 per cent annually and
standards of provision of pensions and health remain in real terms
constant, the share of current income going to contributions will increase
from 10 to 35 per cent between 1980 and 2025.

Governments endlessly speak of the urgent need for reform of the
pension, welfare and health systems, but are severely constrained by the
political resistance to anything which seems likely to reduce the standard

of care for the aged – and thus become a symbol of governmental attempts to escape the social contract which, people suppose, is the attribute of citizenship.

There have been many other attempts simply to lower costs. The British, for example, unilaterally raised the retirement age of women from 60 to 65 with much empty posturing about equality of the sexes. The Japanese changed the relationship of the pension to income from gross to net pay in order to avoid a situation where, because of taxes on income, earners might receive less than untaxed pensioners. The average age at retirement was 58, even though it was officially 60, and the government proposed to raise it to 65. But brute reality was stronger than argument: worn-out workers opted for retirement (40 per cent retired below the age of 60). The Japanese also, more audaciously, proposed to move pensioners to lower-cost locations abroad – to Australia (employing Filipina nurses), Mexico and Spain. But it was difficult for the aged to be separated from their children and grand-children.

The problems are daunting, with governments on the one hand liable to be crushed by the weight of provision, and on the other boxed in by past promises to care for the aged as part of the social contract. Without a means to lower the average age of the labour force (so that contributions to the pension funds can be enhanced), an increased income from abroad, or a way to shift a proportion of the aged out of the country to cheaper locations, the crisis of public finance flowing from ageing challenges the basis of the sovereign state.

Immigrants

It is hardly surprising that at least some people started to revise their views. As we have seen, the North Americans and the Australians are inclined to consider larger numbers of primary immigrants – although limited to the skilled, when as we have argued here it is the unskilled that are more needed. In Europe, we have noted a number of *ad hoc* derestrictions.

On the margins of public debate, counter-arguments did appear. In Germany, only 4 per cent of the ethnic German inflow is over the age of 65 (compared to 21 per cent for the residential population), so that despite much hullabaloo about the flows, some people noted its salutary economic effect. Hans-Ulriche Klose, then-leader of the Social Democrats, argued that Germany needs 300,000 immigrants annually to secure a tax base capable of financing the pension demand of the aged. The Free Democrats pointed out that the 2 million non-German workers in the country contributed 10 per cent of national output and DM90 billion in taxes and contributions. Others suggest that, even on the most narrowly specific basis, 1 million new foreign workers in Germany (or Japan) will increase the tax base and the rate of growth. In the United States, the *Wall Street Journal* and some right-wing Republican Party supporters maintain that a free-market economy requires the unimpeded movement of labour. In Australia, business federations periodically argue that the country booms whenever there is a rapid increase in immigration, but without suggesting which is cause and which effect.

But these were minority voices. They did not touch the perceptions of the mass of the population, schooled from time immemorial to see foreigners in general (if not foreigners in particular) as dangerous and threatening. Few showed that the economic strength upon which sovereignty rested, maintaining the standard of living of the native-born and even keeping the aged in some measure of security, makes the developed countries increasingly dependent upon the developing. Comparative advantages are changing with a vengeance in the new world order.

7

Arguments and Evidence

Introduction

Everyone, as we noted earlier, is an expert on immigration, and imaginative theorization is everywhere current. Consider Senator Strom Thurmond (formerly of South Carolina), on

> the need to limit the rising tide of illegal aliens who, attracted by the many advantages of living or working in the United States, flood across our borders and take jobs from American workers. In many cases, those illegal entrants and their families soon become a welfare burden on our society, supported in one way or another by the American taxpayer.

Or a comparable European summary:

> [Immigrants] alter indigenous traditions and settled values. They compete for jobs and displace indigenous workers. They depress wages. They foster strikes, violence and crime. They lower the general standard of living. They take places in schools, beds in hospitals and seats on trains, depriving needy nationals of them. (reproduced in OECD, 1993)

Was any of this litany of charges valid? By sheer repetition, it gained the appearance of self-evident truth. Yet the quality of its language betrays the fantasies it purveys. Immigrants rarely catch buses or planes; they 'flood', 'flux', 'flow', 'surge', 'pour', 'drain'; they are, in the worthy senator's words, not just a 'tide' but a 'rising' one, and one flowing into areas which are 'saturated'. Water imagery appears irresistible.

Water is not an exclusive discourse. As Hintjins (1992) notes,

> Botanical and zoological analogies are common: immigrants come in hordes, swarms; immigrant communities mushroom in inner cities overnight and so on.

Or, turning up the rhetorical temperature, the language of warfare is often employed: immigrants 'invade', 'overwhelm defences'; they are a 'time bomb', 'dynamite'. Or they are diseases, cancers, threats to hygiene (requiring in the chilling phrase of the Bosnian Serbs, 'ethnic cleansing'). This is not the language of fringe extremists but of the mainstream of politics. It is as if these earnest middle-aged, middle-class European and American politicians retain some folk memory of the Golden Horde, of Goths and Vizigoths, Tatars, Huns, Turks and Celts, battering at the gates of Rome. Their discourse embodies fears that are genuine enough but apparently unrelated to the issue at stake. The same pathological approach occasionally affects elected leaders. Consider President Reagan's claim: 'The simple truth is that we've lost control of our borders; no nation can do that and survive' (1 June 1984). Yet the US government had not in the early 1980s lost control of its borders; and even if it had, why did this affect the survival of 'the nation'? Nations have survived without borders or border controls – if they had not been able to do so, there would be few nations in the world today since border controls are of such recent invention.

Some statements revert, usually unconsciously, to the argument of the Nazis: anti-Semitism only exists because of the existence and behaviour of Jews – that is, the victims are entirely responsible for their persecution. Consider a pair of sophisticated analysts making a similar point: 'anti-immigrant political movements have grown rapidly, *following accelerating inflows of immigrants* [my emphasis] from the East and from the Third World' (Russell and Teitelbaum, 1992: 5). *The Economist* (13 June 1987: 52) in an unguarded moment similarly notes 'the social tensions that significant migrations create'. The one, it seems, is a reflex of the other. It would follow, as it did in the Nazi case on the Jews, that getting rid of the immigrants ends the problem of 'social tensions'. Yet there are numerous cases of 'accelerating migration' without social tensions, and the overwhelming majority of 'social tensions' do not involve immigration. Establishment politicians who – shamefaced or not – champion anti-immigrant political movements claim they do no more than give voice to what the majority are thinking but are too frightened to say. Yet there are a legion of issues where politicians knowingly ignore what 'the majority' of people are thinking, in order, supposedly, 'to lead': politicians choose to play the race card.

Even where popular prejudice is widespread, however, it is never clear whether immigration is the real source of the problem. As Fijalkowski puts it:

> One may think of it in terms of the proverbial drop of water that makes a bucket run over, but one must not forget that the sewage and dirty water that filled the bucket in the first place was generated by the domestic life and internal activities of a society. (855)

Blaming the outsider for current discontents is an ancient dishonourable tradition, and plays an important role in protecting people who might otherwise be held to account. Consider the case of Boris Yeltsin as head of the Moscow Communist Party in the old Soviet Union. Faced, in 1990, with demonstrators deploring the shortage of housing, consumer goods, transport and health facilities in the capital, Yeltsin did not admit that this was because the government had failed to make timely provision; outsiders, he claimed, had entered the city and increased its population by 1.1 million more than planned for the year. He failed to mention that public authorities controlled migration into the city.

Grievances are real enough, and so are fears and insecurities, but it takes a certain kind of leadership to yoke these fears to outsiders as the source of all problems. The rivalries of political leaders lead to the pursuit of scapegoats. Populations, conditioned to blame foreigners for most problems, rarely resist their lead, particularly where the threats are presented as overwhelming. At one stage, '80 to 100 million' Russians and other citizens of the former Soviet Union were, according to the press, poised to sweep into Western Europe (Shevtsova, 1992), 'ten or twenty million' Mexicans and other Latin Americans into the United States. More sober accounts take longer to appear: in the case of Russia and Eastern Europe, Stefan Teloken of the United Nations wearily observes, 'despite all the prognoses and studies, we are still talking about thousands rather than millions of migrants' (*International Herald Tribune*, 23 September 1991).

At their worst, such fears swamp both courage and common sense. Any qualification is seen as foolish and complacent. Furthermore, governments are assumed to be in control (and governments are obliged to pretend that they are). Supposedly they can stop immigration. Yet the evidence suggests that, within tolerable political and social cost, they cannot. It is within this margin – between the supposed omnipotence of government and its increasingly qualified powers – that the secret life of anti-immigrant paranoia flourishes. For if government can do something, as it claims, but does not, it must be because it is corrupt, incompetent – or controlled by foreign forces. The fantasies expressed so poorly and tediously in *Mein Kampf* still lie, conceptually if not necessarily in practice, just below the surface, unexpurgated by the experience of the Nazis.

The fears make the running, and arguments often seem no more than a decorative façade for fear. Thus, invalidating the arguments may do nothing to remove the fears. The fearful disbelieve the consoling counterarguments or swiftly invent new reasons to fear. But for those with a foothold outside the domain of fear, it is useful to identify some of the primary positions and enumerate some of the evidence.

Does Poverty Push Out the Poor?

The persistence of the idea that poverty drives out unskilled migrants from developing to developed countries is extraordinary. They are, it seems, really refugees, expelled by economic pressures. Sometimes the argument is rendered more obscure by dark references to 'demographic' or 'population pressures' in a developing country – sheer numbers jostle each other out of a country. Or, on the assumption that all migrants are farmers, the decline in per-capita land holdings – due to the growth of population – pushes out the landless (regardless of the actual distribution of land holdings or the availability of other occupations).

The case has the merit that it exonerates the government in the destination country of all responsibility other than – regretfully – to resist this inflowing tide of human misery, the detritus of a ruined economy. The idea is similar in form to Washington's argument on narcotic smuggling – which arises primarily not because Americans wish to use hard drugs, but because Colombia, Peru, Mexico, Pakistan and others insist on supplying them. It follows that no reforms at home are required, only resistance to any arrivals from abroad.

Consider the confidence of a few of the commentators and responsible officials concerning migration to the United States:

> Illegal Mexican migration to the United States depends on 'push' factors more than on 'pull' factors. There has always been a big disparity between the standard of living in Mexico and the US.... Only a resumption of economic growth [in Mexico], accompanied by the creation of new jobs, will resolve the problem.
>
> Susan Kaufman Purcell, vice president, Latin American Affairs,
> America Society (US Congress, 1989a: 64)

> We are faced with the fact that some large percentage – and it could be a very large percentage – of the earth's four billion non-US inhabitants would opt, if they could, to leave where they are now and come to this country. If that happened, Lifeboat America would quickly sink.
>
> Roger Lewis, *Wall Street Journal* (30 November 1981: 23,
> cited in Simon, 1989: 49)

> [I]f Mexico's economy is depressed, waves of immigration will continue into the US, building up unmanageable problems. But if Mexico prospers, migration tapers off or at least assumes less dramatic proportions.
>
> Rudiger Dornbusch (Professor of Economics, MIT,
> in US Congress, 1990: 123)

Illegal immigration to the United States from Mexico varies inversely with the level of economic prosperity in Mexico. Thus, a higher rate of economic growth in Mexico, with improved job opportunities there, should help to alleviate the illegal immigrant problem.

Joseph A. McKinney (Professor of Economics, Baylor University, Texas, in US Congress, 1990: 145)

The shift from active demand pull recruitment to supply-push migration is everywhere evident.

Philip L. Martin (1992a: 3)

Since the late 1960s, however, 'push' factors on the Mexican side seem to have been more important [than demand in the USA]. Indeed, there is no other way to explain the large increases in illegal migration from Mexico to the US.

Wayne Cornelius (1978: 36)

These judgements often seem to be offered independent of time period – Cornelius's comment, for example, was made when Mexico's oil boom was already well under way and there was a relative labour scarcity in the country. Peter Gregory's authoritative study (1986) of the Mexican labour market demonstrates convincingly that Mexico was at or close to full employment throughout the late 1970s up to 1985. Indeed, in a recent well-documented article on Mexican rural migration to the USA in the 1980s, Cornelius and Martin themselves link it to a prodigious growth in the demand for labour as the result of a major expansion in the US output of fresh fruit and vegetables.

However, countless studies have shown – as mentioned earlier – that it is not the poor who migrate, particularly internationally where the costs and risks are high. Remittances are commonly used, not for subsistence (as they would be for the poorest groups), but for home improvements, land or vehicle purchase, education, and so on. Furthermore, for illegal migrants, the common experience (particularly in the case of Mexican–US movement) is that they move only for temporary periods to earn enough to return and stay at home.

If mere income differentials produced migration, then the number of exceptions would be extraordinary. European integration should have produced major movements from the poorer countries (Portugal, southern Spain, Greece, southern Italy) to the richer, but in fact there seems to have been a decline in movement. The countries of Southeast and East Asia ought to have been sending people to Japan at least from the 1960s, to Taiwan from the 1970s, to South Korea in the 1980s, and so on. In fact, the experience is that most poor countries produce few, if any, emigrants.

The idea that slump or economic stagnation increases emigration, whereas boom reduces it, is not borne out historically. In the Great Depression of the 1930s, European emigration to the Americas fell off sharply, only reviving with the boom after the Second World War. The demand for labour is weakest in a slump – and is not revived by a readily available supply of labour. Thus the truth seems to be the reverse of the popular wisdom: people are not generally driven to work; they are attracted to it. A boom in the destination area, not a slump in the sending area, stimulates movement. Income differences – if people know about them – may heighten their willingness to move, but they are far from being an effective cause.

The emphasis on poverty-driven expulsion often goes with a comforting but dubious thesis that there is a universal process of maturation for countries. At low levels of income, it is said, a country is forced by poverty to export workers. As economic development proceeds, capital flows into the country, employment rises and migration comes to an end; workers abroad return. 'History teaches', Philip Martin (1992a) confidently affirms, 'that development will ultimately reduce emigration which results from the search for better jobs and wages'. Poland is mentioned, where 1 million emigrants in the 1980s turned to net immigration in the 1990s. However, the most frequently mentioned case is Italy and its transition from net emigration (to Germany) in the 1960s to net immigration in the 1970s. Similar transitions took place in Sweden, Germany and Britain.

However, even a partial examination of the record raises more questions than are answered. For example, Britain was characterized by net emigration in most years between 1950 and 1980 and so was presumably then an immature economy. Ireland moved from net emigration to net immigration – but then back to net emigration in the 1980s. The decline of migration from southern Europe to the north (despite an easing of the conditions for movement) was more the result of the decline of demand (at a given wage) in the north for the types of workers produced in southern Europe than any change in southern Europe.

Saskia Sassen (1988) draws attention to the fact that in Korea and Taiwan, which experienced high rates of economic growth from the early 1960s, migration to the USA and elsewhere increased at the same time. Indeed, she goes further with the sensible thesis that economic development itself generates rising, not declining, migration. This thesis is alarming for proponents of the conventional wisdom. The remedy for illegal immigration was to have been rapid economic growth at home. As the US Commission for the Study of International Migration and Cooperative Economic Development put it: 'It is clear that in the long term, rapid economic development in the Third World would ultimately reduce the pressures for migration' (1992: 62). The Commission followed this line of thought by deploring Washington's restrictions on imports from developing countries which would reduce their capacity to develop.

In Europe, OECD's SOPEMI (1992: 11) reported the most important conclusion of a high-level 1991 conference thus: 'emigration is not the answer to the problems of underdevelopment ... a new form of economic cooperation between the North and the South needs to be established to reduce the incentive to migrate'.

There have even been attempts to assist the transition. US government officer Sally Shelton (US Congress, 1978) claimed that part of US aid to developing countries was directed toward developing labour-intensive work to discourage emigration. The European Council of Ministers urged the same course of action on its members. Abel Malutes of the EC Commission for Relations with Developing Countries formulated a scheme in 1990 for a cooperative strategy to develop joint ventures in 14 Mediterranean countries in order to dissuade emigrants from moving to the European Union (*Financial Times*, 11 March 1990). In September of the same year, the foreign ministers of Spain and Italy called for 0.25 per cent of the European Union's gross output to be devoted to industrializing the countries of the southern Mediterranean rim in exchange for a commitment by the governments there to reduce emigration to the north (*International Herald Tribune*, 25 September 1990).

However, there is a major problem with such policies. Private investment, which must inevitably play the larger role in any development project, makes poor profits out of schemes with such quixotic criteria for investment. Investors insist on their right to make their own decisions on where they will risk their capital, and that may or may not coincide with countries from which emigrants come. There are also doubts about the underlying thesis. The US Commission for the Study of International Migration and Cooperative Economic Development went a little way to meeting Saskia Sassen's point: 'While job-creating economic growth is the ultimate solution to reducing these migratory pressures, the economic development process itself tends in the short to medium term to stimulate immigration by raising expectations and enhancing people's ability to migrate.' But it was only half way – the Commissioners still envisage a world where migration ceases, where the geographical distribution of the world's population by country wonderfully coincides with the optimal location of economic activity.

If it is not poverty but development which induces movement, the more developed the world becomes, the greater the movement. If the aim of governments is to stop movement, then they have to stop economic change and the dynamic transformation of labour demand which leads to the increasing redistribution of the world's workers.

Immigrants and the Employment of the Native-born

Immigrants are conventionally charged with depriving natives of work, driving them out of whole sectors, lowering the incomes received by the low-paid, forcing down working conditions, weakening trade unions, and holding back technical progress by continuing to do jobs which ought to be eliminated. However, the underlying case for this charge – namely, that labour is homogeneous (the 'lump of labour' thesis), that the number of jobs on offer, like the supply of capital, is fixed, and that output is constant, is of doubtful validity. It leads to the false conclusion that an increase in the supply of labour drives down the average price of labour-time, reduces the employment of the more highly priced, the native born, and increases unemployment. The view is popular, even among the supposedly sophisticated. For example, *The Economist* (13 January 1987: 52) observed of Mexico that,

> 82 million people will ... be joined by over two million more this year. For the rest of the century, one million young Mexicans will enter the job market. *Not surprisingly* [emphasis added – NH], Mexico's unemployment rate has doubled since 1982.

But, given the severe economic crisis in Mexico after 1982, unemployment could have doubled even if the population had been shrinking. Unemployment is not created by an expanding supply of workers but by a declining demand – and demand is not a function of supply.

Nonetheless, a favoured argument about illegal immigration is that it deprives the native poor of work which should, by reason of their citizenship, be theirs. Consider, from the United States, the following:

> The native poor – those in marginal menial services and unskilled occupations – must ... compete directly with illegal labor. Since wetbacks [illegal Mexican workers] are willing to work more hours for lower pay and no fringe benefits, the native worker finds himself at a disadvantage and is often completely displaced from his job. Only the poor pay the costs of illegal immigration; the sectors most severely affected by the wetback flow are precisely the ones least able to wield effective political power in defence of their interests. (Portes, 1974: 45)

Or again, from the trade unions:

> [H]is [the illegal worker's] real effect, the real impact, is on lowering the wage standards. He works for less, he is in hiding, he doesn't complain. He

> doesn't demand what other workers get because he is afraid that, if he does, he will be deported. So he is here as a fearful person in hiding, and as such, most easily victimized. (US Congress, 1977: 12)

The logic of the case, if true, would seem to suggest the need to protect the native poor by legalizing illegal immigrants and thus securing the regulation of their employment. But that would be naive. The real demand is to deport the illegal worker – supposedly to make space for unskilled natives.

The evidence contradicts the claim. Borjas – rather grandly – summarizes the findings of a wealth of studies thus:

> [T]he methodological arsenal of modern econometrics cannot find a single shred of evidence that immigrants have a major adverse impact on the earnings and job opportunities of natives of the United States. (OECD, 1993: 191)

In the case of illegal immigrants, the same author (Borjas, 1990: 19) concludes that, 'despite all of the concern about the displacement effects of illegal immigration, the available evidence suggests that illegal aliens ... have a minor impact on the earnings and employment opportunities of the natives.' Other studies reach the same conclusions. Muller and Espenshade (1985) found no evidence that immigration had a significant effect on employment levels; so far as 'disadvantaged' workers are concerned, 'Black unemployment rates are not increased – if anything, they are lowered – by a rise in the proportion of Mexican immigrants in the local labor market' (99). Attonji and Card (in Abowd and Freeman, 1991) found that newer immigrants tend to compete for jobs only with earlier immigrants, but nowhere was there a sufficient concentration to have any large effects. So far as native unskilled workers were concerned, they tend to move out of immigrant-intensive industry.

Some studies suggest that immigrants have a positive effect on native employment by saving industries that would otherwise either close or relocate – for example, the shoe, vehicle, garment and fruit-processing industries in California. In the case of Los Angeles, McCarthy and Valdez (1986) found that when national employment contracted by a total of 5 per cent in the leather-goods, textile and garments, and furniture industries in the 1970s, employment in the city in these industries expanded by 50 per cent, largely, they argued, as a result of the availability of immigrant workers, legal and illegal, which increased the demand for native-born workers as owners, managers, supervisors, technicians, in the input and machine-supplying industries, and in transport. If Los Angeles had contracted in these industries at the national rate, its labour market would have had 83,000 fewer jobs. Straubhaar

(1992) similarly found that an increase in immigration in a locality correlated closely with higher participation rates and higher savings (see also Portes, in OECD, 1993: 43). These calculations omit to include the increase in native employment as a result of immigrants (including illegals) spending the incomes they earn – on housing, foodstuffs, furnishings, journeys to work, and so forth. Harrison (1983) found that this factor was important in reducing native unemployment.

Finally, in many cases, a higher proportion of immigrants than native-born workers start businesses or are self-employed, thereby adding significantly to the net demand for workers and supplies. In Britain, according to the 1991 census, 13 per cent of working whites are self-employed, compared to 15 per cent for ethnic-minorities – and 42 per cent of ethnic minority businesses employ non-immigrant workers, whereas only 34 per cent of white-owned businesses do. In the United States, the business links of ethnic minorities with their countries of origin stimulate trade and hence increase the employment of native workers – 'the larger immigrant links [with their original country] are, the less labor will lose as a result of immigration' (Gould, 1992; see also Light and Bonacich, 1988; and Min, 1989).

Since the share of the workforce which is immigrant is usually so small, its impact at this level cannot be detected very easily. The more important point is that, with unskilled workers, immigrants and natives do not compete for the same jobs; on the contrary, they tend to be complementary, so an expansion in the supply of one may open opportunities for the other. Stahl (1989: 363) makes this point about skills: 'Insofar as skilled and unskilled are complementary factors, a shortage of one will reduce the productivity of the other.' Piore (1976: 25–6) notes the skewed nature of popular perceptions in this respect:

> [T]he heavy emphasis in public policy discussions upon the competition between native and foreign workers is misplaced. Foreign workers are coming essentially to fill jobs which native workers have rejected. To the extent that these jobs are critical to the functioning of industrial society – and, while there are exceptions, the jobs taken as a group do seem to be critical – the aliens are complementary to native workers and to domestic consumption patterns. Any wholesale attempt to end migration is therefore likely to be exceedingly disruptive to the operation of society and to the welfare of a variety of interest groups within it.

The case has a broader significance than present-day America. Even in nineteenth-century America, where native and foreign-born workers seemed to possess similar attributes, in fact immigrants undertook the new jobs (building railways, canals etc.), or the old ones which the natives shunned (domestics and factory work). Once the native-born had deserted these sectors, it was inconceivable that they would return. Kayser (1971: 175) notes the same point in the European case:

> [T]he throng of foreign workers does not form a simple quantitative supple-ment, elastic by definition; on the contrary, it is for the most part an essential force in the economy because of the sectors of which it is in possession. For the main feature of immigrant manpower on the labour market is its practical irreversible specialization: it seems out of the question that, even in a period of crisis, nationals should demand again for themselves jobs which have become considered inferior and abandoned to the foreigners.

The reality does not deflect the ambitious politician and sometimes governments from linking unemployment and immigration. In the United States in the Great Depression, '[i]n the manner of a crusade, the idea was promulgated that aliens were holding down high paying jobs and that by giving these jobs to Americans, the depression could be cured' (Martinez, 1976: 340). The campaign was directed primarily against Mexicans; many left or were driven out, so that the Mexican-born population fell from 639,000 in 1930 to 377,000 in 1940. Despite this, the year 1940 saw the second highest level of unemployment ever recorded in the country (Grebler, 1965: 26). In fact, the expulsion of immigrants, in so far as it reduced the complementary supports for native employment, deepened the slump – just as the reduction of imports to the United States did.

The same spurious connection does good service in modern times. In the late 1970s, the French government threatened the residential status of half a million Algerians and Africans, supposedly to reduce French unemployment. A contemporary government report showed that, since in general immigrants and natives did not compete for work, for every 150,000 immigrant departures only 13,000 jobs for natives would become available. The study did not assess the significant in-crease in native unemployment as a result of the domestic market for goods contracting by the demands of 150,000 consumers.

In 1976 the commissioner for the US government's famous INS (Immigration and Naturalization Service), General L.F. Chapman Jr, reported that 1.5 million illegal immigrants had been arrested in the preceding two years in the 16 largest cities. Furthermore, he argued, if the recruitment of illegal workers could be controlled, 'we could quickly open at least one million jobs for unemployed Americans' (US Congress, 1977). A year later, Villalpondo (1977: 59) reported two experiments to test the thesis that removing illegal immigrants would open job oppor-tunities for the native-born:

1. 2154 illegal immigrants were expelled from California. However, no natives could be found to replace them, partly because some of the employers were paying wages below the legal minimum, but more importantly because the jobs were extremely unattractive, arduous and involved long hours.

2. In April 1976 in San Diego, 340 illegal workers in hotel maintenance, food processing and laundries were deported; the jobs were filled, not from the local unemployed who did not apply, but from daily commuters from Mexico.

This disheartening experience for advocates of the interchangeability of workers, however, did not deflect the government from returning to the same theme whenever unemployment became a political issue. In the recession of the early 1980s, the Reagan administration launched a drive to arrest illegal immigrants (in April 1982) in nine major cities. There were 6000 arrests to 'free' jobs for unemployed Americans. Americans did indeed apply for the jobs, but few pursued the matter when they discovered their 'irreversible specialization' – that is, employers offered the minimum wage (then $3.35 per hour) for a ten-hour shift of heavy and dirty work. The illegals returned to their jobs.

Approaching the issue from a different angle, there are examples of a major increase in labour supply without perceptible long-term effects on the employment situation. Thus, on the occasion of Algerian independence (March 1962), some 900,000 *pieds noirs* (French nationals of former French Algeria) returned to France. By December, the unemployment rate in the areas where the refugees settled peaked at 20 per cent, but was 6 per cent one year later, and 4 per cent in the following year (Layard et al., 1991: 47). When 8 million ethnic Germans arrived in Germany between 1945 and 1950, the national unemployment rate peaked at 10.5 per cent, but fell to 2 per cent by the mid-1950s. With the independence of Portugal's African possessions, the number of returning colonial settlers (in 1977–78) reached some 5 per cent of Portugal's population, yet they were quickly absorbed, despite a recession in the second half of the 1970s (OECD, 1993: 119).

Finally, Card (1990) has shown that the migration of 125,000 Cubans to Miami in 1980 (equal to 7 per cent of the Miami labour market) had no apparent short-term effect on unemployment or wage levels. In the medium term, the half million immigrants (since 1959) had a remarkable effect in saving the city from decline and turning it into a major centre of Latin American trade, investment and tourism. In all these cases it seems that the inflow of assets accompanying the migrants expanded market demand faster than the inflow of workers.

Still the idea persists that increasing numbers of workers leads to unemployment. Yet immigration has never added to the labour force anything like the numbers from domestic sources. Thus, the postwar baby boom in the United States (1945–60) led to some 4 million extra workers entering work in the late 1960s and early 1970s, a figure well over four times the number of immigrant arrivals of those years. Furthermore, the participation rate for women increased between 1960 and 1980, adding a further 8.5 million workers to the American labour force without leading to unemployment. It is solely because immigrants are foreigners that they are made the target of resentments concerning the business cycle.

If the direct effect of immigration on employment and unemployment appears negligible or so small as to be undetectable (and the indirect effect, positive), do immigrants drive down wage levels? This is the instinctive reaction of trade unionists. For example, the representative of the US union AFL-CIO addressed a US congressional committee (cited Otero, 1988: 39) in these terms:

> [T]he AFL-CIO opposes any program that would permit the importation of foreign labor to undercut US wages and working conditions ... we don't favour the new levels of legal immigration.

The idea is probably as old as migration itself, yet in the US context there is again a wealth of evidence that, at best, encourages scepticism. The US Department of Labor (1989) surveyed the many studies of the wage impact of immigration, and found that there was no detectable effect on native-born workers. There was sometimes an effect upon other immigrants or their children, but even this was very small and usually outweighed by the expansion in native employment as a result of immigrant expenditure.

Smith and Newman (1977) found that wages on the US border with Mexico – where there were larger numbers of Mexican-born workers available – were one-fifth below areas further north, but if allowance was made for differences in the local cost of living, the gap was reduced to 8 per cent (and this was further cut if the higher costs of the cities in comparison to small border towns were allowed for). In any case, the differences in regional incomes could not be attributed to differences in the source of labour. De Freitas and Marshall (1983) detected a statistically significant negative impact due to immigration on the rate of growth of hourly earnings in manufacturing in US cities, but again it was very small even when immigration was very large. De Freitas (1986) on the basis of a 1980 census sample found that South American immigrants had no negative earnings effects except possibly on the earnings of black women, but this was very slight. There was, however, a correlation with an *increase* in white male earnings. Bean, Lowell and Taylor (1988) tried to assess the effects of illegal immigration on poor groups in the labour markets of the southwest of the United States, and concluded that '[t]he concern that undocumented immigration may be depressing the earnings of native born workers does not appear to be borne out by these results' (15). Borjas (OECD, 1993: 104) summarized the findings of nine studies of American cities and found that, where immigration was large, native wages were very slightly lower – an increase in immigration of 10 per cent seemed to be related to a reduction in native wages by two- to three-tenths of 1 per cent.

On the other hand, there is some evidence – as seen from the (1986) study mentioned earlier by McCarthy and Valdez – that illegal immigration can increase both the employment and incomes of native-born workers. On the basis of an overwhelming body of evidence, Abowd and Freeman (1991: 17) conclude that the United States can more easily absorb immigrants who stimulate the domestic economy than imports, which supposedly do not (although, in so far as imports are inputs to domestic output and exports, they may also stimulate domestic production).

Even if the net effect of migration is positive, there are still people who lose their jobs. But this is even more true in the ordinary evolution of economies without immigration. Economies are in continuous flux, with jobs turning over, and immigration plays a very marginal role in this process of change. However, if, as a worker, you are part of the 'negative effects', it is little comfort to know that society as a whole has gained. On the other hand, the gain of society certainly justifies a demand for proper compensation for the damage – short of keeping unwanted jobs alive at the cost of everybody else.

In sum, the overall impact of immigration appears to be associated with increasing incomes for the native-born – as the President's Council of Economic Advisers concluded in 1986:

> [T]he net effect of an increase in the labour supply due to immigration is to increase the aggregate income of the native born population.

The conclusion from these American studies has been repeated elsewhere – for example, in Canada by Swan and others (1991); in Australia by Nevile (1991), McMahon (1993) and Withers (1987); and in New Zealand by Poot (1992).

A broader argument blames unskilled immigration for slowing down the technical modernization of the economy. Unskilled immigrants, it is said, keep alive industries which should die – an argument that contradicts those who accuse immigrants of stealing jobs which rightfully belong to poor natives. The case is used also in relation to domestic migration. For example, in the old Soviet Union, *Trud* (the trade-union daily newspaper) attacked the practice of allowing temporary workers into Moscow as follows:

> *Limitchiks* [temporary residence permits] are also convenient for the negligent economic planner. Why should he bother about liquidating heavy and dangerous technology or worry about improving the living and working conditions of workers if it is easy to get people from out of town to fill unpopular jobs? (*Financial Times*, 21 January 1987)

Coleman (1992: 456), in the European context, puts the issue bluntly: 'The availability of cheap labour impedes modernization of the economy and the substitution of capital for the less skilled labour.' Suzanne Payne (1974) also argues that large-scale immigration reduces the rate of growth of productivity by delaying the introduction of labour-saving devices. Examples are offered – in the German garment industry and coalmining – to suggest that cheap foreign labour made possible expansion without investment in the technical upgrading of the industry. As we have seen, the Singapore government was sufficiently taken with these arguments to seek to drive up labour costs in order to purge the city of low-skilled workers.

Finally, Martin (1993a: 2) suggests that, in so far as declining labour-intensive industries are kept alive by the availability of cheap labour, this gives employers the basis for demanding protection against imports. Thus, it seems, the poor immigrant obstructs the growth of free trade and – especially if illegal – has become the source of technical decline. The foreign worker is a narcotic that, like Shakespeare's Cleopatra, increases the desire even in satisfying it – but ultimately produces disaster.

Without immigrants, the general case implies, employers would be obliged to pay higher wages and to increase investment in labour-saving innovations. The argument is plausible only if employers are free to determine wages and to choose between combinations of capital and labour without reference to markets at large. Again, neither evidence nor theory suggests employers have this freedom, particularly in those sectors employing most unskilled workers. Furthermore, Kuhn (1974) shows that no reduction in capital investment takes place where labour is relatively abundant – that is, the abundance or scarcity of workers does not determine the nature of production, but rather market demand.

In practice, the jobs in question are usually not susceptible to mechanization or to significant wage increases, let alone what some call 'job enrichment'. If labour is not available at an appropriate price, firms go out of business and, in so far as it is feasible, imports replace their former output. If the jobs that disappear are the precondition for other employment, the reduction can have knock-on effects in sectors which employ the native-born. Thus, the idea that controlling immigration can, as the Singapore government tried to do, force employers into technical change is almost certainly wrong, particularly in an open economy where domestic employers are governed by the imperatives of external markets.

The alternative case is by now familiar. Other things being equal, immigrants respond to the demand for labour, filling specialized roles in the economy which are no longer being manned by native-born workers. In doing so, they make possible expanded employment and incomes for the native-born both where they work and in other related activities. They expand demand, and allow economies of scale and greater capacity utilization – that is, they have the same disproportionate effects on output as any increase in the population (Chenery, 1960; Clark, 1967: 265). The position is summarized in a 1986 statement by Beryl Sprinkel, then chairman of the US President's Council of Economic Advisers. Justifying his opposition to financial sanctions on employers who hired illegal immigrants, Sprinkel said:

> To the extent that sanctions are effective in banning illegal aliens from employment, aggregate income and output will also be reduced. (*The Economist*, 1 February 1986: 341)

The same issues arise in many discussions of immigration. Take, for example, the British parliamentary consideration of whether British passports should be extended to people in Hong Kong in the approach to the 1997 return of the city to China. The *Financial Times* (21 December 1989) meditated:

> A more liberal immigration policy would almost certainly be in the best interests of the country [Britain], but the fact is that no government, Conservative or Labour, could contemplate presenting to parliament any proposals to issue passports to the entire Hong Kong population.

Samuel Brittain of the same newspaper reflected that the numbers involved were small – equal to 5.6 per cent of the British population (substantially less than the 'ethnic Germans' being admitted to Germany), and if entry were staggered over eight years, the population increase in Britain could be reduced to 0.7 per cent annually (or close to the rates of natural increase in developed countries). In terms of the skills involved, the Hong Kong labour force was concentrated in some of the sectors of greatest scarcity in Britain, with a high proportion in the younger age groups and with high levels of education. They were likely to expand the British economy, increase the number of jobs for the native-born, as well as government revenue and spending capacities; they could be used as a powerful force to regenerate the relatively backward north of the country. Why did the Conservative government not rush to capture such a desirable population? 'It would be kinder not to speculate, but the reasons can have little to do with Britain's economic performance' (ibid., 10 August 1989).

The Pursuit of National Homogeneity

At least some figures can be produced to discipline the argument on wages and employment. But the search for, or the defence of, a social homogeneity, a national identity or common set of values allows anyone to claim anything, with scarcely a token nod at the need for evidence. Culture allows people to escape from the rocky terrain of what passes for the facts into whatever imagination suggests. It also permits prejudice free rein. Consider a sample of opinions:

> [One] reason we are beset with conflict is that since 1965 a flood tide of immigration has rolled in from the Third World, legal and illegal, and our institutions of assimilation – public schools, popular culture, churches – disintegrated.
>
> Patrick Buchanan, a candidate for the Republican presidential nomination in 1991 (*Far Eastern Economic Review*, 26 March 1992: 31)

> It is with grave concern that we observe the infiltration of the German nation by million-fold waves of foreigners and their families, the infiltration of our language, our culture and our national characteristics by foreign influences.
>
> Biologically and cybernetically, nations are living streams of a higher order, with different systemic qualities that are transmitted genetically and by tradition. The integration of large masses of nonGerman foreigners and the preservation of our nation thus cannot be achieved simultaneously; it will lead to the well-known ethnic catastrophe of multi-cultural societies.
>
> An 'association of German professors' in 1982
> (*Population and Development Review*, vol. viii, no. 3, 1982: 636–7)

> Japan's racial homogeneity has helped us become a more 'intelligent society' than the United States, where there are blacks, Mexicans and Puerto Ricans and the level is still quite low.
>
> The then Japanese Prime Minister Nakasone in 1986
> (*Wall Street Journal*, 13 November 1986)

The fears and fantasies attached to cultural differences are quite extraordinary. Yet supposedly sober commentators also pay deference to the incredible as if it were self-evidently true (even down to the silliness of Japan's 'racial homogeneity', whatever that might mean, or the German pseudo-scientific humbug).

What are these 'cultures' or values so vulnerable to subversion? Why is the discussion apparently dominated by people of such peculiar cultural insecurity? Why is it that *culture* is the issue in dispute, when social conflict, without cultural differences, is everywhere apparent? In this discussion, no one is under an obligation to identify what, out of the extraordinary heterogeneity of real society, *the* culture is supposed to be. To define common elements, we would have to start from culture as a continually changing bundle of practices and beliefs, differentiated by class, origin, locality, language and dialect, religion and inheritance and no doubt many other things. In practice, we take heterogeneity for granted: it has no inevitable implications for conflict. People travel the world and even settle in other countries for their lifetimes without feeling their 'culture' is under threat – indeed, in an important sense, we are unable to shed the cultures in which we grew up, regardless of our wishes.

It seems that the terms – culture, values, identity – refer to something else, something more powerful. Their very vagueness allows the unscrupulous to trade on prejudice, even to lie – as when Mrs Thatcher, as we noted earlier, found it 'understandable' that British people would feel they were 'rather swamped by people of a different culture' when, at the time, just four people in every one hundred in Britain were 'from the New Commonwealth' (the local euphemism for black).

As we have seen, some governments endeavour to take the term 'culture' more seriously as a test of membership of the nation. The German government administers a detailed questionnaire to establish the rightfulness of 'ethnic German' claims. But the definition of German culture is not based upon what those who are German do, but upon one selection of the past. It is inevitably arbitrary and personal, and, since cultures are continually changing, always out of date. Indeed, the act of defining a culture is designed to exclude; it is a pre-emptive strike in the struggle for power, not the summary of the shared practices of a people.

Being undefined, culture or values cannot be employed to identify who rightly belongs to the citizenry and who should be excluded. In practice, so far, the United States has eschewed such an approach, allowing the ordinary processes of social change to continue to change what is an 'American'. Sooner or later, the Europeans and the Japanese will be obliged to learn the same flexibility – if the employment and incomes of their citizens are to grow.

An Inferior People?

If poverty is supposed to drive people to emigrate, then immigrants – at least those in unskilled occupations – are seen as poor. All the contempt of class society comes to be attached to them. As we saw earlier, this is a continuing phenomenon – in a country of traditional immigration like the United States, each new generation of immigrants is seen as inferior to its predecessor. The 1907 Dillinger Commission took 42 volumes to demonstrate the declining quality of immigrants, and drew up a Dictionary of Races to prove it. Yet, historically, the 'quality' of immigrants is almost inevitably improving – those moving from Mexico to the United States today are certainly much better educated than the Europeans who arrived in the nineteenth century.

Immigrants tend to be bunched at either end of the skill/education spectrum (in terms of the status ranking of the destination society). But even at the lowest end, by the standards of the sending society, they are far from 'the wretched refuse' of foreign countries (in the phrase on the base of the Statue of Liberty, from the poem by Emma Lazarus). The poor only rarely gather the resources to migrate any distance. Most often they are not among the poor even in the destination society. This has, contrary to popular perceptions, always been broadly true – as Peter Hill (1975: 48) notes for nineteenth-century America:

> [A]lmost all the empirical evidence leads one to a conclusion in direct opposition to that reached in most of the historical literature ... immigrants, instead of being an underpaid, exploited group, generally held an economic position that compared very favourably to that of the native-born members of the society.

Yet the myth persists even among those with claims to expertise in migration. For example, Thomas Straubhaar (1992: 462) speaks of the 'invasion of the poor [which] challenges Western Europe'. It is allied to the idea of an invasion by the poor of the world sweeping away the civilization of the rich. But here we retreat again into the fantasy where fears become disconnected from reality. There are no modern cases where foreigners, poor or otherwise, have been able peacefully to subvert the modern state (even if 'foreigners' had any common interest in doing so).

Do Immigrants Live on Welfare?

A favoured argument is that immigrants draw disproportionately on welfare services, without matching contribution; the mass of the native-born therefore subsidize them. Senator Thurmond repeats this in the statement at the beginning of this chapter, and Leonard Chapman, as then-head of the US government's INS, repeats the allegation with reference to illegal immigrants: 'We spend millions every month supporting people who are not supposed to be here' (US Congress, 1977).

Successive governors of particular American states make the same charge as the basis for demanding subventions from federal sources. The same proposition occurs in Europe and in Japan – thus, a Japanese Labour Ministry study in late 1990 argues that the cost of housing, training and other social benefits is greater than the contributions made by immigrants, particularly since immigrant labour, it said, depresses Japanese wages and working conditions (*Financial Times*, 25 January 1991). The accusation strikes at the essence of the idea of a social contract between government and people. Supposedly, the prerogative of citizenship is that citizens in need should be cared for by the state. It is, in this view, politically outrageous that non-citizens should gain access to the same privileges without being obliged to share the same responsibilities.

However, the evidence suggests otherwise. The primary motive for migration is to earn, so that in general, migrants are unwilling to be unemployed for any length of time – and more willing than the natives to accept a reduction in pay by changing jobs or moving elsewhere in search of work. This in turn suggests a low dependence on unemployment support. For other social provisions, the demographic character of immigrants (age, relatively low number of disabled, sick, etc.) implies a low take-up rate; those drawing most on social services are the very young, the aged, female-headed households, the disabled, and so on. Thus, in theory, immigrants would seem to be less likely to draw on social provisions than the average (which includes all these special groups).

Furthermore, in response to popular suspicions, governments often take special measures to prevent immigrants – or at least illegal ones – from drawing on social funds. In the United States, illegals were excluded from major federal public-assistance programmes in 1971 (Supplementary Security Income for the Aged, Blind and Disabled; Aid to Families with Dependent Children; Medicaid; Food Stamp Programmes etc.). Efforts were also made to exclude them from State-level programmes. At the same time, it was notorious that illegal immigrants generally avoided applying for public programmes lest they be identified and deported.

Numerous studies confirm this conclusion. North and Houston (1976) found that, in the case of illegal immigrants to the United States, a majority paid direct taxes to finance public-support programmes, but were rare users of tax-supported programmes (a conclusion reiterated in the US Congress (1978: 549–51). In the case of Caribbean migration to Britain, Jones and Smith (1970: 104) found that in the 1960s few immigrants drew retirement pensions (one of the largest items in the national insurance and benefit systems), and their use of other provisions was slightly lower than that of the native-born. In California, McCarthy and Valdez (1986) found that under 5 per cent of Mexican immigrants received any assistance from public welfare services (that is, well below all other low-income groups). In all sectors, except education, they paid more than they received; however, the authors also mentioned that their sample underenumerated single Mexicans, so the contributions to education may have been higher than their estimates suggest. Simon (1989: 115–23) found considerable variation in immigrant use of different social programmes, but generally the more recent the immigrant, the less they benefited. Even up to the age of retirement, immigrants drew less than the natives, so that the system operated to transfer resources from immigrants to natives (the transfer was greatest for illegal immigrants who drew least). However, as Freeman notes (1986: 52), it is not always clear what should be included in assessing social provisions, so the evidence is less than conclusive.

The distribution of American fiscal revenues and expenditures does nevertheless create a problem so far as illegal immigrants are concerned. A US Federal Department of Labor study of illegal immigrants in the early 1980s (*The Economist*, 8 May 1982: 58) estimated that 73 per cent had income taxes deducted from their pay, and 77 per cent paid social-security taxes, but only 0.5 per cent received welfare benefits. The lion's share of the payments are made to Washington, whereas most of the costs are born by the local state. In Los Angeles, it seems that large immigrant families call on the educational system to a far greater extent than is covered by their local contributions (a point confirmed by Weintraub and Cardenas, 1984). This is the basis for state claims for compensation from the federal budget.

However, with time, the difference between the immigrant and the native-born disappears. Immigrants acquire families with young children and some retire. Second-generation immigrants may, as we have seen in Europe, have higher than average rates of unemployment. Borjas and Trejo (1991) also relate the drawing of welfare to the demographic character of immigrants – thus, while for adult workers benefits may be minimal, in so far as immigration controls are skewed in favour of family reunification with a larger number of children and old people, there will tend to be a greater call on welfare provisions. There seems also to be a variation according to country of origin. While the evidence does not show immigrants as net beneficiaries, the surplus that the natives used to gain from the contributions of immigrants in the past has tended to decline (Borjas and Trejo, 1990).

Overall, then, despite the complexities and qualifications, it seems that the evidence suggests immigrants are not net beneficiaries from most social welfare programmes. In any case, their status under welfare schemes does not settle their net economic contribution. That is shown only in conjunction with the product of their work. As Böhning (1974) concludes on European experience:

> There is a lot of talk about the 'problems caused by migrants' – that it costs money to house them, to school their children etc. – as though these problems would not arise if the labour were of national rather than foreign origin.... If there were no migrants, there would be few of the problems attributed to them; but there would also be fewer of the goods they provide which enhance the welfare and comfort of all residents.

Do Immigrants Damage the Host Society?

The continuing structural change of the economies of developed countries confuses perceptions of the role of immigrant workers, reversing cause and effect. Because immigrants initially take work at incomes and in conditions that most natives shun, it is assumed they are driving native workers out. Furthermore, being desperate for work, they supposedly allow employers to drive down wages and reduce working conditions. In the same way, immigrants are accused of reducing the quality of the housing stock into which they move, when in fact, as the housing stock deteriorates (and native families move out), low-income immigrants can afford to move in (and in practice often make radical improvements in the condition of the housing stock). Economic change in our times certainly gives rise to increasing instability and insecurity – the problem is genuine and painful enough – but immigrants have no causal role in this change. They are as much, or even more so, victims of processes outside their control.

There are a variety of other charges, not all of which are easy to specify. One, for example, is that foreign workers send part of their pay abroad to their families, and this constitutes a drain on the domestic economy. In the 1970s, INS Commissioner Chapman repeated the charge in relation to illegal immigrants, who, he said, 'send about $3 billion each year out of the country (US Congress, 1977: 7; see also Shelton in US Congress, 1978: 31). The argument makes no more sense than that against imports (which likewise require money to be sent abroad). Immigrants would not be employed if there were no net benefit to the employer; the gains to the country must, therefore, be greater than any outflow of remittances.

Immigrants are also accused, as we have seen, of carrying diseases, being unhygienic or corrupt, causing crime, and so forth. For illegal immigrants, the case is a moral one; a US 1981 select committee argues that 'illegality breeds illegality', although it is not clear why (in practice, illegal immigrants avoid illegal acts lest they lead to their detection and expulsion):

> It is this undermining of national values that poses the greatest threat to US society, not the displacement of US workers or use of social services by undocumented workers. (US Congress, 1983: 560)

For a country that has bequeathed the world one of the richest traditions of criminal gangs, it is bizarre to see any distinctive contribution in this respect by the poor Mexican farmworker. Furthermore, a report for the select committee (by Steinberg: 44) found no evidence of a higher rate of crime by immigrants. Popular perceptions have been influenced by immigrant gangs – for example, the New York Colombians or Miami Cuban narcotics dealers. But these were no more representative of Colombians or Cubans in the United States than Bonnie and Clyde are representative of all native-born Americans.

In Europe, crime rates among immigrant groups tend to be lower than those among the natives. For Italians, Greeks, Spaniards and Turks in Germany in the 1970s, the level of crime was under half that for the German-born (Bourguignon et al., 1977: 151). On the other hand, the association of illegal immigration with the gangsters of Japan, the Yakuza, leads to popular opinion blaming the luckless foreigners for the sins of their brokers.

The environmental movement has produced, on the margins, a different set of arguments. Increasing the population from immigration goes beyond the 'natural carrying capacity' of local natural resources. Members of the Australian Green movement have suggested that the shortage of water and fertile land makes it necessary to curb immigration. The case is old prejudice in new clothes. To escape the charge it would be necessary to call for the removal of Australians too, if 'carrying capacity' was exceeded. Where the argument is most popular – in Australia and the United States – population densities are very low compared to the rest of the world (Japan, with 125 million people, is smaller than Montana), so there is far to go before the threat, if such it is, becomes real. In fact, as the population of the world has grown, efforts to protect the environment have increased as well, so that today the quality of food, water and air is purer in most of the world than ever before (a purity correlated not with the numbers of people, but with the wealth of society). As Australian Senator Ray responded to Green activists:

> All our ecological disasters occurred when we had only six or seven million people. You protect the environment through growth. (*The Economist*, 10 March 1980)

Finally, there is an argument that is not anti-immigrant as such, but rather expresses apprehension about the gullibility of the majority population. Continued immigration, it is said, gives a greater opportunity to the extreme right and racists to threaten the status quo. This is not because the extreme right has, in present circumstances, any opportunity to come to power, but rather because it has a handle on the fears of the population, and in this way pushes the Establishment to the right. As we have seen, this has been a recurrent problem in virtually all developed countries – as the surges of hysteria on immigration control illustrate. Few have the courage to risk defending a minority.

However, the argument is mistaken. Immigration is going to be increasingly important in sustaining the livelihood of the native majority; if the majority is mistaken in its opinions, the sooner the argument is in the public domain the better for the majority. The fight is inevitable, and to avoid it is to add aid and comfort to those forces that, if successful, would destroy all that is best in modern society.

Do Emigrants Damage the Sending Society?

There are several arguments here, but two have particular appeal for people on the political left or of liberal persuasion. The first is that emigration removes the domestic pressure in the home society for reform. Briggs (1984: 144), in the United States, puts it in this way:

> By encouraging emigration, Mexico's leaders have been able to avoid making internal changes that are needed to eliminate political corruption, to improve the distribution of the nation's income and to develop a comprehensive job creation strategy.

On illegal workers, Charles Knapp (Special Assistant to the Secretary of Labor, US Congress, 1978: 21) repeats the point: '[I]llegal immigration acts as a safety valve for the employment problems of sending countries.' The case is a political variant on the 'push' thesis examined earlier, but it has other elements. The metaphor of a 'safety valve' is dubious: do Mexican villagers in Michoacán or Turkish small-town craftsmen exercise such detectable pressure upon their respective governments as to require their emigration? Indeed, is there any connection between ending emigration and domestic reform? Have the developed countries followed Briggs's agenda?

An alternative argument stresses the supposed economically deleterious effects of emigration on the home country in terms of the loss of skilled labour and the 'brain drain'. Bhagwati in the 1970s endeavoured to assess the costs to developing countries of the loss of human capital. Böhning and Maillat (1974: 93) also argue that immigrant labour in a developed country cheapens its exports and therefore intensifies competition with the exports of the home economy:

> Manufactured exports ... continue to draw a disproportionate benefit from the employment of foreigners in terms of export prices.... From the viewpoint of the labour sending country, this means that it suffers from a permanent disadvantage which derives from its own emigration. In other words, the beneficial effects of labour import under conditions of external turnover widen the competitive gap between the sending country and the receiving country.

However, as argued earlier, the economic evaluation of migration is equivocal. Is it an unrequited transfer of human capital from the sending to the receiving country? Is it a gaining of access to the high-productivity conditions of the destination country without meeting the costs of reproduction? Or should we regard the costs of reproduction (the human capital costs) as historic or sunk costs, with no bearing on current issues – the gain at the destination does not indicate a loss at the sending point? The argument about competing *countries* – or governments – leads inevitably to arbitrary conclusions. Alternatively, it might be argued that to move workers from areas of low to areas of high productivity represents a gain for the world economy even if one country loses. Or we can consider the issue in terms of individual welfare, refusing to accept that governmental interests should be privileged.

So far as the argument of Böhning and Maillat is concerned, it is most unlikely that the two countries are in competition. It is more likely that the sending country will import capital goods from the destination country, capital goods made cheaper by the use of immigrant labour – and perhaps paid for out of remittances.

At its worst, the argument about damaging the sending society is hypocrisy. The answer proposed for the poverty of the poorer country is not to allow its citizens access to the means to be more productive, but to exclude them altogether. In empirical terms, as we have seen, while the short-term effects of emigration may be perceptible, the medium-term ones appear slight. An increase in the relative scarcity of particular workers has had a beneficial effect in raising incomes, as suggested for the Philippines by Golafant (cited in Amjad, 1989). The effects are even more beneficial when there is local overproduction of particular skills, leading, as in parts of India, to high levels of graduate unemployment. The return stream of remittances often represents for the country concerned a significant strengthening of the balance of payments – and a much enhanced income compared to what the emigrant would have earned by staying at home.

Emigration is neither for the individual nor for the country what Tapinos (OECD, 1993: 175) calls 'a solution of despair, an individual response to the impossibility of national development'. On the contrary, it is one of the most successful mechanisms for redistributing the world's income in favour of poorer countries and for making possible much higher productivity for the workers concerned.

Conclusions

The arguments against immigration are elaborate and not easily refuted. Furthermore, the grounds are often swiftly changed, for the arguments are not always what the case is about. There is a supposedly 'hard-nosed' case for rejecting immigration, especially that of the unskilled (and especially the illegal migrants), and there are liberal arguments which are supposedly directed to protecting oppressed minorities – whether the native poor or the migrants themselves – or the interests of poor countries. But whatever the broader stance, all the arguments end up denying migrants access to the means to raise their own and the world's productivity.

The specific arguments do not matter in the general political debate because the case is not so much about whether migration damages the interests of some or all. Capitalism is a system of change, so that regardless of whether migration takes place or not, there are continually losers. The real question is whether migration increases significantly the number of losers. The weight of evidence suggests it does not. If we see the inexorable decline of employment in the developed countries in, say, the garment and textile industry, or in agriculture through the ordinary operation of markets, the direct impact of migration is, at most, trivial. Indirectly, the effect has been to expand the overall economy – and therefore the incomes and employment of the natives in developed countries.

The real case is not here. That is about the betrayal of the social contract by the state, about sovereignty and the powerful old distinction between citizen and noncitizen. In the old order, it is supposed, society was based upon trust – among the mass, that their ultimate interests would be honoured as against those of outsiders. Now not only do immigrants seem to threaten this position, but the incomes and employment of the poorest natives have declined over two decades, and governments themselves are busily reforming the structure of social provision to reduce costs. It is hardly surprising that the case against immigration sometimes takes on a tone of tragic betrayal, of high treason. Those who laboured long and loyally in the lord's vineyard, who feel they made great sacrifices uncomplainingly for so long – and, after all, two world wars are not inconsiderable sacrifices – are now deserted in favour of outsiders. Migration becomes the symbol of the internationalization of the economy, and the supposed source of all the problems generated by that process. The fact that immigrants do the worst work is unseen in comparison with their competition for scarce resources – of housing, schooling, health facilities.

Thus the emotional logic of the case against immigration is far more powerful than any of the specific arguments suggest – and citing evidence and logic against the arguments does not touch the well-springs of the emotions. Fortunately, the emotional reaction is relatively rare – confined to a sudden sweeping vote for a racist candidate, a momentary riot – and for much of the time the economic benefits loom larger.

Yet while the transition to a fully open international economy takes place, the dangers are real enough. Society is periodically swept by gusts of insecurity, gusts which are related to real material crises in the world at large. Each country produces ambitious and hungry contenders for power who can link current crisis with the old conditioned reflex of hostility to foreigners making their fortune. The contenders do not have to be as extreme as Adolf Hitler, who did something similar.

History does not repeat itself, but that should not encourage complacency. The developed world remains vulnerable to the adventurer who trades upon the ancient hatred of the foreigner to lever himself or herself into power. Governments themselves exploit precisely the same prejudice in order to avoid the real problems of material scarcity – and the media generally collude in this – which is why society remains vulnerable.

The prejudice is not just about foreigners. It is also about unskilled workers, the mass of people at the base of the occupational hierarchy who, largely unseen and unthanked, make it possible for the rest to work. After all, the United States employs one and a half times as many janitors as lawyers, accountants, investment bankers, stockbrokers and computer programmers put together. Part of the counterargument must include a recognition that the citizens of the developed countries depend for their livelihood and their future on the labour both of foreigners, some of them at home, most of them abroad, and on the unskilled natives.

Furthermore, the illusion that there are options freely available is false. National economies can be well or badly steered by governments, but not planned in detail, especially now with global integration. The factors of production are not subject to much intersubstitution, particularly in conditions of open competition. As a result, the discussion of alternatives to immigration – the substitution of imports; of capital for labour; of investment in the home countries of immigrants to discourage emigration (is there a shred of evidence that such a policy has ever worked?); the search to expand the utilization of the existing labour force – has a utopian character. It is not within the power of government, in an open world system, to make such choices and implement them.

On the other hand, the cost of immigration controls is high. Leaving aside the gains which might accrue in terms of higher growth – and as we have seen, Hamilton and Whalley (1984) suggest a possible doubling in world output as the result of an end to all migration controls – the immediate cost is not inconsiderable, and it is rising.

Only rarely does a little common sense break through, as when, for example, the *Wall Street Journal* (7 May 1985) observes wryly that 'Throughout the south east [of the United States], the idea of life without illegal immigration is as alarming as the idea of life without the rays of the sun.' Or when *The Economist* (17 August 1991: 12) urges on Europe's statesmen 'their duty ... to support a general good that costs a particular discomfort' and urges an increase in legal immigration in order to eliminate illegal movements and asylum-jumping. Yet in both cases, it is business which presses the case, so automatically it is assumed to be solely in the interests of employers. Where is the brave and bold argument that the incomes and jobs of the mass of people depend upon expanding the labour supply? The left, so often hiding in its slit trench, gazing in fear at the foreigner, has grown accustomed to its alignment with the state, so there are few to argue the case for a popular and material internationalism.

8

The Freedom to Move

Introduction

In 1944, Karl Polyani wrote that the history of capitalism from the late eighteenth to the third quarter of the nineteenth century was a long-drawn-out struggle to subordinate society to a completely self-regulating market. In his view, the simultaneously absurd and oppressive character of this endeavour was embodied in the attempt to make land and labour simply marketable commodities. However, from the depression of the years 1873–86, he saw a sustained and successful campaign to reverse this process and establish national (or state) regulation of land and labour as well as of finance and trade. In the case of labour, this process was embodied in the creation of strong trade unions which sought to regulate labour markets and, in alliance with the government, to regulate hours and conditions of work, and create measures of popular welfare, education and health.

From the vantage point of 1944, the achievements seemed impressive. The trade unions had moved from the status of barely tolerated marginal organizations to that of great corporations of state. With the settlement of the Second World War, many governments established more comprehensive systems of welfare than ever before, in effect guaranteeing a minimum level of livelihood for all.

Yet half a century later, what then seemed permanent accomplishments, now appear as temporary victories. And those victories were only the by-product of a larger process in which the Great Powers settled their domestic class struggles in order the better to fight each other. The other side of the coin to Polyani's triumphs of 1944 was, not growing social sanity, but total war. What we have called the fully 'socialized state', in which the mass of inhabitants became citizens and, in return for complete loyalty to the state, were accorded both consultative and welfare rights – a kind of social contract – now appears as a temporary phase in the evolution of the system. It is as if world capitalism needed a period of national incubation, and that for nearly a century up to about 1960 this was indeed what occurred – with all the attendant horrors of war implied by the unification of capital and the state within a system of competitive Great Powers.

The creation of the modern national state, however, opened a gulf between those who were legitimate citizens – members of the 'social homogeneity' – and the rest of the world, the vast majority of people. Access to full participation became a precious privilege, a route to what was presented as participation in the exercise of national sovereignty. It was not that national loyalty or sentiment was created by the change – they had existed to some degree and for various classes for a long time – but the sentiment was now armed with specific legal privileges and material benefits.

The project of building a national state of self-governing citizens in which all have rights and duties is now part of the past. It implied a strict control of the economic and political boundaries of the state, consistently discriminating between native and foreigner in trade, in capital movements and in people. The process of postwar rapid economic growth forced the governments of the developed countries – and latterly, those of the developing countries – to decontrol if they were to enjoy the benefits of growth. For the best part of 30 years, the developed states have been dismantling trade and currency regulations, capital and finance, and more recently, of domestic labour markets, conditions of work and the structure of social support (welfare, health and education). Thus, the profound difference between citizens and foreigners upon which the socialized state was founded, is being progressively blurred. Indeed, so great is the complexity of the system that no one can any longer be sure where a commodity is made or to what country a unit of capital belongs – or even if the question any longer makes sense (although the newspapers and popular discussion still assume it does).

As we have seen, with economic growth the developed countries have always experienced serious labour scarcities – that is, their economies have rapidly exceeded the potential of the domestic labour market and demand has spilled out to other countries. This has been an even more extreme phenomenon in the postwar period: labour demand in the developed countries has not only invaded areas formerly outside the normal labour market (housewives, for example), not only drawn in legions of new immigrants, but also swept into production the labour forces of a mass of developing countries, particularly in East and Southeast Asia. Indeed, what the labour demand of the developed countries started has by now assumed an autonomous momentum.

In the end, these processes will lead to the creation of a single integrated global economy with geographically diversified sources of growth. We can already envisage what has long existed for the higher professions (doctors, engineers, airline pilots, etc.): world labour markets setting the prevailing pay rates in each national economy. The full emergence of that process is still blocked by more or less elaborate immigration controls, some of the few systematic barriers remaining to obstruct the mobility of workers as a 'factor of production', and a form of protectionism still accepted by liberals and non-liberals alike.

Thus, as governments have been driven, to different degrees, to end the old social contract with their citizens, to dismantle the socialized state, so has the emergence of global labour markets made for continuously increasing rates of worker mobility – whether this means settlers, internal company movements, temporary migrants or whatever. The operation of global markets is thus imposing a crisis on the state system, seen at its most dramatic in the old Soviet Union, but no less severely felt wherever the state structure is vulnerable – as in, among other places, sub-Saharan Africa, the Balkans, the Caucasus, former Soviet Central Asia and parts of the Middle East. The movement of unprecedented numbers of refugees across international borders is one painful index of that crisis.

In developing countries, the old project of national economic development – usually founded upon the aspiration to create a socialized state – has also come to an end. Growth now implies increased integration and specialization, not increased economic independence. One sign of this change is the collapse of the vigorous movements of economic nationalism of the 1950s and the rise of alternative ideologies, preeminently religious fundamentalism, which try to nurture alternative forms of nationalism, without an economic agenda.

For the unskilled workers of the developed countries, prospects are alarming. On the one hand, the old social contract has been unilaterally scrapped by what was supposed to be their patron and protector, the state. On the other hand, the material foundations of their existence are radically contracting, represented by high levels of unemployment in Europe, and declining relative incomes in North America. By the standards of society at large, many of the jobs on offer in these economies do not provide anything like adequate subsistence, even though they can be the basis for immigrant workers, by means of prodigious effort and an abstemious life, to attain some prosperity.

Prospects for the future appear worse still. For the rest of the world, the entry into production in an open world economy of, say, China and India seems capable of not only transforming world technology (by profoundly changing the factor endowment of the world economy) but also of making possible pay levels that will marginalize sections of the world's workforce far more drastically than anything Polyani envisaged. He, after all, was discussing market imperatives in a relatively isolated national economy. Some observers think the process of equalizing wages between developed and developing countries has already begun and that this accounts for the decline in the relative position of the unskilled worker in the developed countries (Wood, 1994). But the evidence is not clear cut, and the time period is still short to draw such drastic conclusions.

The old working class, on the appalling experience of the nineteenth century, rejoiced at the new security offered by the state in a turbulent and dangerous world. The decline in this sense of security induces both periodic panic and continuing resentment at the harsh regime which has replaced it. At the other extreme, for the new cosmopolitan worker, nationality is a garment to be donned or shed according to convenience. Income and class, as well as mobility, divide the cosmopolitan and the local. For one the freedom to move is the threatening insecurity of the other. Immigration controls are thus equivocal – as *The Economist* (18 April 1987) put it:

> [U]niversal immigration controls keeping people out are tantamount to a Berlin Wall shutting them in. It is time to recognize that the right to freedom of movement implies a duty to permit immigration.

The idea that people of necessity are permanently located in one national entity is also under challenge. World economic integration continually increases rates of mobility, so that in future it is going to be as difficult internationally to give an unequivocal answer to the question 'Where are you from?' as it already is in developed countries. Native places are in decline and often the complexity of origins is well beyond the conventional mythology. The marks of identity may remain individual, ancestral, tribal, occupational – and even religious – rather than national.

The fears of the competition of workers from developing countries are misplaced, even though Western politicians are adept at reinventing this threat when it suits their purpose. The scale of exports from developing to developed countries is still too small for it to have had profound effects (cf. Lawrence and Slaughter, 1993; Bhagwati and Kosters, 1994). In any case, the differences in the productivity of workers are so great that mere differences in wages tell us little either about where production should be located or the tactics of bargaining. There is no inevitable downward auction in wages, and the record for unskilled

Table 8.1 Output of highly qualified workers, USA compared to six major developing countries (thousands)

	Total college graduates	Scientists	Engineers	Ph.D.s
United States	979.5	180.7	77.1	394.3
The 'six'	1053.1	153.8	172.6	66.2

Source: UNESCO, 1988: Tables 3-10, 3-306.

workers in Europe and North America is affected not only by labour-intensive imports but also by the choices of employers in terms of technology and management. Since simultaneously the incomes of the majority have increased, unskilled workers have a powerful claim for full compensation if they alone bear the costs of an adjustment which is benefiting everyone else.

The Structure of the World's Labour Force

The need for increased movement of workers as the world economy grows is exaggerated by the changing demography of the world's labour force. As noted earlier, the world's young workers are becoming increasingly concentrated in developing countries. This is shown in the distribution of those who enter the labour force. For the developed countries (the OECD group), there are 13 under the age of fifteen for every 10 over the age of sixty-five, while in sub-Saharan Africa, the region with the fastest growth of population, there are 156 for every 10.

If the distribution of the working population is changing, so too is the highly educated sector of the population. In the late 1980s Asia produced annually some 9 million graduates compared to 3.5 million in the developed countries. Or to look at the issue from a different angle, between 1970 and 1985 the developed-country share of particular categories of the world's educated people declined from 44 to 30 per cent for high-school enrolments; and from 77 to 51 per cent for college students (Johnston, 1991: 121). If we compare the 1986 output of the highest qualified workers in the United States with six major developing countries (Brazil, China, the Philippines, Korea, Mexico and Egypt), then the differences are narrowing (and if we include others – India, Indonesia, Bangladesh, Pakistan – then the difference disappears) (see Table 8.1).

Indeed, as we have noted earlier, developing countries appear to be becoming major suppliers of engineers and medical doctors to the developed countries – or, rather, to the world as a whole. Students and staff from developing countries tend also to be predominant in these fields in the universities of the developed countries. In 1987, in US universities, 51 per cent of doctorates in engineering were awarded to students from developing countries (compared to 48 per cent in mathematics, 32 per cent in business studies, and 29 per cent in physical sciences) (Johnston, 1991: 124).

The emergence of national specializations in the higher skills is already advanced, and this parallels specialization in the provision of unskilled labour. It could be that in the future all engineers working in developed countries will be recruited from developing countries, that consumers of medical services will go primarily to developing countries to receive treatment, and so on. Thus, developing countries will not be simply suppliers of unskilled labour to the world; nor will the developed countries be able to monopolize the higher skills. Nor are the flows simply of workers travelling from developing to developed countries – consumers will increasingly travel in the opposite direction. This is what a single world economy means.

Morality and Migration

The overwhelming majority of the world's population are foreigners, and all of us are part of that great majority. Even for someone from China, 79 per cent of the world's people are foreign; and the figure is 84 per cent for someone from that other population giant, India. For a small country like Britain, over 99 per cent of the world's people are foreigners. The figures put in some perspective the awful egotism of nations who see themselves as the centre of the known universe.

Discussions on immigration do not start from the interests of the world, the universal, but from those of the minority, the country. There is no political lobby for the majority, no agency to press for internationalism. Yet in the shift from semi-closed national economies to an open world economy, the principles by which issues should be judged are also under revision, especially so in the field of labour, where moralizing is most developed. Of course, this does not mean abandoning the specific interest of a people, regardless of how big or small it is, but rather placing that interest in a universal context. This is no more than following the standard practice in morality or the law – few try to justify murder on the simple grounds of egotism, but rather acknowledge that it is universally wrong to murder, even though in this particular case a plea for an exception may be made.

Yet all discussions of immigration policy start from the monopoly position of government, without even a nod at a universal interest. Public debate assumes a level of state egotism and particularism which would never be tolerated in an individual. No government is required to justify its immigration policy in terms of the interests of the world; no properly constituted tribunal is empowered to judge the state. Not even a forum like GATT exists to apply some common principles or adjudicate disputes. It seems that for governments, people are very much less important than traded commodities – or else too important to allow foreigners to be involved in deciding their fate.

Yet the need for common policies is inexorably emerging. At the moment, as we have seen, virtually all governments cheat on the agreed rules for accepting refugees, and do so with impunity. Those who by geographical or other accident find themselves receiving a disproportionate number of those in flight – as Germany did in the early 1990s – complain and demand a sharing of the burdens. So far this has not led to any common position, and governments continue to subordinate issues of international compassion to often the most trivial questions of local parochialism. Yet sooner or later, common policies will be required to protect any individual power, at which stage the possibility of both developing some higher set of principles and bringing practice into some relationship with those principles may arise. Then building higher walls round the country – and the most shameless cheating – to avoid lending help to those in flight might give way to collective mechanisms either to make flight no longer necessary or help to accommodate all who wish to flee (on the not unreasonable assumption that no one embarks on such an intrinsically dangerous option without being seriously threatened by disaster). Indeed, it seems that most people do not want to move, and if they are obliged to do so, do it with great reluctance and, if at all possible, return as soon as feasible. Only in the fantasies of paranoid governments are foreigners assumed to be guilty until they can prove their innocence, assumed to be desperate at any cost to break in to the destination country.

A world economy cries out for a world morality and a world system of law. The first existed in the great religions of the world. But the rise of the modern state subverted that universalism – in Christianity, the duty to love thy neighbour was displaced by one's duty, if the state so willed, to kill him or her. The military chaplain became the symbol of this subversion.

The Future

The regulation of immigration assumes that the norm is either a citizen or a foreigner, and the distinction is clear cut. The citizen has rights, normally lives at home and is relatively immobile; the foreigner has no rights (other than those agreed under bilateral arrangements between governments), is mobile and temporarily in the country concerned. The transition from foreigner to citizen is difficult; but, if made, then the former foreigner is presumed to become immobile with the acquisition of rights.

However, the norm is coming to include – albeit still a very small minority – mobile workers for whom nationality is no more than a means to facilitate travel. The rights of citizens are no longer needed, only the right to work. In Germany, with its rather more strict distinction between the two notions, the concept of *Gastarbeiter* is the intermediate form. Those intermediate forms are now multiplying as national economies come to need a growing number of imported workers, even if only for a day or a week. Entry provisions must be rendered increasingly elastic to allow in those who are wanted but exclude those who are not, and immigration law becomes both opaque and hypocritical (at least Singapore is honest in its sharp distinction between a class of desired professional migrants and a class of resisted manual workers). Lionel Castillo, President Carter's Commissioner of the INS, noted this paradox in US immigration regulations:

> The actual policy of the US government is quite different from its stated policy, which is the strict control of the border and strict restriction of entry. The de facto policy is to keep the door half open. (US Congress, 1989)

The half-open door allows the recruitment of foreign workers for particular jobs – New York hospitals advertise for nurses in the Irish or Philippine press; British hospitals send recruitment officers to the Caribbean. The system allows a growing mass of workers to move frequently for short visits, a type of international commuting. It allows the recruitment of seasonal unskilled workers – Caribbean workers to the apple orchards of Florida or the farms of western Ontario, Polish workers to Germany. It obliges all governments from time to time to acknowledge the failure of their controls by legalizing illegal immigrants.

Most of the legal exceptions are for the highly skilled. The unskilled – those who make possible the work of the skilled – must rely on illegality to help the output of the developed countries grow. They therefore, potentially, undergo the most pernicious regimes of oppression in sectors the natives shun. In some cases – but sadly too few – trade unions have wisely campaigned to protect illegal immigrants, since the toleration of bad conditions undermines the position of both legal immigrants and native-born workers.

In the present political climate, particularly in Europe, it is difficult to believe the numbers of unskilled foreign workers admitted could be expanded without public outcry – or, rather, political challenge from the extreme right – even though the economic arguments for doing so are strong. Furthermore, the numbers of immigrants required to make up for the decline in the size of the labour force and, particularly, the decline in the younger age groups, would have to be large. Zlotnik (in Kritz et al., 1992) estimates that over 1 million immigrants would be required in Europe annually for the first half of the next century to compensate for the declining rate of natural increase in the population.

However, once we separate the question of citizenship from that of work, and accept that in increasingly flexible economies temporary workers are likely to be the most rapidly expanding groups, the issue is no longer one of large permanent transfers. Indeed, if immigration controls were less draconian, fewer immigrant workers would be obliged to seek citizenship. For the unskilled, the right of settlement is little more than a route to security which eases the crossing of borders. In other words, immigration rules in their current form produce a high demand for the right to settle and secure citizenship. Furthermore, once a worker is obliged to settle in order to work, he or she then has a powerful interest in bringing in a spouse and children. If there was less of a difference between resident alien and citizen – as in the United States – fewer would bother to move permanently.

Reforming the law to ease crossing borders would make for a considerable increase in temporary migration without settlement or the acquisition of citizenship rights. In the future, this might allow foreign workers to tender for, for example, city or hospital cleaning services, for computer programming or data loading. The work would then be undertaken in the host country for set periods per month or per year while remaining based at home. Agricultural subcontracts might be run in the same way. Construction companies might be permitted to recruit foreign work teams, or foreign construction companies bid for contracts, on a project basis. Already entertainers, singers, dancers, and so forth, are hired on a seasonal basis on international circuits. Cheap and rapid foreign travel makes it possible for a growing variety of jobs to be turned into temporary subcontracts, legal – and legally regulated – tasks which allow people to remain based in their home country.

For jobs which cannot be defined in discrete time periods – preeminently domestic service, staffing in hospitals, hotels and restaurants

– longer-term but still temporary contracts might be feasible (although 'temporary' should not mean without normal rights, access to pensions, etc.). Again, this might be organized by companies which bid to supply labour for set periods, as Korean companies have done on Middle Eastern contracts. In principle, such companies could be legally obliged to operate according to the local standards of pay and working conditions and sued if these standards are not adhered to. Government authorities have too little power to protect *individual* workers, and the home country governments are even less well equipped to ensure tolerable conditions for the immigrant. In time, international trade unions – unions with an international membership, rather than simple federations of national unions – might be able to check the maintenance of standards and represent workers in international negotiations, but in the short term company regulation appears the only means to protect workers.

The horrors of indentured and contract labour are notorious. Images of Indian and Chinese serfs in Africa, of South African miners, colour the images of the nineteenth century. Not dissimilar occurrences have recently been noted in the Middle Eastern oil-producing countries. Yet such conditions are not intrinsic to contract labour, only to systems allowed to operate completely without regulation. It is for this reason that it is worth preparing in advance for growing numbers of migrant workers, rather than thinking that controls can stop movement. Even the horrors of unregulated contract work are superior to unemployed hunger (and very superior to working conditions already taken for granted in many developing – and some developed – countries). Conditions can be improved provided migrant workers have the same rights to act against their employers as the natives do, and trade unions make it their business to facilitate this.

A company-organized system of immigration (whether organized by governments, voluntary organizations or private companies) would make normal immigration controls unnecessary. The market demand for workers as shown in the attempt to secure the contract would determine the numbers. There would be no need for arbitrary quotas or limits, since in conditions of local economic contraction no new arrangements would be created. It would also serve to reassure citizens that whatever privileges supposedly attached to their nationality were not being arbitrarily ignored or diluted.

With no legal restrictions on migration, the second phase would involve proper – and fair – procedures to allow the minority which might wish to change status from temporary contract worker to resident (with a right to change jobs), and so to citizen, to apply to do this.

Again, there is no reason to believe that, if immigration regulations are eased and the numbers crossing borders increased, the numbers requiring this change of status would be large. But no doubt some would wish to marry locally or make some longer-term commitment. The issue of facilitating a mobile migrant workforce which maintains its home base would have become separated from the issue of nationality. In theory the German *Gastarbeiter* system took this form, except that the workforce was kept on a lifetime basis while controls on movement grew steadily more strict, leading to workers needing to bring their families and become, in all but legal status, German.

With increased movement, there needs to be an international forum where governments can negotiate, as they do in GATT and now the new World Trade Organization, mutual concessions on the restrictions to movement – a General Agreement on Migration and Refugee Policy. Such a forum could also provide a body capable of reprimanding governments which seek to use resident foreigners as scapegoats for domestic discontents or cats-paws in their foreign policy. It could also seek to secure standard rights to protect foreign workers, procedures of entry and exit, standardized taxation rules, rules for the transfer of remittances and goods, pension transfer procedures etc. (see *The Economist*, 16 March 1991; Straubhaar, 1992: 478).

In the future, an increasing number of jobs meeting demand in developed countries will be undertaken in developing countries, and an increasing number of foreign workers will work in developed countries. These two processes may make it possible, first, to avoid the disasters which seem implicit in the declining size of labour force and ageing in the developed countries, and second, to give growing access to workers in developing countries to the means to earn and to learn in the developed countries. Both sides would gain from such arrangements. Furthermore, the overall expansion of the economies of the developed countries as a result of expanded immigration should produce a general expansion of labour demand to the benefit of the unskilled native-born, allowing an upgrading of their position (as we saw earlier in the case of the Los Angeles garment industry).

This is a second-best remedy which compromises on the essential underlying principle that the inhabitants of the world ought to be free to cross borders in the world as they decide – and that they can be as trusted to do so sensibly in this field as in any other activity beloved of advocates of free markets. But it is a compromise that offers a way of reconciling the fears and interests of the citizens, settled in one territory, and the need for the income and output of the world to be expanded and for workers to get work.

Such arrangements would do nothing for refugees. Here different procedures are required. Funds need to be established to offset the financial implications of sudden large-scale movements of those in flight, to mobilize the power to protect the persecuted and to strengthen the volunteer agencies that currently are the most effective in reacting to emergency. To treat refugees as illegal immigrants, as many governments are now doing, is disastrous. Those seeking refugee status are denied the right to work, and since the numbers applying often exceed the capacity of governments to deal with their case, people are interned – imprisoned without charge – for long periods at high cost. If those in flight are allowed to work, the burden on the public purse would be relieved (and hence the supposed resentments of the natives eased), the refugees would avoid the demoralization of long imprisonment, and the local demand for labour would be met.

Sooner or later the world's governments will be forced to tax themselves in order to establish a global fund to cover the transitional costs of refugee flight. This would make funds available to bribe governments to be more compassionate than is currently the case. A powerful international agency responsible for refugees can seek to link refugee skills with acknowledged labour deficits, so that temporary work permits become available for them in places that need workers. Indeed, such a scheme could become so important that governments would compete for access to refugee workers. Would making it easier to flee war or persecution encourage illegal immigrants? It might, but is that issue of such moment that it should allow the ending of the supposed compassion of governments – and the current brutal hypocrisy?

For worker migrants, the suggestions here imply an increasing separation of place of work and residence, a dissociation long established for long-distance commuting. Internationally, this pattern is quite common, with workers moving between countries on a regular basis. It is even more established in border areas, with commuters travelling daily between the USA and Mexico, Poland and Germany, France and Germany, Hong Kong and China, and so on. As transport grows faster and cheaper, geographical distance becomes less of an obstacle to such movement. Might we expect people who live in Bombay to work in New York (as some software programmers already do), or residents of San Francisco to go to an office in Shanghai?

Some countries might come to employ more foreigners than natives. At an extreme, the entire labour force might live outside the country, while the natives work abroad. Within countries, this has long been the case: central business districts in important cities employ a labour force which commutes from outside the employment area. Internationally this would affect the political order. The idea of democracy – residents or citizens having the exclusive right to vote – would have to be redefined to give some rights of participation to commuters. At an extreme we can imagine a country which is no more than a junction in flows, where no one 'belongs', where there is neither polity nor electorate corresponding to the national economy. It would be a perverse embodiment of Marx's principle of a communist administration – simply the administration of things, a transport terminal, not people. However, unlike communism, this would be a market-driven society (if it could be called a 'society'), not subject to an egalitarian democracy. The sanction against its survival would not be an adverse vote by the citizens – for there are none – but travellers failing to use it.

Prediction is hazardous, as the 1950s judgement of Brinley Thomas illustrates:

> [M]igration is ceasing to be a major factor in the rise of per capita incomes, not because of legal barriers to movement but because of its reduced economic significance. (1958: 360)

The argument here has been the exact opposite. Global integration is making the movement of commodities, of finance and of workers, greater and greater – movement increases far faster than output. The world economy, it seems, has by now passed the point of no return, and we are set upon the road to a single integrated global economy, regardless of the wishes of governments or citizens. Indeed, any efforts to reverse the process spell catastrophe – and particularly for the central project, the employment at tolerable incomes of all those in the world who wish to work.

By whatever route, workers will come to secure the same 'liberation'. The costs are already apparent – as always – for the poor and the insecure. But that was always true, even within the illusory security of one national state, as the most cursory glance at either the history of nineteenth-century Europe or contemporary developing countries shows. The promise of the open world economy is growth on a scale which will allow many more of the world's workers to get work. The demonstration that this is possible has come in East and Southeast Asia, but is still a far prospect in sub-Saharan Africa. Nonetheless, there is no hope in an attempt to return to the old world.

Economic growth is not an alternative utopian programme which will meet all aims simultaneously. It will not eliminate the great historic inequalities of the world, let alone achieve universal justice. It may make some inequalities worse. But equality is a different political agenda. In the short term, the capacity to produce and earn is the immediate aim. Those with work gain the confidence to pursue these other issues. But without work, there is demoralization.

The promise is also for an end to the devastating world wars which were the product of the heyday of national egotism. Fierce nationalisms have reappeared even as economic integration proceeds – indeed, economic fusion seems to be making possible a greater degree of political fission and a downsizing in the scale of political management. But the disjuncture of political and economic power makes for a decreasing scale of war, and that is some advance on the epoch of world wars.

In the new world economic order, global markets are temporarily swamping national politics. Governments have decreasing power to determine what happens in their domestic economies, so that the key focus of politics in the old order is declining. The old left became almost completely submerged in the issues of national power, and the decline in the state now robs them of the supposed means to change the world. But this is not the end of politics. Younger generations take for granted that problems of state power are only one element in the new politics. There are a bewildering array of other issues, from the defence of the new rapidly growing working classes of the developing countries, to issues of human rights, of animal welfare, the environment, road transport, and the future of the world. There is no programme, as there was for the old left, linking a diagnosis of current disorder with the means to transform it, and a comprehensive programme for the construction of a new world. The vehicle of social transformation, the old state, is weakening before global markets, producing a sense of helplessness in those who used to work for change. It will be a long time before any similarly comprehensive programme becomes possible. But it will be reconstructed, since the struggle for the freedom of the majority – including that freedom to decide collectively the material means of existence, rather than just what is left over after markets have settled all the important questions – is a stubborn theme of all human history. But the transition to a global politics involves the painful destruction of the old national politics of right and left, of corporatism and state socialism. There remains an intellectual vacuum within which the old left shrivels, shell-shocked by the completeness of its reversals. Trade unions in the developed countries are grateful to be still alive, preoccupied with individual grievances rather than collective action, with few aspirations beyond immediate interests. The bold promises of universal freedom which still blazon out on their banners mock the humdrum reality. The outcome of the long confrontation between capitalist nationalism and socialist internationalism sliced the wrong way, leaving confident capitalist internationalism and defensive socialist étatism. Thus the world made mock of the dreams.

If the world economy in its new guise seems to be restoring elements of the economic order of the nineteenth century (particularly that which occurred in the surge of cosmopolitan growth between 1840 and 1870), the world polity seems to be emulating the order of fifteenth-century Europe, a mass of principalities and city-states, based upon many different principles of foundation. History does not repeat itself; it offers us only paradoxical echoes. The world today has no earlier parallels simply because of both the extraordinary wealth of the system and the even greater potential to overcome the severe material constraints on the lot of the majority of people. All endeavours to change that state of affairs are fraught with dangers, but the dangers are still less than those offered by the past. If it is true that 40 million people died in the Soviet Union in the Second World War, that 12 million perished in the concentration camps, there is a long way to go before those triumphs of European civilization are superseded by the horrors of the new world order.

An antiquated national political system is being dragged along by a world economy. There are many cruelties and injustices involved in that process. But within this, world interest and a universal morality – like Hegel's Spirit of Reason – are likewise struggling to be reborn after the long dark night of nationalism and the God-like state which incubated world capitalism. There are grounds for cautious optimism.

References

Abadan-Unat, Nermin (1992), 'East–West versus South–North migration: effects upon the recruitment areas of the 1960s', *IMR*, 98, 26/2, Summer, pp. 401–12.

Abowd, John M., and Freeman, Richard B. (eds) (1991), *Immigration, Trade and the Labor Market*, National Bureau of Economic Research, University of Chicago, Chicago.

Aird, John S. (1990), *Slaughter of the Innocents: Coercive Birth Control in China*, AEI Press, Washington DC, 1990.

Altonji, Joseph G., and Card, David (1991), 'The effects of immigration on the labor market outcomes of less-skilled natives', in John M. Abowd and Richard B. Freeman (eds), *Immigration, Trade and the Labor Market*, National Bureau of Economic Research, University of Chicago, Chicago, pp. 201–34.

Amjad, Rashid (ed.) (1989), *To the Gulf and Back: Studies on the Economic Impact of Asian Labour Migration*, ARTEP, ILO/UNDP, Bangkok.

Anti Slavery Society (1990), *A Pattern of Slavery: India's Carpet Boys*, Anti Slavery Society, London.

Appleyard, Reginald (ed.) (1989), *The Impact of International Migration on Developing Countries*, Development Centre seminar, OECD, Paris.

——— (1991), 'Summary Report, International Migration', Ninth IOM Seminar on Migration, xxix/2, June, pp. 333–40.

Archdeacon, Thomas J. (1992), 'Reflections on immigration to Europe in the light of US immigration history', *IMR*, 98, 26/2, Summer, pp. 525–48.

Arnold, Fred (1992), 'The contribution of remittances to economic and social development', in Mary M. Kritz, Lean Lim and Hania Zlotnik (eds), *International Migration Systems: A Global Approach*, Clarendon Press, Oxford, pp. 205–20.

Athukorala, Premachandra (1993), 'Improving the contribution of migrant remittances to development: the experience of Asian labor-exporting countries', *International Migration*, xxxi/1, Geneva, pp. 103–24.

Bacci, Massimo Livi (ed.) (1972), *The Demographic and Social Patterns of Emigration from the Southern European Countries*, University of Florence, Florence.

Baison, Richard, and Weinstein, David (1994), *Growth, Economies of Scale and Targeting in Japan, 1955–1990*, Harvard Institute of Economic Research Discussion Paper 1644, Harvard University, Cambridge, Mass.

Bakan, Abbie (1978), *The New Immigration Act: What's in It and Where It Came From* (mimeo), Canadian IS, Toronto.

Balassa, Bela (1989), *US Trade Policy towards Developing Countries: Policy, Planning and Research (Development Economics)*, WPS 151, World Bank, Washington DC, January.

Banerjee, S. (1979), *Child Labour in India*, Anti Slavery Society, London.

Baneth, Jean (1993), *'Fortress Europe' and Other Myths about Trade: Policies towards Merchandise Imports in the EC and in Other Major Industrial Economies and their Impact on Developing Countries*, WPS 1098, The World Bank, Geneva, February.

Basson, P. (1984), 'Male emigration and authority structure of families in North West Jordan', unpublished paper, Irbid, Yarmouk University, Jordan.

Bean, Frank D., Lowell, B. Lindsay and Taylor, Lowell J. (1988), 'Undocumented Mexican immigrants and the earnings of other workers in the United States', *Demography*, 25(1), pp. 35–52.

Bean, R. (ed.) (1989), *International Labour Statistics: A Handbook, Guide and Recent Trends*, Routledge, London.

Beggs, John J., and Chapman, Bruce J. (1991), 'Male immigrant wage and unemployment experience in Australia', in John M. Abowd and Richard B. Freeman (eds), *Immigration, Trade and the Labor Market*, National Bureau of Economic Research, University of Chicago, Chicago, pp. 369–84.

Bernard, W.S. (1953), 'The economic effects of immigration', in B.M. Zeigler, *Immigration: An American Dilemma*, DC Heath, Boston, Mass., pp. 42–67.

Bhagwati, Jagdish (1978), 'Incentives and disincentives: International migration', *Weltwirtschaftliches Archiv*, 130/14, pp. 678–701.

Bhagwati, Jagdish, and Dehejia, Vivek H. (1994), 'Free trade and wages of the unskilled: is Marx striking again?', in Jagdish Bhagwati and Marvin H. Kosters, *Trade and Wages: Levelling Wages Down?*, American Enterprise Institute, AEI Press, Washington DC.

Bhagwati, Jagdish and Kosters, Marvin H. (1994), *Trade and Wages: Levelling Wages Down?*, American Enterprise Institute, AEI Press, Washington DC.

Birks, J., and Sinclair, C. (1978a), 'Kuwait, Country Case Study', Pt. 1 (mimeo), International Migration Project, Department of Economics, University of Durham, Durham.

———— (1978b), *Egypt: Country Study*, International Migration Project, MEP/ILO, Geneva, March.

Bisharat, R.T. (1975), 'Yemeni farmworkers in California', *MERIP Reports*, 34, January, pp. 22–6.

Blanchet, Didier, and Marchand, Olivier (1991), 'Horizons 2000', in *Economie et Statistique* 243, Insée, Paris, July.

Blaschke, Jochen (1993), 'Gates of immigration into the Federal Republic of Germany', *International Migration*, xxxi/1/2/3, pp. 361–88.

———— (1994), 'East–West migration in Europe and the role of international aid in reducing the need for emigration', in W.R. Böhning and M.-L. Schloeter-Paredes (eds), *Aid in Place of Migration*, International Labour Office, Geneva, pp. 75–106.

Blau, Francine D. (1984), 'The use of transfer payments by immigrants', *Industrial and Labor Relations Review*, 37/2, January, pp. 222–39.

Böhning, W.R. (1970), 'Elements of a theory of international economic migration to industrialized nation states', in Mary M. Kritz, Charles B. Keeley and Silvaro M. Tomasi (eds), *Global Trends in Migration: Theory and Research on International Population Movements*, Centre for Migration Studies, New York, pp. 28–43.

Böhning, W.R., and Maillat, D. (1972), 'The social and occupational apprenticeship of Mediterranean migrant workers in West Germany', in Massimo Livi Bacci (ed.), *The Demographic and Social Patterns of Emigration from the Southern European Countries*, University of Florence, Florence.

———— (eds) (1974), *The Effects of the Employment of Foreign Workers*, OECD, Paris.

Böhning, W.R., and Schloeter-Paredes, M.-L. (eds) (1994), *Aid in Place of Migration*, International Labour Office, Geneva.

Borjas, George J. (1990), *Friends or Strangers: The Impact of Immigrants in the US Economy*, Basic Books, New York.

——— (1991), 'Immigration and Self-Selection', in John M. Abowd and Richard B. Freeman (eds), *Immigration, Trade and the Labor Market*, National Bureau of Economic Research, University of Chicago, Chicago, pp. 29–76.

——— (1993), 'The impact of immigration on employment opportunities for natives', in OECD, *The Changing Course of International Migration*, OECD, Paris, p.191.

Borjas, George J., Freeman, Richard B. and Lang, Kevin (1991), 'Undocumented Mexican-born workers in the United States: How many, how permanent?', in John M. Abowd and Richard B. Freeman (eds), *Immigration, Trade and the Labor Market*, National Bureau of Economic Research, University of Chicago, Chicago, pp. 77–100.

Borjas, George J., and Trejo, Stephen J. (1991), *Immigrant Participation in the Welfare System*, National Bureau of Economic Research, Reprint No. 1600, University of Chicago, Chicago.

Börsch-Supan, Axel (1991), 'Aging: problems and policy options in the United States and Germany', *Economic Policy: A European Forum*, No. 12, April, pp. 103–40.

Bourgeois-Pichat, J. (1988), 'Du XXe au XXIe siècle: l'Europe et sa population après l'an 2000', *Population XLIII*, Paris, pp. 9–42.

Bourguignon, François, Gallais-Hamong, Georges, and Ferret, Bernard (1977), *International Labour Migration and Economic Choices: The European Case*, OECD Development Centre Studies, OECD, Paris.

Bovenkerk, Frank, and Ruland, Loes (1992), 'Artisan entrepreneurs: two centuries of Italian immigration to the Netherlands', *IMR*, 99, 26/3, Fall, pp. 927–39.

Briggs, Vernon S. (1984), *Immigration Policy and the American Labor Force*, Johns Hopkins University Press, Baltimore, Md.

Brubaker, W. Rogers (ed.) (1989), *Immigration and the Politics of Citizenship in Europe and North America*, University Press of America, Lanheim/New York/London.

——— (1992), 'Citizenship struggles in the Soviet successor states', *IMR*, 98, 26/2, Summer, pp. 269–91.

Buchan, James, Seccombe, Ian and Bull, Jane (1992), *The International Mobility of Nurses: A UK Perspective*, Institute of Manpower Studies, Report 230, University of Sussex, Brighton.

Burchall, Brendan, and Rubery, Jill (1989), *Segmented Jobs and Segmented Markets: An Empirical Investigation*, ESRC Working Paper 13, London.

Burki, S.J. (1984), 'International migration: implications for labor exporting countries', *Middle East Journal*, 38/4, pp. 668–84.

Burtless, Gary (ed.) (1990), *A Future for Lousy Jobs? The Changing Structure of US Wages*, Brooking Institute, Washington DC.

Butaud, J.Ph. (1971): 'Le logement des étrangers en France', Ministére de l'Equipement et Société des exploitations des Données (mimeo), February.

Card, D. (1990), 'The impact of the Mariel boatlift on the Miami labor market', *Industrial and Labor Relations Review*, 43, January, pp. 245–57.

Cárdenas, Gilberto (1974), 'United States immigration policy towards Mexico: an historical perspective', *Chicano Law Review*, 2, UCLA, Summer.

Carr-Saunders, A.M. (1960), *World Population: Past Growth and Present Trends*, Oxford University Press, London (originally published 1936).

Castles, Stephen (1992), 'The Australian model of immigration and multiculturalism:

is it applicable to Europe?', *IMR*, 98, 26/2, pp. 549–67.

Castles, Stephen, and Miller, Mark J. (1993), *The Age of Migration: International Population Movements in the Modern World*, Macmillan, London.

Catholic Institute for International Relations (1987), *The Labour Trade: Filipina Migrant Workers Around the World*, Catholic Institute for International Relations, London.

Chenery, H.B. (1960), 'Patterns of industrial growth', *American Economic Review*.

Chiswick, B. (1982a), 'The impact of immigration on the level and distribution of economic well being', in B. Chiswick, (ed.), *The Gateway: US Immigration and Policies*, American Enterprise Institute for Public Policy Research, Washington DC.

Chiswick, B. (ed.) (1982b), *The Gateway: US Immigration and Policies*, American Enterprise Institute for Public Policy Research, Washington DC.

Clark, Colin (1967), *The Conditions of Economic Progress*, 3rd edn, Macmillan, London.

Cohen, Robin, and Mottero-Cohen, Selina (1981), 'Habituating agricultural labour in the US: the roles of state and the grower', in J. Henderson (ed.), *Working for Capital: Studies in Working Class Habituation and Resistence*, Routledge, London.

Coleman, David A. (1992), 'Does Europe need immigrants? Population and workforce projections', *IMR*, 98, 26/2, Summer, pp. 413–61.

Consumers' Association (1983), *Which: Book of Money*, Consumers' Association, London.

Cornelius, Wayne A. (1978), *Mexican Migration to the United States: Causes, Consequences and US Responses*, Center for International Studies, MIT, Cambridge, Mass., July.

——— (1979), 'Mexican immigration: causes and consequences for Mexico', in A.S. Bryce-Laporte (ed.), *Source Literature on the New Immigration: Implications for the United States and the International Community*, Transaction Books, New Brunswick, N.J.

Cornelius, Wayne, and Martin, Philip (1993), 'The uncertain connections: free trade and rural Mexican migration to the US', *IMR*, 103, 27/3, Fall, pp. 484–512.

Cross, G.S. (1983), *Immigrant Workers in Industrial France: The Making of a New Labouring Class*, Temple University Press, Philadelphia.

Davis, Kingsley (1974), 'Migration of Human Populations', *Scientific American*, 231, September.

Davis, Steven J., Haltiwanger, John and Schuh, Scott (1993), 'Small business and job creation: dissecting the myth and reassessing the facts', unpublished paper, MIT, Cambridge, Mass., 25 October.

De Freitas, Gregory (1986), 'The impact of immigration on low wage workers', (mimeo).

De Freitas, Gregory, and Marshall, Adriana (1983), 'Immigration and wage growth in US manufacturing in the 1970s', Proceedings of the 36th Annual Meeting of the Industrial Relations Research Association, Madison, Wis., pp. 149–56.

Department of Employment (UK) (1983), *Employment Outlook*, DoE, London, September.

——— (1986), *New Earnings Survey*, DoE, London, April.

——— (1993), *Employment Gazette*, DoE, London, May.

Despres, Leo A. (1990), *Manaus: Social Life and Work in Brazil's Free Trade Zone*, State University of New York Press, Albany, N.Y.

Dillinger (1911), The 'Dillinger Commission' Report, in Abstract of Report of the Immigration Commission, US Senate, 61st Congress, 3rd Session, Document No. 747, Government Printing Office, Washington DC.

Divine, Robert A. (1957), *American Immigration Policy, 1924–1952*, Yale University Press, New Haven, Conn.

Domenach, H., and Picouet, M. (1989), 'Typologies and the likelihood of reversible migration', in Reginald Appleyard (ed.), *The Impact of International Migration on*

Developing Countries, Development Centre seminar, OECD, Paris, pp. 26–37.

ECE (1964), *Some Factors in the Economic Growth in Europe during the 1950s*, Economic Commission for Europe, United Nations, Geneva.

Economic Planning Agency (1983), 'Japan in the Year 2000: preparing Japan for an age of internationalization, the aging society and maturity', *Japan Times* (English version), Tokyo.

Elbadawi, Ibrahim A., and de Rezende Rocha, Robert (1992), *Determinants of Expatriate Workers Remittances in North Africa and Europe*, Policy Research, Transition in Macro Adjustment (Country Economics Dept.), WPS 1038, World Bank, Washington DC, November.

Emmerji, Louis (1993), 'The international situation, economic development and employment', in OECD, *The Changing Course of International Migration*, OECD, Paris, pp. 123–30.

European Commission (1977), *Foreign Employees in Employment 1976*, EC, Brussels, December.

Fawcett, J.T. (1987), *The New Immigration from Asia and the Pacific Islands, Pacific Bridges*, Center of Migration Studies, Staten Island, New York.

Fawcett, J.T., et al. (1984), 'Asian Immigration in the United States: Flows and Processes' (mimeo), East–West Population Institute, Honolulu.

Feketekuty, Geza (1988), *International Trade in Services: An Overview and Blue Print for Negotiations*, Ballinger Publications, Cambridge, Mass.

Fijalkowski, Jurgen (1993), 'Aggressive nationalism, the problem of immigration pressure and asylum policy disputes in today's Germany', *IMR*, 104, 27/4, Winter, pp. 850–969.

Fong, Pang Eng (1993), 'Labour migration to the newly industrializing economies of South Korea, Taiwan, Hong Kong and Singapore', *International Migration*, xxxi, 2/3, pp. 300–313.

Foot, Paul (1965), *Immigration and Race in British Politics*, Penguin, London.

Freeman, Gary P. (1986), 'Migration and the political economy of the welfare state', in *Annals of the American Academy of Political and Social Sciences*, 485, May, pp. 51–63.

Freeman, Richard (1988), 'Union density and economic performance: an analysis of U.S. States', *European Economic Review*, 32.

—— (1994), *New Economics*, Institute for Public Policy Research, London, Spring.

Fröbel, Folker, Jurgen, Heinrich and Kreye, Otto (1980), *The New International Division of Labour: Structural Unemployment in the Industrialized Countries and Industrialization in the Developing Countries*, translated by Peter Burgess, Cambridge University Press, London.

Frost, G. and Spence, F. (1991), 'British employment in the 1980s: the spatial, structural and compositional change of the workforce', *Progress in Planning*, 35, part 2, Pergamon, Oxford.

Galaleldin, M. Al-Awad (1979), *Migration of Sudanese Abroad*, Council on Economic and Social Research, Khartoum.

Galbraith, J.K. (1979), *The Nature of Mass Poverty*, Harvard University Press, Cambridge, Mass.

Ghosh, Birmal (1992), 'Migration, trade and international economic co-operation: do the interlinkages exist?', *International Migration*, xxx/3–4, pp. 377–95.

Gilani, G. et al. (1981), *Labor Migration from Pakistan to the Middle East and its Impact on the Domestic Economy*, Final Report of the Research Project on the Export of Manpower from Pakistan to the Middle East, World Bank (South Asia Country

Programmes Dept.), World Bank, Washington DC, June/July.

Gilbert, Geoffrey (1994), 'Tackling the causes of refugee flows', in Sarah Spencer (ed.), *Strangers and Citizens: A Positive Approach to Migrants and Refugees*, Institute for Public Policy Research, Rivers-Oram Press, London, pp. 18–43.

Glytsos, N. (1990), 'Measuring the income effects of migrant remittances: an empirical analysis for Greece' (mimeo), Centre for Planning and Economic Research, Athens, September.

Gould, David M. (1992), *Immigration Links to the Home Country: Implications for Trade, Welfare and Factor Rewards*, Paper No. 9203, Research Dept., Federal Reserve Bank of Dallas, Texas, March.

Gould, W.T.S., and Findlay, A.M. (1994), *Population Migration and the Changing World Order*, Wiley, Chichester.

Government of Japan, Ministry of Foreign Affairs (1993), 'Problems associated with foreign labor in Japan', *International Migration*, xxxi/1/2/3, pp. 437–41.

Grebler, Leo (1965), *Mexican Immigration to the United States: The Record and Its Implications*, Mexican–American Study Project, Advance Report 2, December.

Grecic, V. (1991), 'East–West Migration', *International Migration*, xxix/2, June.

Greenwood, Michael J., and Hunt, G.L. (1984), 'Migration and interregional employment redistribution in the United States', *American Economic Review*, 74/5, December, pp. 957–69.

Gregory, Peter (1986), *The Myth of Market Failure: Employment and the Labor Market in Mexico*, World Bank Research Publications, Johns Hopkins University Press, Baltimore, Md.

Gregory, R.G., Anstie, R. and Klug, E. (1991), 'Why are low-skilled immigrants in the United States poorly paid relative to their Australian counterparts? Some of the issues illustrated in the context of the footwear, clothing and textile industries', in John M. Abowd and Richard B. Freeman (eds), *Immigration, Trade and the Labor Market*, National Bureau of Economic Research, University of Chicago, Chicago, pp. 385–404.

Gulati, Leela (1987), 'Coping with male migration', *Economic and Political Weekly*, Bombay, 31 October, pp. WS41–6.

Halbronner, Kay (1989), 'Citizenship and Nationhood in Germany', in W. Rogers Brubaker (ed.), *Immigration and the Politics of Citizenship in Europe and North America*, University Press of America, Lanheim/New York/London, pp. 67–80.

Hakim, Catherine (1984), 'Employers use of homework, outwork and freelancers', *Employment Gazette*, DoE, London, April, pp. 144–50.

Hamilton, B., and Whalley, J. (1984), 'Efficiency and distributional implications of global restrictions on labor mobility: calculations and policy implications', *Journal of Development Economics*, 14, pp. 61–75.

Harrell-Bond, Barbara (1993), 'War Report', *Bulletin of the Institute for War and Peace*, London.

Harris, Nigel (1972), *Competition and the Corporate Society: British Conservatives, the State and Industry, 1945–1964*, Methuen, London.

——— (1987), *The End of the Third World: Newly Industrializing Countries and the Decline of an Ideology*, I.B. Tauris/Penguin/Viking, London and New York.

——— (1990), *National Liberation*, I.B. Tauris/Penguin, London.

——— (1993), 'Mexican trade and Mexico–US economic relationships', in Neil Harvey (ed.), *Mexico: Dilemmas and Transitions*, Institute of Latin American Studies (University of London) and British Academic Press, London.

Harrison, David S. (1983), *The Impact of Recent Immigration on the South Australian Labour*

Market, Report to the Committee for the Economic Development of Australia, Canberra, May.

Heer, D.M. (1979), 'What is the annual net flow of undocumented Mexican migrants to the United States?', *Demography*, 16, pp. 417–24.

Heller, G., et al. (1986), *Aging and Social Expenditure in the Major Industrial Countries, 1980–2025*, IMF Occasional Paper 47, IMF, Washington DC, September.

Henderson, Jeffrey (1989), *The Globalisation of High Technology Production: Society, Space and Semi-Conductors in the Restructuring of the Modern World*, Routledge, London.

Heyden, H. (1991), 'South–North Migration', *International Migration*, xxix/2, June.

Hill, Peter J. (1975), 'Relative skill and income levels of native and foreign born workers in the US', *Explorations in Economic History*, 12/1, pp. 47–60.

Hintjens, H.M. (1992), 'Immigration and citizenship debates: reflections on ten common themes', *International Migration*, xxx/1, March, pp. 5–18.

Hollifield, James F. (1992), 'Migration and international relations: cooperation and control in the EEC', *IMR*, 98, 26/2, Summer, pp. 568–95.

Honekopp, Elmar (1993), 'East–West migration: recent developments concerning Germany and some future prospects', in OECD, *The Changing Course of International Migration*, OECD, Paris, p.55.

Hong Kong Government, Education and Manpower Branch (1990), *A Statistical Projection of Manpower Requirements and Supply for Hong Kong*, Hong Kong Government, Hong Kong.

Houte, Hans van, and Melgert, Willy (1972), *Foreigners in Our Community: European Problem to be Solved*, Institut Internationale d'Études Sociales, Keesing, Amsterdam.

Hurstfield, Jennifer (1987), *Part Timers under Pressure: The Price of Flexibility*, Low Pay Unit, London.

Huws, Ursula, Hurstfield, Jennifer and Holtmaat, Riki (1989), *What Price Flexibility? The Casualization of Women's Work*, Low Pay Unit, London.

International Labour Organization (ILO) (1949), *Migration for Employment: Recommendations*, International Labour Organization, Geneva.

ILO–ARTEP (1988), *Manual on International Labour Migration Statistics*, Asian Regional Programme on International Migration, ARTEP–ILO, New Delhi.

International Monetary Fund (IMF) (1989), *World Economic Outlook*, IMF, Washington DC, October.

Incomes Data Services (1993), *Pension Service Bulletin* 70, IDS, London, November.

Intergovernmental Interior Ministers (1992), *Report*, Secretariat, Geneva.

International Union of Foodworkers (IUF) (1978), *News Bulletin*, 6–7, IUF, Geneva.

Johnson, Paul, Conrad, Christopher and Thomson, David (eds) (1989), *Workers against Pensioners: Intergenerational Justice in an Aging World*, Centre for Economic Policy Research, Manchester University Press, Manchester and New York.

Johnston, William B. (1991), 'Global workforce 2000: the new world labor market', *Harvard Business Review*, March–April, pp. 115–27.

Jones, Charles A. (1987), *International Business in the Nineteenth Century: The Rise and Fall of a Cosmopolitan Bourgeoisie*, Harvester Wheatsheaf, Brighton.

Jones, K., and Smith, A.D. (1970), *The Economic Impact of Commonwealth Immigration*, Cambridge University Press, Cambridge.

Jones, Randall, King, Robert and Klein, Michael (1992), *The Chinese Economic Area: Economic Integration without a Free Trade Area*, OECD Economics Department, Working Paper 124, OECD Development Centre, Paris.

Joseph Rowntree Foundation (1992), *Social Policy: Research Findings*, No. 31, November.

Julius DeAnne, S. (1990), *Global Companies and Public Policy: The Growing Challenge of*

Foreign Direct Investment, Royal Institute of International Relations, Pinter Publications, London.

Kamiar, M.S., and Ismail, H.F. (1991), 'Family ties and economic stability concerns of migrant labour families in Jordan', *International Migration*, xxix/4, Geneva, December, pp. 561–72.

Kayser, Bernard (1971), *Manpower Movements and Labour Markets, Report under the Auspices of the Working Party on Migrant Manpower and Social Affairs Committee*, OECD, Paris.

Khan, Aga, and Talal, H. Bin (1986), 'Forward to an independent commission on international humanitarian issues', in *Refugees: The Dynamics of Displacement*, Zed, London.

Kindleberger, Charles (1967), *Europe's Postwar Growth, The Role of Labour Supply*, Harvard University Press, Cambridge, Mass.

Korale, Raja B.M. (1986), 'Migration for employment to the Middle East: its demographic and socio-economic effects on Sri Lanka', in Fred Arnold and Nasra M. Shah (eds), *Asian Labor Migration: Pipeline to the Middle East*, Westview Press, Boulder, Colo.

Kowahara, Y. (1992), *To Tie the United String: Migrant Workers and Japanese Economic Cooperation*, World Employment Programme, International Labour Organization, Geneva.

Kritz, Mary M. (ed.) (1983), *US Immigration and Refugee Policy: Global and Domestic Issues*, Lexington Books, Lexington, Mass.

Kritz, Mary M., Keeley, Charles B., and Tomasi, Silvaro M. (eds) (1981), *Global Trends in Migration: Theory and Research on International Population Movements*, Centre for Migration Studies, New York.

Kritz, Mary M., Lim, Lean Lin and Zlotnik, Hania (eds) (1992), *International Migration Systems: A Global Approach*, Clarendon Press, Oxford.

Kuhn, W.E. (1974), 'Guest workers as an automatic stabiliser of cyclical unemployment in Switzerland and Germany', *IMR*, 12, pp. 210–24.

Kushner, S. (1975), *Long Road to Delaho: A Century of Farm Workers' Struggle*, International Publications, New York.

Kwan, C.H. (1994), *Economic Interdependence in the Asia-Pacific Region: Towards a Yen Bloc*, Routledge, London and New York.

Kynaston, David (1994), *The City of London, Vol. 1, A World of Its Own, 1815–1890*, Chatto and Windus, London.

Lane, Barbara (1992), 'Filipino-born domestic workers in Hong Kong', *Asian Migrant*, V/1, Manila, January–March, pp. 24–32.

Lawrence, Robert Z. and Slaughter, Mark (1993), *International Trade and American Wages in the 1980s: Giant Sucking Sound or Small Hiccup?*, Microeconomics (Brookings Papers on Economic Activity), Brookings Institution, Washington DC.

Layard, Richard, Blanchard, Oliver, Dornbusch, Rudiger and Krugman, Paul (1991), *East–West Migration: The Alternatives*, MIT Press, Cambridge, Mass.

Layton-Henry, Zig (1990), *The Politics of Immigration*, Institute of Contemporary British History/Blackwell, Oxford.

Lee, Arthur Rogers (1988), *Economics of Changing Age Distribution in Developed Countries*, Clarendon Press, Oxford.

Leh, Anthony Gar On (1990), *Foreign Labour in Hong Kong: Trends, Impacts and Implications*, University of Hong Kong, paper for UNCRD Expert Meeting, 5–8 November 1990, Hong Kong.

Lerner, A.P. (1953), *Factor Prices and International Trade: Essays in Economic Analysis*, Macmillan, London.

Levy, F., and Murnane, Richard J. (1992), 'US earnings levels and earnings inequality: a review of recent trends and proposed explanations', *Journal of Economic Literature*, xxx, September, pp. 1333–81.

Light, I., and Bonacich, E. (1988), *Immigrant Entrepreneurs*, University of California Press, Berkeley and Los Angeles.

Lindbeck, Assar, and Snower, Dennis J. (1988), *The Insider–Outsider Theory of Employment and Unemployment*, MIT Press, Cambridge, Mass.

Long, C.D. (1958), *The Labor Force under Changing Income and Employment*, National Bureau of Economic Research, Princeton University Press, New York.

Low Pay Unit (1987), *A Cut Below the Rest: Pay and Conditions in Hairdressing*, Low Pay Unit, London.

Low Pay Unit and Open University (1985), *Working Children*, Low Pay Unit, London.

Lucas, R.E.B. (1987), 'Emigration to South Africa's Mines', *American Economic Review*, 77/3.

Lumsdaine, Robin L., and Wise, David A. (1990), *Aging and Labor Force Participation: A Review of Trends and Explanations*, National Bureau of Economic Research Working Paper No. 3420, Cambridge, Mass., August.

Lustig, Norah (1992), *Mexico: The Remaking of an Economy*, The Brookings Institution, Washington DC.

Lutz, Vera (1963), 'Foreign workers and domestic wage levels with an illustration from the Swiss case', *Banca Nazionale del Lavero Quarterly Review*, 16, March.

Ma, Rudy (1983), *Employment and Multinationals in Asian Export Processing Zones*, Asian Regional Team for Employment Promotion (Bangkok), International Labour Organization, Geneva.

Macdonald, John S., and Leatrice D. (1964), 'Chain migration, ethnic neighbourhood formation and social networks', *The Millbank Memorial Fund Quarterly*, xlii/1, London, January.

Mahmud, Wahiddudin (1989), 'The impact of overseas labour migration on the Bangladesh economy', in Rashid Amjad (ed.), *Gulf and Back: Studies on the Economic Impact of Asian Labour Migration*, ARTEP, ILO/UNDP, Bangkok, pp. 55–94.

Manfrass, Klaus (1992), 'Europe: North–South or East–West migration?', *IMR*, 98, 26/2, Summer, pp. 388–400.

Manolo, I. Abella (1992), 'Contemporary labor migration from Asia: policy and perspectives of sending countries', in Mary M. Kritz, Lean Lin Lim and Hania Zlotnik (eds), *International Migration Systems: A Global Approach*, Clarendon Press, Oxford, pp. 263–78.

Martin, Philip L. (1991), *The Unfinished Story: Turkish Labor Migration to Western Europe (with special reference to the Federal Republic of Germany)*, World Employment Programme, ILO, Geneva.

—— (1992a), *International Economic Insights*, Institute for International Economics, Washington DC, March–April.

—— (1992b), 'Foreign direct investment and migration: the case of Mexico's maquiladores', *International Migration*, xxx/34, 1992, pp. 399–422.

—— (1993a), 'Migration and development, conference report', *IMR*, 99, 26, Fall, pp. 1000–1012.

—— (1993b), 'Migration and trade: the case of the Philippines (conference report)', *International Migration Review*, 103, 27/3, Spring, pp. 639–45.

Martin, Jean, and Roberts, Ceridwon (1984), *Women's Employment: A Lifetime's Pursuit*, HMSO, London.

Martinez, Vilma S. (1976), 'Illegal immigration and the labor force: an historic and legal view', *American Behavioural Scientist*, 19, January/February.

Massey, D.S. (1990), *International Migration in Comparative Perspective*, Working Paper for the Commission for the Study of International Migration and Co-operative Economic Development, No. 1, US Government Printing Office, Washington DC.

Masson, Paul R., and Tryon, Ralph W. (1990), *Macroeconomic Effects of Projected Population Aging in Industrial Countries*, IMF Staff Papers, 37/3, IMF, Washington DC, September.

Mathew, E.T., and Nair, P.R. Gopinathan (1978), 'Socio-economic characteristics of emigrants and emigrant households: a case study of two villages in Kerala', *Economic and Political Weekly* (Bombay), 15 July, pp. 1141–53.

Maw, Leila (1974), *Immigration and Employment in the Clothing Industry: The Rochdale Case*, Runnymede Trust, London.

McCarthy, Kevin F., and Valdez, R. Burciaga (1986), *Current and Future Effects of Mexican Immigration in California* (R-3365–CR), California Round Table/ Rand Corporation, Santa Monica, Calif., May.

McKinley, L., Blackburn, L., Bloom, David and Freeman, Richard (1990), 'The declining economic position of less skilled American men', in Gary Burtless (ed.), *A Future for Lousy Jobs? The Changing Structure of US Wages*, Brooking Institute, Washington DC, pp. 31–76.

McMahon, V. (1993), 'Immigrant integration and the labour market in Australia', paper presented to the Conference on Migration and International Cooperation, OECD, Paris.

McWilliams, Douglas (1992), *Will the Single European Market Cause European Wage Levels to Converge?*, London Economics, London.

Mendelevitch, E. (1979), 'Child labour', *International Labour Review*, 118/5, September.

Mertens, L. (1986), *Employment and Stabilisation in Mexico*, World Employment Research Programme, WP 10, International Labour Organization, Geneva.

Michie, Jonathan and Grieve Smith, John (eds) (1994), *Unemployment in Europe*, Academic Press, London.

Miller, Mark J. (1992), 'Evolution of policy modes of regulating international labour migration', in Mary M. Kritz, Lean Lin Lim and Hania Zlotnik (eds), *International Migration Systems: A Global Approach*, Clarendon Press, Oxford, pp. 300–314.

Min, P. (1989), *Korean Immigration in Los Angeles*, Institute of Social Science Research, Working Paper 2(2), University of California at Los Angeles.

Mines, R. (1985), 'Workers in California's furniture manufacturing: domestic and immigrant workers', unpublished paper, Berkeley, Calif.

Mishel, Lawrence (1992), 'The end of the white collar boom', *International Economic Insights*, Washington DC, September/October.

Mitchell, Gary David (1992), 'The impact of US immigration policy on the economic "quality" of German and Austrian immigration in the 1930s', *IMR*, 99, 26, Fall, pp. 940–67.

Mitchell, Olivia S. (1993), *Trends in Retirement Systems and Lessons for Research*, Policy Research: Education and Employment, WPS 1118, World Bank, Washington DC, May.

Muller, Thomas, and Espenshade, Thomas J. (1985), *The Fourth Wave: California's Newest Immigrants, A Summary*, Urban Institute Press, Washington DC.

Muus, Philip J. (1993), *Employment and Vocational Training of Young Immigrants in the Netherlands, West Germany and Belgium*, OECD, Paris.

Mytelka, Lynn K. (ed.) (1991), *Strategic Partnerships and the World Economy*, Pinter Publishers, London.

Natapat, M.D., and Radakrishnan, K. (1978), *Kerala Engulfed in Prosperity*, Mathrubhunu Pvt. and Pbg. Co., Calicut, January.

Nevile, J. (1990), *The Effect of Immigration on Australian Living Standards*, Australian Government Publishing Services, Canberra.

———— (1991), 'Immigration and macro economic performance in Australia', *Growth, (The Costs and Benefits of Immigration)*, 39, September.

Nolan, Peter (1993), 'Economic reform, poverty and migration in China', *Economic and Political Weekly* (Bombay), 26 June, pp. 1369–73.

North, David S. (1970), *The Border Crossers: People who Live in Mexico and Work in the US*, Trans Century Corporation, Washington DC.

———— (1979), *Worker Migration: A State of the Art Review*, prepared for the Bureau of International Labor Affairs, US Department of Labor, 11 January.

North, David S., and Houston, Marian F. (1976), *The Characteristics and Role of Illegal Aliens in the US Labor Market: An Exploratory Study*, Linton, Washington DC.

O'Brien, Peter (1992), 'German–Polish migration: the elusive search for a German nation-state', *IMR*, 98, 26/2, Summer.

Oberai, A.S., and Singh, H.K.M. (1980), 'Migration, remittances and rural development: findings of a case study in the Indian Punjab', *International Labour Review*, 19/2, Geneva, pp. 229–41.

OECD (1978), *Migration, Growth and Development*, OECD, Paris.

———— (1991), *Migration: The Demographic Aspects; Demographic Change and Public Policy*, OECD, Paris.

———— (1992a), *Structural Change and Industrial Performance: A Seven Country Growth Decomposition Study*, OECD, Paris.

———— (1992b), *Historical Statistics*, 1960–1990, OECD, Paris.

———— (1993), *The Changing Course of International Migration*, OECD, Paris.

OECD–SOPEMI (Permanent Observation System on Migration) (1976), *Continuous Reporting System on Migration*, OECD, Paris.

———— (1992), *Trends in International Migration*, OECD, Paris.

Office of Technology Assessment (1991), *Competing Economies: American, European and the Pacific Rim: Summary*, Congress of the United States, US Government Printing Office, Washington DC.

Ogata, Sadako et al. (1993), *Towards a European Immigration Policy*, The Philip Morris Institute for Public Policy Research, Brussels, October.

Ohlin, Bertil (1967), *Interregional and International Trade*, Harvard University Press, Cambridge, Mass. (originally published 1933).

Orr, Akiva (1983), *The UnJewish State: The Politics of Jewish Identity in Israel*, Ithaca Press, London.

Osterman, O. (ed.) (1984), *International Labor Markets*, MIT Press, Cambridge, Mass.

Otero, J.F. (1988), 'A labor view of US immigration policy', *The Humanist*, 41/6, pp. 39–46.

Palomares, L., and Mertens, L. (1987), 'Programmable automation and new work contents: experience of the electronic, metal engineering and secondary petrochemicals industries in Mexico, and evolving skill profiles and new technology in the Mexican electronics industry', unpublished paper, International Labour Organization, Mexico City.

Papademitriou, D.G. (1991), 'South–North migration in the western hemisphere and the US reaction', *International Migration*, xxix/2, IOM, Geneva, June, pp. 291–316.

———— (1993), 'Illegal Mexican migration in the US and the US responses', *International Migration*, xxx 1/2/3.

Park, Young-bum (1993), 'Conditions of Filipino workers in Korea', *Asian Migrant*, V/1, Manila, January–March, pp. 17–24.

Payne, Suzanne (1974), *Exporting Workers: The Turkish Case*, Cambridge University Press, Cambridge.

Perotti, Rosanne (1992), 'ICRA's anti-discrimination provisions: what went wrong?', *IMR*, 99, 26/3, Fall, pp. 732–53.

Piore, Michael J. (1976), *Illegal Aliens: An Assessment of the Issues*, National Council on Employment Policy, Washington DC, October.

——— (1979), *Birds of Passage: Migrant Labour in Industrial Societies*, Cambridge University Press, London.

Piore, M.J., and Sabel, C.F. (1984), *The Second Industrial Revolution: Possibilities for Prosperity*, Basic Books, New York.

Polyani, Karl (1944), *The Great Transformation*, Beacon Press, Boston, Mass. (1957 edn).

Poot, J. (1992), 'International migration in the New Zealand economy of the 1980s', in A.D. Tolim and P. Spoonley (eds), *New Zealand and International Migration: A Digest and Bibliography*, No. 2, Massey University, Palmerston North.

Portes, Alejandro (1974), 'Return of the wetback', *Society*, March–April, p. 45.

Prakash, B.A. (1978), 'Impact of foreign remittances: a case study of Chavakkad village in Kerala', *Economic and Political Weekly* (Bombay), 8 July, pp. 1107–12.

Proudfoot, M.J. (1957), *European Refugees, 1939–52: A Study in Forced Population Movements*, Faber, London.

Quibria, M.G. (1986), 'Migration and remittances in Asian developing countries', *Asian Development Review*, 4/1, Manila, pp. 78–99.

Ransome, Roger L., and Sutch, Richard (1988), 'The decline of retirement and the rise of efficient wages: US retirement patterns, 1870–1940', in R. Ricardo-Campbell and E. Lazear (eds), *Issues in Contemporary Retirement*, Hoover Institution, Stanford, Calif., pp. 3–37.

Reder, Melvin W. (1982), 'Chicago economics: permanence and change', *Journal of Economic Literature*, March.

Reynolds, Clark W. (1979), 'Labor market projections for the United States and Mexico, and their relevance to current migration controls', *Food Research Institute Studies*, No.17, Stanford University, Stanford, Calif.

Rhee, Yung Whee, and Belot, Therese (1990), *Export Catalysts in Low Income Countries: A Review of Eleven Success Stories*, Discussion Paper 72, World Bank, Washington DC.

Richmond, Anthony H. (1981), 'Immigrant adaptation in a post-industrial society', in Mary M. Kritz, Charles B. Keeley, and Silvaro M. Tomasi (eds), *Global Trends in Migration: Theory and Research on International Population Movements*, Centre for Migration Studies, New York, pp. 298–319.

Richmond, Anthony H., Lam, Lawrence, Mata, Fernando and Wong, Lloyd (1989), 'Some consequences of Third World migration to Canada', in Reginald Appleyard (ed.), *The Impact of International Migration on Developing Countries*, Development Centre seminar, OECD, Paris, pp. 335–60.

Riveros, Luis A. (1989), *International Differences in Wages and Non-wage Costs*, Policy, Planning and Research (Macro Adjustment and Growth, Country Economics Dept.), WPS 188, World Bank, Washington DC, April.

Robinson, Olive (1985), 'The changing labour market: the phenomenon of part time employment in Britain', *National Westminster Bank Quarterly Review*, November.

Rodrigo, Chandra, and Jayatissa, R.A. (1989), 'Maximising benefits from labour migration: Sri Lanka', in Rashid Amjad (ed.), *To the Gulf and Back: Studies on the*

Economic Impact of Asian Labour Migration, ARTEP, ILO/UNDP, Bangkok.

Rogers, Rosemarie (1981), 'Incentives to return: patterns of policies and migrants' responses', in Mary M. Kritz, Charles B. Keeley, and Silvaro M. Tomasi (eds), *Global Trends in Migration: Theory and Research on International Population Movements*, Centre for Migration Studies, New York, pp. 338–64.

—— (1992), 'The future of refugee flows and policies', *IMR*, 100, 26/4, Winter, pp. 1112–43.

Rose, E.J.B. et al. (1969), *Colour and Citizenship, A Report on British Race Relations*, Oxford University Press, London.

Russell, Sharon Stanton (1992), 'Migrant remittances and development', *International Migration*, xxx/3/4, Geneva, pp. 267–88.

Russell, Sharon Stanton and Teitelbaum, M.S. (1992), *International Migration and International Trade*, World Bank Discussion Paper 160, World Bank, Washington DC.

Saggar, S. (1992), 'Race and politics in Britain', in J. Benyon (ed.), *Contemporary Political Studies*, Harvester Wheatsheaf, Hemel Hempstead.

Salomon, Kim (1991), *Refugees in the Cold War: Towards a New International Refugee Regime in the Early Postwar Era*, Lund University Press, Lund.

Salt, J., and Kitching, R.T. (1990), 'Labour migration and the work permit system in the United Kingdom', *International Migration*, 28/3, September, pp. 267–94.

Samuelson, P.A. (1948), 'International trade and the equalisation of factor prices', *Economic Journal*, 58, June, pp. 163–84.

Sassen, Saskia (1988), *The Mobility of Labor and Capital: A Study in International Investment and Labor Flow*, Cambridge University Press, Cambridge.

Schuck, Peter H. (1989), 'Membership in the liberal policy: the devaluation of American citizenship', in W. Rogers Brubaker (ed.), *Immigration and the Politics of Citizenship in Europe and North America*, University Press of America, Lanheim/New York/London, pp. 51–65.

Selangor Graduates Society (1978), *Plight of Malaysian Workers in Singapore*, Selangor Graduates Society, Petaling Jaya.

Select Committee on Immigration and Refugee Policy (1989), *US Immigration Policy: Staff Report*, US Congress, US Government Printing Office, Washington DC.

Serageldin, I., et al (1983), *Manpower and International Labor Migration in the Middle East and North Africa*, Oxford University Press for the World Bank (Final Report, 30 June 1981), New York.

—— (1985), *Simulating Flows of Labor in the Middle East and North Africa*, World Bank Staff Working Paper 736, World Bank, Washington DC.

Shahid, S. (1979), 'Homes remittances', *Pakistan Economist* (Karachi), 1–7 September.

Shamshur, Oleg V. (1992), 'Ukraine in the context of the new European migration', *IMR*, 98, 26/2, Summer, pp. 258–68.

Shevtsova, Lilia (1992), 'Post Soviet emigration today and tomorrow', *IMR*, 98, 26/2, Summer, pp. 241–57.

Simmons, Alan B., and Guengant, Jean Pierre (1992), 'Caribbean exodus and the world system', in Mary M. Kritz, Lean Lin Lim and Hania Zlotnik (eds), *International Migration Systems: A Global Approach*, Clarendon Press, Oxford, pp. 94–114.

Simon, Julian L. (1989), *The Economic Consequences of Immigration*, Basil Blackwell for Cato Institute, Oxford.

Simons, Henry C. (1948), *Economic Policy and a Free Society*, University of Chicago Press, Chicago.

Singhanetra-Renard, Anchalee (1992), 'The mobilisation of labor migrants in Thailand: personal links and facilitating networks', in Mary M. Kritz, Lean Lin Lim and Hania Zlotnik (eds), *International Migration Systems: A Global Approach*, Clarendon Press, Oxford, pp. 190–204.

Sklair, Leslie (1989), *Assembling for Development: The Maquila Industry in Mexico and the United States*, Unwin Hyman, London.

Skeldon, Ronald (1992), 'International migration flows within and from the East and Southeast Asian region: a review essay', *Asian and Pacific Migration Journal*, 1/ 1, Manila, pp. 19–63.

Smith, Barton and Newman, Robert (1977), 'Depressed wages along the US–Mexican border: an empirical analysis', *Economic Inquiry*, xv/1, pp. 51–66.

Soltwedel, Rudiger (1993), 'Structural Adjustment, Economic Growth and Employment', in OECD, *The Changing Course of International Migration*, OECD, Paris, pp. 55–66.

Spain, Ernst (1994), 'Taikong's and Calo's: the role of middlemen and brokers in Javanese international migration', *IMR*, 105, xxviii/1, Spring, pp. 93–113.

Spencer, Sarah (ed.) (1994), *Strangers and Citizens: A Positive Approach to Migrants and Refugees*, Institute for Public Policy Research, Rivers-Oram Press, London.

Spencer, Stephen A. (1992), 'Illegal migrant labourers in Japan', *IMR*, 99, 26, Fall.

Stahl, Charles W. (1989), 'Overview: Economic Perspectives', in Reginald Appleyard (ed.), *The Impact of International Migration on Developing Countries*, Development Centre seminar, OECD, Paris, pp. 361–90.

—— (1991), 'South–North migration in the Asia Pacific region', *International Migration*, xxix/2, June, pp. 163–94.

Stark, Oded (1991), *The Migration of Labour*, Basil Blackwell, Oxford.

Stola, Dariusz (1992), 'Forced migration in Central European history', *IMR*, 98, 26/ 2, Summer, pp. 324–41.

Straubhaar, Thomas (1992), 'Allocational and distributional aspects of future immigration in Western Europe', *IMR*, 98, 26/2, Summer, pp. 448–62.

Streeck, W. (1991), 'On the institutional conditions of diversified quality production', in E. Matzner and W. Streeck (eds), *Beyond Keynesianism: The Socio-Economics of Production and Full Employment*, Edward Elgar, Aldershot.

Swamy, Gurushni (1981), *International Migrant Worker Remittances*, World Bank Staff Working Paper 481, World Bank, Washington DC, August.

Swan, B.R., et al. (1991), *Economic and Social Impact of Immigration*, Research Report, Economic Council of Canada, Ottowa.

Szoke, Laszlo (1992), 'Hungarian perspectives on emigration and immigration in the new European architecture', *IMR*, 98, 26/2, Summer.

Tapinos, Georges (1993), 'Can international co-operation be an alternative to the emigration of workers?', in *The Changing Course of International Migration*, OECD, Paris, pp. 175–82.

Tienda, Marta, and Jensen, Leif (1986), 'Immigration and public assistance participation: dispelling the myth of dependency', *Social Science Research*, 15/4, December, pp. 372–400.

Teitelbaum, Michael S. (1993), 'Effects of economic development on emigration pressures in sending countries', in *The Changing Course of International Migration*, OECD, Paris, pp. 161–4.

Thoburn, John and Takashima, Makoto (1993), 'Improving British industrial performance: lessons from Japanese sub-contracting', *National Westminster Bank Quarterly Review*, February, pp. 2–12.

Thomas, Brinley (ed.) (1958), *The Economics of International Migration*, Macmillan, London, 1958.

———— (1961), *International Migration and Economic Development*, UNESCO, Paris.

Tinker, Hugh (1977), *The Banyan Tree: Overseas Migration from India, Pakistan and Bangladesh*, Oxford University Press, London.

Titmuss, R.M. (1958), *Essays on the Welfare State*, Allen and Unwin, London.

Tsay, Ching-Lung (1992), 'Clandestine labor migration in Taiwan', Institute of Economics, Academia Sinica Special Reprint Service (originally *Asian and Pacific Migration Journal*, 1/3–4, 1992, pp. 637–55), Taipei.

United Nations High Commission for Refugees (UNCHR) (1993), *The State of the World's Refugees: The Challenge of Protection*, UNCHR, Geneva.

United Nations Development Programme (UNDP) (1991), *Human Development Report 1991*, UNDP, New York.

———— (1992), *The Human Development Report 1992*, UNDP, New York.

UNESCO (1988), *Statistical Yearbook 1988*, UNESCO, Paris.

United Nations (1978), *Immigration: Trends and Prospects*, Department of Economic and Social Affairs, United Nations, New York.

———— (1980), *Child Prostitution, Report of the Working Group on Slavery* (E/CN.4/Sub 2/447), New York, August.

———— (1982), *Exploitation of Child Labour, Final Report of the Sub Commission on Prevention of Discrimination and Protection of Minors* (E/CN.4/Sub 2/479/Rev.1), New York.

US Bureau of the Census (1984), *Detailed Population Characteristics, US Summary, 1980 Census of Population, Pt. I, Vol. 1*, US Government Printing Office, Washington DC, March.

US Commission for the Study of International Migration and Co-operative Development (1990): *Unauthorised Migration: An Economic Development Response*, US Government Printing Office, Washington DC, July.

US Congress (1977), *Illegal Aliens: Analysis and Background*, Committee on the Judiciary, US House of Representatives, 95th Congress, 1st session, US Government Printing Office, Washington DC.

———— (1978), *Undocumented Workers: Implications for US Policy in the Western Hemisphere*, Subcommittee on Inter-American Affairs of the Committee on International Relations, House of Representatives, 95th Congress, US Government Printing Office, Washington DC.

———— (1983), *Immigration Reform and Control Act of 1982*, Senate Committee on the Judiciary (Subcommittee on Immigration, Refugees and International Law) and the House Committee on the Judiciary, US Government Printing Office, Washington DC.

———— (1989a), *Hearings: Overview of US–Mexican Relations, before the Subcommittee on Western Hemisphere Affairs*, Committee on Foreign Affairs, House of Representatives, 7 June, US Government Printing Office, Washington DC.

———— (1989b), *US Immigration Policy*, Select Committee on Immigration and Refugee Policy, Staff Report.

———— (1990), *US–Mexican Economic Relations: Hearings*, the Subcommittee on Trade of the Committee on Ways and Means, House of Representatives, Serial 101–108, US Government Printing Office, Washington DC.

US Department of Justice (1979), *Immigration and Naturalization Service, Annual Report and Statistical Yearbook for 1979*, US Government Printing Office, Washington DC.

US Department of Labor (1989), *President's Comprehensive Triennial Report on Immigration*, US Government Printing Office, Washington DC.

US Senate (1976), *Immigration 1976: Hearings*, Subcommittee on Immigration and Naturalization, Committee of the Judiciary, 94th Congress, Government Printing

Office, March–April.

Valcarenghi, Marina (1981), *Child Labour in Italy*, Anti Slavery Society, London.

Vasileva, Darina (1992), 'Bulgarian Turkish Emigration and Return', *IMR*, 98, 26/ 2, Summer, pp. 342–52.

Vialet, Joyce C. (1977), *Illegal Aliens: Analysis and Background*, Subcommittee on Immigration, Citizenship and International Law (Report No. 5), US Congress, US Government Printing Office, June.

Villalpondo, M. Vic., et al. (1977), *A Study of the Socio-economic Impact of Illegal Aliens*, County of San Diego, Human Resources Agency, San Diego, Calif., January.

Wasserstein, Bernard (1979), *Britain and the Jews of Europe, 1939–45*, Oxford University Press, London.

Wehler, Hans Ulrich (1972), 'Polenpolitik im Deutschen Kaissereich, 1871–1918', in E.W. Boeckenfoerde (ed.), *Modern Deutsche Verfassungsgesichte (1815–1918)*, cited by Peter O'Brien, 'German–Polish migration: the elusive search for a German nation-state', *IMR*, 98, 26/2, Summer, pp. 373–387.

Weintraub, Sidney and Cárdenas, Gilberto (1984), *The Use of Public Services by Undocumented Aliens in Texas*, Policy Research Project Report, Lyndon B. Johnson School of Public Affairs, University of Texas, Austin.

Wells, D.A. (1889), *Recent Economic Changes*, Airdlie, New York.

Werner, Heinz (1993), 'Migration movements in the perspective of the single European market', in *The Changing Course of International Migration*, OECD, Paris, pp. 79–86.

White, P. (1986), 'International migration in the 1970s', in A. Findlay and P. White (eds), *Western European Population Change*, Croom-Helm, Beckenham.

Widgren, Jonas (1992), *Intergovernmental Consultations on Asylum, Refugee and Migrant Policies in Europe, North America and Australia*, OECD, Paris.

——— (1993), *Movement of Refugees and Asylum Seekers: Recent Trends in Comparative Perspective*, OECD, Paris.

Wilpert, Czarina (1992), 'The use of social networks in Turkish migration to Germany', in Mary M. Kritz, Lean Lin Lim and Hania Zlotnik (eds), *International Migration Systems: A Global Approach*, Clarendon Press, Oxford, pp. 177–89.

Wilson, D. (1992), 'Overseas students in the UK private sector', *International Journal of Education*, 3/2, July.

Withers, G. (1987), 'Migrants and the labour market: the Australian evidence', in OECD, *The Future of Migration*, OECD, Paris.

Wood, Adrian (1994), *North–South Trade, Employment and Inequality: Changing Fortunes in a Skill-driven World*, Clarendon Press, Oxford.

Wood, Harold (1976), 'Future labor supplies for lower level occupations', *Monthly Labor Review*, 99/3, pp. 22–31.

World Bank (1992), *Global Economic Prospects and the Developing Countries*, World Bank, Washington DC.

Zeigler, B.M. (ed.) (1953), *Immigration: An American Dilemma*, DC Heath, Boston, Mass.

Zolberg, A. (1983), 'Contemporary transnational migrations in historical perspectives: patterns and determinants', in Mary M. Kritz (ed.), *US Immigration and Refugee Policy: Global and Domestic Issues*, Lexington Books, Lexington, Mass., pp. 15–51.

Index

on, 224; racial, 122; seizure of, 81; status, 103 (rejection of, 127); treated as illegal immigrants, 225; Vietnamese, 70, 71, 129, 130
refuse collection, 12, 43
registration drives for illegal immigrants, 69
religious associations of migrants, 139
relocation: of populations, 92, 93, 121; of production, 45, 175, 176; of work, 174 *see also* manufacturing
remittances of migrants, 66, 68, 91, 107, 141, 143, 144, 146, 147, 152, 153, 155, 190, 207, 211; as source of foreign exchange, 60; decline of, 144; flows of, 147 (estimated scale of, 141, 142; fluctuations of, 145); of Mexican workers, 143; regulation of, 66, 224; to Korea, 61; transfer of, 141
repatriation, 61, 75, 126, 128; incentives, 11
Replenishment of Agricultural Workers (RPA) (USA), 38
reproduction, 153, 157–8; costs of, 30, 165–72, 176
residence permits, 200
residency rights, 107, 196; in USA, 97
resident, category redefined, 99
restaurant work, 12, 14, 35–6, 109, 175, 222
restaurants, ethnic, 35
retirement age: early, 163; extension of, 52, 109, 182; of women, raised, 184
right to vote *see* vote, right to
rights of entry, 112
robots, 52; introduction of, 25
Rocard, Michel, 114
Romania, 121, 122, 123
Roosevelt, F.D., 95
Russia, 5, 65, 118
Russian nationality, 117
Russification, 121
Rwanda, 129

Sabah, 67
Sarawak, 67
Sassen, Saskia, 191
Saudi Arabia, 59, 60, 68, 123, 124, 143, 156
Save Our State initiative (California), 99
savings of migrants, 10, 141, 154
Saztec company, 63
school truancies, 48
Schuck, Peter, 112
Scott, W.L., 87
sea captains, picking up boat people, 130
seamen, 43–5, 65, 66, 176; 'non-domiciled', 44

seasonal labour, 106, 109, 134, 149
self-employment, 17, 42, 139, 195
semi-skilled workers, 35, 105
Senegal, 106
service industries, 21, 64, 72, 73
services: personal, 176; pricing of, 21 (overpricing, 22); public, 43; relocation of, 25
sex industry, 49
shanty towns, 60
Shelton, Sally, 192
ships, carrying migrants, 68, 122, 126; turned round at sea, 128
shoemaking, 24, 28, 73, 194
Silicon Valley, 34
Simon, Julian, 159
Simons, Henry C., 158
Simpson, Alan, 85, 88
Simpson–Kennedy bill, 100
Simpson–Mazzoli bill, 85
Singapore, 8, 11, 15, 24, 67, 75–81, 92, 125, 126, 133, 134, 135, 148, 179, 183, 200, 201; productivity of, 76
single men, as immigrants, 9, 61, 119
single mothers, 170
single-women-headed households, 31, 164
skilled workers, 11, 25, 72, 103, 137, 147, 184, 221
skills, 168, 169, 171, 195, 201, 219; loss of, 152; overproduction of, 150, 211 *see also* skilled, unskilled *and* semi-skilled workers
Slovakia, 14
Snakeheads, 69
social contract, 19, 171, 184, 205, 212, 214
social contributions, role of, 26
social networks of migrants, 132–56
social security, 23, 25, 99, 168, 169, 183–4; barriers to, 173; cuts in, 19, 26, 115
social services, costs of, 22
social spending, shift towards health, 180
socialism, 20
software programming, 21
Somalia, 120, 127
South Africa, 93, 102, 223
sovereignty, 87, 94, 102, 109, 110, 111, 114, 118, 121, 212, 215
Spain, 9, 112, 178, 184, 190, 192
Spanish language, in USA, 89
Sprinkel, Beryl, 201
Sri Lanka, 57, 77, 83, 117, 124, 127, 128, 144, 147, 148, 150, 152
SS *Struma*, 122
St Patrick's Day parade, New York, 140
state: and immigration, 85–131; decay of system, 120; decline of, 227; intervention of, 170; left's attitude to,